SARAH RUHL

SARAH RUHL
A Critical Study of the Plays

JAMES AL-SHAMMA

McFarland & Company, Inc., Publishers
Jefferson, North Carolina, and London

LIBRARY OF CONGRESS CATALOGUING-IN-PUBLICATION DATA

Al-Shamma, James.
    Sarah Ruhl : a critical study of the plays / James Al-Shamma.
        p.   cm.
    Includes bibliographical references and index.

    ISBN 978-0-7864-5887-5
    softcover : 50# alkaline paper ∞

    1. Ruhl, Sarah—Criticism and interpretation.   I. Title.
    PS3618.U48Z55   2011
    812'.6—dc22   2010054396

BRITISH LIBRARY CATALOGUING DATA ARE AVAILABLE

© 2011 James Al-Shamma. All rights reserved

No part of this book may be reproduced or transmitted in any form or by any means, electronic or mechanical, including photocopying or recording, or by any information storage and retrieval system, without permission in writing from the publisher.

Cover image: Joseph Parks as Orpheus, Maria Dizzia as Eurydice and Charles Shaw Robinson as Father in a concluding scene of *Eurydice*, Yale Repertory Theatre, 2006 (photograph by Joan Marcus)

Manufactured in the United States of America

McFarland & Company, Inc., Publishers
    Box 611, Jefferson, North Carolina 28640
    www.mcfarlandpub.com

To William Davies King

Table of Contents

Preface	1
Introduction	5
I—Navigating Sorrow in *Eurydice*	13
II—Joke as Incantation in *The Clean House*	38
III—Melancholy Plague	68
IV—Falling in Love with Long Distance: *Dead Man's Cell Phone*	84
V—A Cowboy Stew	99
VI—Apocalypse Deferred: *Passion Play*	111
VII—Alternating Currents of Desire: *In the Next Room or the vibrator play*	141
VIII—Other Works	177
IX—Conclusion	186
Appendix: Chronology of Play Premieres	197
Chapter Notes	199
Bibliography	203
Index	215

Preface

This book is the first full-length, comprehensive study of the plays of Sarah Ruhl, who is one of the most important American playwrights working today. It not only introduces readers to Ruhl—it also provides an in-depth analysis that will benefit students, theater practitioners, reviewers, librarians, and scholars. Ruhl is widely staged in regional theaters in the United States and globally, made her Broadway premiere in 2009, and is unsurpassed among female playwrights in the United States for frequency of production. Her success is critical as well as commercial; although still only in her 30s, Ruhl has received widespread recognition and commendation. Most noteworthy is her status as a two-time Pulitzer finalist (*The Clean House*, *In the Next Room*), a Tony award nominee (*In the Next Room*), and a MacArthur Fellowship recipient. Other awards include the Kennedy Center Fourth Forum Freedom Award, the Helen Merrill and Whiting Writers' awards, the Susan Smith Blackburn Prize, and a PEN Award. Theaters that have staged her work include the Goodman Theatre, Arena Stage, Lincoln Center Theater, Second Stage, Yale Repertory Theatre, Woolly Mammoth Theatre Company, Berkeley Repertory Theatre, the Wilma Theater, Cornerstone Theater, Madison Repertory Theatre, Clubbed Thumb, the Piven Theatre Workshop, and Steppenwolf Theater. Her plays have been translated into German, Polish, Korean, Russian, and Spanish, and have been produced outside of the United States in Great Britain, Canada, Germany, Latvia, New Zealand, Australia, and Poland.

This study consists of an analysis of Ruhl's plays both as literature and in performance, accomplished through the examination of her scripts, both published and unpublished, a survey of production reviews, and attendance at major productions. This has been supplemented by Ruhl's own thoughts as culled from interviews and articles. I have attempted to meet each play on its own terms, drawing on literary theory and research in other fields where appropriate. Ruhl's approach is eclectic and she frequently conducts in-depth research herself, so in order to illuminate her plays I have delved into such varied topics as Greek mythology, the psychology of bereavement, the semiotics of humor, the American cowboy, magic realism, wet nursing, and the history of the vibrator.

The introduction provides a biography and an analysis of her style, and discusses her status as a woman playwright. A chapter is devoted to each of Ruhl's full-length, completed plays, exclusive of adaptations. They are *Eurydice*, *The Clean House*, *Late: a cowboy song*, *Melancholy Play*, *Dead Man's Cell Phone*, *Passion Play*, and *In the Next Room or the vibrator play*. Each of these has been published and will therefore be readily available to the reader. Ruhl's full-length adaptations of *Orlando*, after Virginia Woolf's novel, and Chekhov's *The Three Sisters*, receive mention in the chapter on other works along with her one-acts, as does *Demeter in the City*, which the playwright considers a work-in-progress. The conclusion situates Ruhl historically as an American dramatist in the non-realist tradition, following Thornton Wilder, John Guare, and Tony Kushner. The appendix provides a chronology of Ruhl premieres, inclusive of director and theater.

Many individuals contributed to the writing of this book, whom I will attempt to thank here; my apologies to any I might have overlooked. I owe much to the theater faculty at the University of California, Santa Barbara, for their multiple contributions to this project. Simon Williams and Judith Olauson provided crucial feedback, and William Davies King's invaluable guidance at every step led directly to this publication. Catherine Cole transmitted her keen understanding of historiography and methodology, and Leo Cabranes-Grant shared his expertise in postcolonial studies, which informs the discussion of magic realism in *The Clean House*. Jody Enders's insights into critical writing have proved extremely helpful, and Maggie Mixsell has provided unflagging encouragement.

The conveners of and participants in the Contemporary Women Playwrights Working Session at the 2009 American Society for Theatre Research Conference provided a forum in which to develop ideas about *In the Next Room*, and to situate Ruhl as a woman playwright. The conveners were Anna Birch, Penny Farfan, and Lesley Ferris. Apart from the working session, Beth Conklin contributed significantly to the formulation of the chapter on this play, and Carol Gilligan unlocked the ending.

I would like to thank the students, staff, and faculty at Belmont University, especially in the department of theatre and dance, for their interest in and support of this project. Specifically, Brandy Austin granted access to the Chicago theater scene as I pursued photo rights, and Claire Syler, Don

Griffiths, and Jessika Malone shared in my enthusiasm for Ruhl. Department Chair Paul Gatrell and Cynthia Curtis, dean of the School of Visual and Performing Arts, provided a supportive academic home as I researched and wrote. Bill Feehely and Vali Forrister, artistic directors of Actors Bridge Ensemble of Nashville, allowed the opportunity to dramaturg *Dead Man's Cell Phone*.

Sarah Ruhl graciously supplied unpublished scripts of her plays and her agent, Bruce Ostler, has been most helpful. Kathy Kehoe Ruhl provided valuable input on the introduction. Marisa Smith of Smith and Kraus generously permitted the inclusion of portions of *Ruhl in an Hour* here. Last but not least, credit is due Kate Al-Shamma for providing an example with her fearless research, and to my family for always being there: my mother, Anne Saunders, brothers Nabeel and Robert, sons Orion and Steven, and in-laws Hala, Anne, John and Diane, and those present in spirit if not in body, namely my sister Suzan and father Abid.

Introduction

Currents

Currents of desire transport Sarah Ruhl's characters to extraordinary places, and transform them in remarkable ways. They deposit her characters on strange and distant shores, such as the nether bank of the river Styx inhabited by talking stones, or into an afterlife in which the residents do their laundry in the nude. They sweep parents back from the dead, and they inspire doctor and patient to sing a medieval love duet in Latin during the course of a mastectomy. The currents elicit speech from a dog, and install a deceased father in the moon to have tea with a Renaissance queen. They transform the melancholic into almonds, and a welfare mother into a Greek goddess. They deliver snow to comfort a world ravaged by global warming, and dissolve a house. They unite a mother and her invisible child with a female cowboy and, on a Renaissance ship, sail a Vietnam War veteran into the sky. Ruhl's currents of desire whirl and eddy into fantastical shapes not to distract, but rather to reveal as she follows Emily Dickinson's dictum to "tell all the truth—but tell it slant." Her metamorphoses of magic uncover inner states of being in modes unavailable to the realist.

Her currents of desire alternate, in the senses of a shift in direction, of reciprocity, and of ambivalence. A husband's attention is diverted from wife to mistress, or a wife's to a lover. The alluring melancholic turns suddenly, inexplicably, repulsively happy. In the reciprocal sense, a father's and daughter's mutual love pulls her to him, even though he resides in the underworld. A Victorian housewife demands an open flow of communication with her husband even though its force blows away their house. An accidental tourist to the afterlife discovers that the object of her desire fails to reciprocate her affection, and she is repulsed back into the world of the living and the arms of his doting brother. In terms of ambivalence, Ruhl captures the complexities of life in her onstage relationships. The love between a young book enthusiast and her musical beau shows signs of strain even as she accepts his marriage proposal. Unable to nurse, a young mother finds her adoring feelings for her infant tainted with frustration and fear; grieving her own child, the hired wet nurse expresses an even greater range of emotions, from love to hate. Reenactors of the passion of Christ struggle to reconcile their own personalities with those of the biblical figures that they portray. Ruhl's characters scrabble for their bearings in a world that is rarely as it seems, and that often shifts beneath their feet. More often than not, as in the case of the veteran wafted into the sky, they discover within themselves the strength, intelligence, and courage required to navigate the winds of change.

Bagging Medusa's Head

Ruhl directs the flow of her alternating currents with a touch as light as air. In *Six Memos for the Next Millennium* (1988), Italo Calvino describes how Perseus conquers Medusa:

> The only hero able to cut off Medusa's head is Perseus, who flies with winged sandals; Perseus, who does not turn his gaze upon the face of the Gorgon but only upon her image reflected in his bronze shield.... To cut off Medusa's head without being turned to stone, Perseus supports himself on the very lightest of things, the winds and the clouds, and fixes his gaze upon what can be revealed only by indirect vision, an image caught in a mirror [4].

He is careful never to look at the bagged head and employs it as a weapon, turning its ossifying stare against his enemies. His strength "always lies in a refusal to look directly, but not in a refusal of the reality in which he is fated to live; he carries the reality with him and accepts it as his particular burden" (5). Like Perseus, Sarah Ruhl carries a particular burden—that of the loss of her father to cancer when she was 20, and also like the Greek hero, she handles it with lightness. Heavy issues of life, love, and death lie at the heart of her drama, but she treats them with a deft touch, keeping humor close at hand even while plumbing the depths of despair and bereavement. Ruhl admires Calvino's *Memos*, specifically his first chapter titled "Lightness." She regards lightness as containing wisdom, as a "philosophical and aesthetic viewpoint" that enables one to step back and "laugh at horrible things" even as they are being experienced (qtd. in Lahr, "Surreal"). Ruhl has worked through her grief across a number of plays, and this grief is characterized by a strong desire to reunite with the lost loved one. The pain of this longing is lightened through mechanisms of fantasy and magic realism, informed by a poetic sensibility and erudite intelligence.

Ruhl began to charm the snakes on Medusa's head in 1995, shortly after her father's death, as an undergraduate in a playwriting class conducted by Paula Vogel at Brown University (Lahr, "Surreal"). Vogel's esteem for her student cannot be overstated. She claims that her "most significant contribution to the American theatre" has been to encourage Ruhl's playwriting (qtd. in Wren, 31). Vogel is, herself, an accomplished playwright, counting among her accolades a Pulitzer Prize for *How I Learned to Drive*. During her 20-year tenure as director of the playwriting programs at Brown University, Vogel mentored numerous young talents including Nilo Cruz, who went on to win his own Pulitzer (Rizzo, "Allen Stars"; Robertson, "Paula Vogel").[1]

Sarah Ruhl (courtesy Walter McBride).

Nevertheless, Vogel considers Ruhl uniquely talented amongst her many accomplished protégés (Reid) and predicts that Ruhl is "going to become her own vocabulary word" (Wren, 31). When Ruhl first entered Vogel's advanced playwriting seminar as a sophomore, Vogel assumed she was a senior due to her quiet and serious demeanor and unique approach to aesthetics. She asked her to write a short play with a dog as protagonist. Ruhl's father had recently passed away, and she wrote about this loss from the perspective of the family dog, who is unable to comprehend the situation in human terms. The play incorporates kabuki techniques, and the rich, vivid language stunned the playwriting teacher, who broke down sobbing as she read the work for the first time (Vogel, "Sarah Ruhl," 54). When Ruhl later approached Vogel with the idea of writing her thesis on "the representation of the actress in the nineteenth-century novel" (Ruhl qtd. in Svich, 39), unsurprisingly Vogel insisted upon a play instead.

The writing exercise described by Vogel gives an early indication of Ruhl's style and thematic concerns. Composed only a few months after her father's passing, it introduces the themes of death and bereavement that would continue to absorb Ruhl for years to come. It demonstrates her ability to elicit a strong emotional response and the element of fantasy, initiated through the assigned canine protagonist, is advanced through inclusion of elements from Kabuki theater (Goodman). Ruhl's poetic sensibility is on display as well, alluded to in Vogel's description of her "emotionally vivid language" (Vogel, "Sarah Ruhl," 54). Indeed, Ruhl wrote poems before she wrote plays, publishing a collection of verse, "Death in Another Country," at the age of 20 (Lahr, "Surreal"). The collection was bundled with the work of two other poets in a volume titled *Troika VI*, published by Thorntree Press in 1995 and now out of print. Ruhl celebrates the white space in the margins of both poetry and plays, insisting that a good writer knows when to keep his or her mouth shut so that the line can sing (Svich, 39). She carefully crafts every line and delights in surprising juxtapositions. Richard Corley, who directed *Eurydice* at Madison Repertory, observes that she "has a reason (and a vision) for every line," and advises directors to pay attention to her "fierce intelligence" (Wren, 32). In "The Golden Ruhl," Celia Wren concisely summarizes Ruhl's style as one of "steely lyricism," whimsy, "deceptive spareness," "metaphysical intensity," and "compassionate humor," alongside "deep sadness" (31). Les Waters, who has directed three productions of *Eurydice* and the world and Broadway premieres of *In the Next Room or the vibrator play*, praises her rare aptitude for advancing plot with lyrical dialogue "where the poetry is welded to the action" (qtd. in Wren, 32).

In addition to Vogel, Ruhl has studied playwriting with Mac Wellman, Nilo Cruz, and Maria Irene Fornes (Weckworth, 35; Vogel, "Sarah Ruhl," 58). The influence of Fornes is evident in Ruhl's essay "Six Small Thoughts on Fornes, the Problem of Intention, and Willfulness," which appeared in the September 2001 issue of *Theatre Topics*. In it, Ruhl examines the concepts of intention and will in current theatrical practice. Ruhl sides with Fornes, who questions the prevalent Stanislavskian insistence on character objectives. Both legitimize the depiction of emotional states of being in the absence of willfulness, and protest a psychological realism in which action and emotion are traced exclusively through cause and effect. Elsewhere, Ruhl has expressed a preference for a type of drama based on Ovid rather than Aristotle, one abounding in small transformations rather than one in which a protagonist pursues a goal and then learns from the experience of either overcoming or being defeated by an obstacle (Lahr, "Surreal"). This does not mean that Ruhl's plays are plotless. She does leave space, however, for small transformations and unprovoked emotional states. As playwright Caridad Svich notes, Ruhl's characters "are in the 'real' world but also live in a more suspended state" (Svich, 36).

A Life in the Theater

Born on January 24, 1974 (Ruhl, "Re: A Request"), Ruhl grew up in the Chicago suburb of Wilmette (Wren, 31) and also spent considerable time visiting her family's home state of Iowa (Gurewitsch). As Ruhl was growing up, her mother, Kathy Kehoe Ruhl, acted in and directed plays while teaching high school English; she now holds a Ph.D. in Language, Literacy, and Rhetoric from the University of Illinois. Ruhl's late father, Patrick, marketed toys for a number of years. He loved "puns, reading, language, and jazz," and, according to his daughter, "should have been a history professor" (qtd. in Lahr, "Surreal"). Her older sister, Kate, is a psychiatrist (Lahr, "Surreal"). Raised Catholic, Ruhl abandoned the faith as a teenager "after she'd decided it was unfair that priests, but not nuns, were the only ones allowed to communicate directly with God" (Goodman). She began telling stories before she could write, which she would dictate to her mother ("A Conversation"). The first story she wrote was about two vegetables from opposite sides of the refrigerator who get married (Gianopulos). As a child, Ruhl thought that she would grow up to be a teacher and writer of stories, rather than plays. She did write "a courtroom drama involving landmasses," which her fourth grade teacher, Mr. Spangenberger, refused to stage (Svich, 39). The topic of her first play demonstrates both her sense of whimsy and her love of language; within that work, she particularly liked the words "isthmus" and "peninsula" ("Playwright Sarah Ruhl").

Ruhl spent time in the theater from an early age. When she was five years old, her mother would take her to rehearsals at which Ruhl would take notes to give to the actors (D. Smith). She started taking classes at the Piven Theatre Workshop while in the fourth grade. Located in Evanston, Illinois, and founded over 35 years ago by Joyce Piven and her late husband, Byrne Piven, the workshop boasts such alumni as John Cusack, Joan Cusack, Jeremy Piven, Aidan Quinn, Lili Taylor, Harry Lennix, Kate Walsh, Hope Davis, and Polly Noonan, the last of whom has appeared in many of Ruhl's plays (*Piven Theatre Workshop*). The Pivens founded the workshop in order to continue the improvisational work of Viola Spolin (Gianopulos). Joyce Piven identifies source materials as "stories, myths, fairy tales, folk tales, and literary tales—Chekhov, Eudora Welty, Flannery O'Connor, Salinger" (qtd. in Lahr, "Surreal"). The emphasis was on language, not scenery, and on transformation: the theater they created was without props and sets, depended upon language, and ignored the fourth wall (Lahr, "Surreal"). Ruhl claims that this focus on transformation, language, and playfulness helped shape her aesthetic (Reid). Jessica Thebus, who directed *The Clean House* at the Goodman Theatre and *Melancholy Play* at the Piven Workshop, agrees with Ruhl's assessment, and she discerns "structures of improvisation and theatre games" in *Melancholy Play* (qtd. in Reid). The workshop was also involved in the development of *The Clean House*, staging its first sit-down reading and three performances as a workshop presentation (Reid). It also commissioned and premiered *Orlando*, Ruhl's adaptation of the Virginia Woolf novel ("Sarah Ruhl"), as well as her adaptations of two of Chekhov's stories (Ruhl, "The Lady," 1).

As referenced above, when Ruhl was 20, in August of 1994, her father died of cancer (a sub-mandibular salivary gland tumor that metastasized to the bones) after fighting the disease for two years, an event that would have a profound impact on her and her art. She graduated from Brown University in Providence, Rhode Island, with a B.A. in English in 1997 (Pressley; Goodman); her undergraduate work included a year spent studying English literature at Pembroke College in Oxford (Lahr, "Surreal"). She worked a variety of jobs for the next two years, including teaching arts education in public schools (Pressley), before returning to Brown for an M.F.A. in playwriting, which she completed in 2001. After graduating, she lived in New York, Chicago, and Los Angeles before eventually returning to New York; she now resides in Manhattan. With Paula Vogel and Anne Fausto-Sterling officiating, she and Anthony Charuvastra, now a child psychiatrist (Crowley, 110), were married on a mountaintop outside of Los Angeles in 2005 after a seven-year courtship (Goodman; Lahr, "Surreal"). Ruhl gave birth to their daughter Anna in the spring of 2006, and to twins in early 2010.

Ruhl as Woman Playwright

Although the playwright's gender is certainly taken into consideration in the analysis that follows, this is not primarily a study of Ruhl as woman playwright; in other words, the writer's gender is not considered to be the overriding factor in shaping her worldview. Nevertheless, it is certainly a significant one and therefore it is helpful to situate her within current trends in playwriting by women. In her introduction to the reissued edition of Sue Ellen Case's groundbreaking *Feminism and Theatre* (2008; first issued in 1988), Elaine Aston provides an overview of feminist theater and feminist theater theory since the 1980s. She notes that younger generations are less apt to identify themselves as feminist for a number of reasons. She speculates that these include a fear of being identified with the media image of bra-burning women's libbers of the 1970s, and the "appeal of the new style of sexualized, non-politicized, girl-power 'feminism' of the 1990s" (xx). Women playwrights also are reluctant to identify as such, for fear of being ghettoized, which in fact they are in terms of production. For example on Broadway, fewer than one out of eight shows are written by women (Cohen).[2]

Rather than focusing primarily on women's or feminist issues, Aston points out that women playwrights today consider complex issues involving nation, class, race, gender, and sexuality and Ruhl is no exception. Aston refers to a feminist residue, to gains of second wave feminism now taken for granted or perhaps overlooked, and these gains appear most significantly in Ruhl in her frequent employment of a female protagonist and her depiction of female agency, and her consistent valuation of community over the individual. Additionally, her dramatic structure tends to be relational or character-based; she herself has expressed a strong affinity for Chekhov and has adapted a number of his works. She has also stated that she prefers a theater of small transformations over one that builds to an Aristotelian climax, and this assertion is borne out in her plays. In the view of some feminist theater critics, the single Aristotelian climax is associated with masculinity and male sexuality; Ruhl's dramaturgy may be considered feminist to the extent that it resists this model. Ruhl thus conforms to current trends in women's playwriting without, however, being conformist. The issues of concern to women playwrights listed by Aston cover an extraordinary range and are of interest, as well, to male playwrights and audience members of either gender. To conform to current trends means to be open to addressing a multitude of complex and interrelated issues, framed globally. Ruhl addresses a subset of issues within this wide field, and does so in her own unique voice.

Issues of primary concern to Ruhl are those of loss and bereavement. In writing *Eurydice*, she shouldered the terrible burden of her father's passing. Ruhl relates that the task failed to have a cathartic effect. She "felt terrible" after she finished writing it, and even while watching it "until at least 10 productions in" (qtd. in D'souza). Nevertheless, she handles her heavy subject matter with light touches of humor. The result is a play that entertains through its whimsical reimagining of the myth even as it plunges the viewer into depths of grief through its precise and compassionate depiction of the process of bereavement.

I

Navigating Sorrow in *Eurydice*

Even the Stones Wept

Time and again since its premiere at Madison Repertory Theatre in September 2003 under the direction of Richard Corley, Ruhl's *Eurydice* has wrung strong emotion from its audiences. Symbolic of grief, the images of the downward flow of water evoked by the play's dialogue and realized onstage in many of its productions have unleashed rivers of tears even amongst that most obdurate group of theatergoers, the critics. In the *San Francisco Chronicle*, critiquing the 2004 Berkeley Repertory Theatre production as directed by Les Waters, Robert Hurwitt rhapsodizes that "pangs of longing strike heartbreaking chords"; furthermore, the scenes between father and daughter are "rich in beautifully observed tenderness" and the conclusion is "as poignantly rewarding as it is luminously ambiguous" (Hurwitt). In the *East Bay Express*, Lisa Drostova finds the production "beautifully sad" and notes that the father's "wistful dancing provoked sniffling from the audience," while the actor playing Orpheus "does his share of tear-jerking too." Overall, she rates the production as "assured, powerful, [and] heart-wrenching" (Drostova). Michael Scott Moore observes, in the *SF Weekly*, that at the conclusion, "half the audience was crying" (Moore). The *East Bay Express* unequivocally states, "there wasn't a dry eye in the house at the end of each show" ("Most Memorable").

The 2006 Yale Repertory Theatre production, also directed by Waters, evoked similar responses. Although Frank Rizzo of *Daily Variety* found the production "not a fully satisfying experience," he nevertheless discerned "individual scenes of exquisite beauty" and "moments of aching beauty"

(Rizzo, "Eurydice"). In *The Stamford Advocate*, Jonathan Rougeot puzzles, "I've never laughed so much at a production that I left feeling so devastated," and concludes that, "'Eurydice' offers a heartbreaking exploration of the theme of loss" (Rougeot). Anita Gates of the *New York Times* was startled by its sudden impact:

> I cry at the theater, sometimes even when the play isn't very good. But normally I know when it's coming; it starts with a little mistiness, allowing me time to dig out the Kleenex. But on Tuesday night, as I watched the final minutes of the Yale Rep's knockout production of Sarah Ruhl's "Eurydice," the tears came with the suddenness of grief [Gates].

She praises its universality, asserting that "it is about every death, every loss, every paralyzing pang of grief" (Gates). Her colleague at the *New York Times*, Charles Isherwood, exalts, "devastatingly lovely—and just plain devastating." He hypothesizes that it might "just be the most moving exploration of the theme of loss that the American theater has produced since the events of September 11, 2001," and that he "fought off tears for half the play, not always successfully" (Isherwood, "A Comic Impudence").

In *The Boston Globe*, Louise Kennedy details her intimately personal reaction after the curtain fell. She leaves the theater excited about the review she is to write, but her mood changes suddenly when she reaches her car:

> I get in, put the key in the ignition, and break down into heaving, wracking sobs. All I can think about is the image of Eurydice's father....
> I saw this play on Oct. 3; my father had died Sept. 7. Ours was a complicated relationship—whose isn't?—and though I had gone through the rituals of mourning I have been troubled by finding myself unable to cry more than about five tears at a time. But now ... I cry for a long time.... [T]his play, more than most I have seen this year, continues to haunt me [Kennedy].

She speculates that the play's impact may owe something to the public mourning for strangers that followed the collapse of the World Trade Center, and the ensuing struggle between "remembering and forgetting, between turning back and moving on" (Kennedy). As argued below, the lachrymose effect of *Eurydice* owes more to the playwright's skill than the aftermath of 9/11. Ruhl conveys the process of bereavement while artfully balancing a series of thematic dualities, sweeping her characters ever downward only to arrest them in a final tableau that captures the finality of death. Before examining the thematic complications and psychological dimensions of the play, it will be situated within a brief history of the origins and stagings of the myth, and the playwright's debt to a poem by Rilke will also be explored.

Orpheus Ascending

In *Descent and Return: The Orphic Theme in Modern Literature* (1971), Walter A. Strauss chronicles the origins of the myth of Orpheus. Scholars generally agree that the poet-god dates to the sixth century B.C., appearing as a shaman-musician capable of subduing all of nature. Associated with the cult of Dionysus, he founds his own so-called Orphic cult. The myth receives its first, albeit brief, written confirmation in Euripides' *Alcestis* (438 B.C.). Virgil and Ovid provide full versions, the former in his *Fourth Georgic* (29 B.C.), the latter in books 10 and 11 of *Metamorphoses* (c. 2–8 A.D.). The Roman poets relate that Orpheus's wife, Eurydice, dies of a snake bite on her wedding day. Grief-stricken, the groom descends to the underworld where, moved by his exquisite, musical lamentation, Hades and his wife Persephone allow him to retrieve his bride. They prohibit him, however, from glancing back at her on the way out; the urge, of course, proves irresistible and Eurydice is whisked back to the underworld. In some versions, Orpheus is then immediately torn apart by the Maenads (Bacchantes), female followers of Dionysus; in others, he first eschews the company of women and introduces homosexuality to Greece. Ultimately, his head floats down the river Hebros, singing and prophesying, accompanied by his lyre, until both wash ashore on the Isle of Lesbos. Strauss divides the myth into three parts: "(1) Orpheus as a singer-prophet (shaman) capable of establishing harmony in the cosmos ...; (2) The descent into Hades [to retrieve Eurydice] ...; (3) The dismemberment theme ..." (6). Most adapters, including Ruhl, have been drawn to the second part.

The story has been retold numerous times in literature, poetry, opera, and theater. It has proved an attractive subject for opera due to its musical and romantic subject matter—indeed, it inspired the very first three operas. Jacopo Peri and Giulio Caccini both composed their 1600 versions on Ottavio Rinuccini's libretto; Claudio Monteverdi adopted Alessandro Striggio's libretto in 1607. In "*Orfeo* and *Eurydice*, the First Two Operas" (1982), Timothy J. McGee dismisses Caccini's as an inferior attempt. As the operas were written for happy occasions, they required upbeat endings. Accordingly, both librettos resolve in visions of connubial bliss. In Striggio, Apollo reunites the couple in heaven whereas in Rinuccini, Orpheus easily succeeds in rescuing his bride because he is allowed to look back (McGee, 163–5).

One particularly noteworthy operatic version is that of Christoph Willibald Glück. Glück began his reformation of opera with *Orfeo ed Euridice* in 1762. He broke from the serious Italian opera of his time, introducing such innovations as integrating the overture into the dramatic structure of the work and abandoning unaccompanied recitative (Howard). Glück's librettist, Calzabigi, follows the precedent set by Striggio, reuniting the couple through the intervention of a *deus ex machina*, in this case personified love (*Amor*). On the journey from the underworld, Orpheus and Eurydice are allowed to speak to one another on the condition that Orpheus must not mention the prohibition. Feeling neglected, she eventually convinces him to turn around (Krieger, 295). Thus, blame for the failure is shifted onto her, although this blame is somewhat obviated by her ignorance of the conditions; a parallel may be drawn with Eve's temptation of Adam (297).

Non-operatic versions have been staged by Jean Anouilh, Tennessee Williams, and Mary Zimmerman, and a recent operatic version by Rinde Eckert premiered in 2006. In *Eurydice (Legend of Lovers)* (1952), Anouilh has added a parental figure, in his case the father of Orpheus rather than Eurydice. Itinerant musicians, father and son play in cafés for pocket change. Allowed to visit Eurydice in the afterlife, Orpheus gazes into her eyes in order to determine her faithfulness, and thereby loses her. A mysterious stranger grants him a second chance to be reunited with his love in the afterlife, an opportunity that he pursues, presumably by committing suicide. In Williams's *Orpheus Descending* (1957), a young, guitar-toting man alights in a moribund Southern town, bringing sexual rebirth to the proprietress of a dry-goods store. Her husband shoots and kills her upon discovering that the stranger has impregnated her; in the meantime, the local authorities attack the stranger with a blowtorch. The poet-musician has temporarily enlivened his Eurydice in, while failing to remove her from, a metaphoric underworld. In *Metamorphoses* (1998), Zimmerman retells the moment of the backward glance in two different ways, first as found in Ovid, then as in Rilke's poem, "Orpheus. Eurydice. Hermes" (1904). Robert Woodruff directed the premiere of Eckert's operatic *Orpheus X* at American Repertory Theatre in 2006. Orpheus is a rock star whose cab runs over Eurydice, a poet and a stranger to him. As in Ruhl, Eurydice acts as the agent that foils Orpheus's plan, in Eckert's version by ripping off his blindfold at the critical moment.

Although Eurydice appears as a fully-developed character in Anouilh and Williams, Eckert and Ruhl grant her greater agency as the spoiler of Orpheus's plan. Zimmerman retells the story through direct quotation of her sources, Ovid and Rilke, and therefore mirrors their handling of Eurydice. In Ovid, she serves merely as Orpheus's love interest, cryptic and without personality. In Rilke, she assumes greater importance; the poet describes her inner state as one of fullness and completeness. She no longer needs or even desires Orpheus, and has even forgotten who he is by the time he turns around. As reviewed by Terry Byrne in the *Boston Herald*, the Eurydice of *Orpheus X* actually becomes more powerful in the underworld and ultimately chooses to remain there. Nevertheless, although Orpheus must share the power of art with Eurydice-as-poet, he remains the central figure. Finally, in Ruhl, Eurydice claims the role of active protagonist.

Rilke and the Fullness of Death

Although, unlike Zimmerman, Ruhl does not quote directly from Rilke's "Orpheus. Eurydice. Hermes.," she nonetheless looks to it for inspiration. In an interview with Caridad Svich, she identifies the poem as the single adaptation of the myth in which Eurydice has "anything" going on inside her head and she follows Rilke's lead in that death has altered Eurydice's perception by the time Orpheus arrives (Svich, 36). Ruhl also evokes the pastoral quality of the poem by lacing her dialogue with words that reference nature and agriculture. Furthermore, she borrows the characterization of Orpheus's physique, a contrast of senses of perception, and peculiar hair imagery.

In Rilke's poem, Orpheus, Eurydice, and Hermes pass through a pastoral landscape on their way out of the underworld. The German poet describes woods, a lake, a rain-filled sky, soft meadows, and a shadow world of grief that arises out of Orpheus's song of lamentation. The generative quality of the music refers to the first stage of the myth as outlined by Strauss—that of the "singer-prophet capable of establishing harmony in the cosmos." Indeed, early sources not only associate Orpheus with harmony in the cosmos, but with the very origin of the cosmos. As examples, a parody of a religious Orphic cosmogonic poem occurs in Aristophanes's *Birds*, and Apollonius of Rhodes places Orpheus on the Argos, where he quiets the drunken sailors with a song describing the origin of the world (Segal, 8). Rilke's poem inspires the creation of a pastoral world in Ruhl's play, not so much in its setting, but through the dialogue. This imagery consists of sky, clouds, and stars, farming and hunting, dirt, fruit and vegetables, duck hunting, and all manner of animals: birds, dogs, fish, bulls, bees, elephants, reindeer, worms, horses, and gazelles. In Ruhl, the pastoral landscape has been fragmented and dispersed, hinted at rather than openly displayed. The language carries a promise of nature, or a nostalgia for it. Eurydice dwells in the shade of her father, who is imagined as a tree only briefly, before the dripping emptiness of the underworld reasserts itself. One can trace nature through the dialogue, but its insubstantiality renders it uninhabitable. It is as if the cosmos has been dispersed, rather than distorted, by grief; or as if nature, rather than Orpheus, has been torn apart and scattered in an act of *sparagmos*.

Rilke seems to have influenced Ruhl's characterization of Orpheus as well. Rilke describes him as "gazing in dumb impatience" as he leads Hermes and Eurydice out of the underworld; the god stands mute at the beginning of Ruhl's play as well, gesturing to Eurydice his offer of the sky and the stars. When Orpheus does speak, in Rilke, to reassure himself that the two are following, he "[says] it aloud and [hears] it die away," an action that suggests the impermanence of language. Ruhl couples memory with language, demonstrating the transient nature of both. As language and memory "die away," so does life.

Rilke's description of Orpheus as a "slender man" (stanza 4) also appears in the play. As the Nasty Interesting Man attempts to seduce Eurydice, he contrasts his own robustness with Orpheus's slim fragility:

> You need to get yourself a real man. A man with broad shoulders like me. Orpheus has long fingers that would tremble to pet a bull or pluck a bee from a hive ... a man who can put his big arm around your little shoulders as he leads you through a crowd ... a man with big hands, with big stupid hands like potatoes, a man who can carry a cow in labor [355].

The Nasty Interesting Man positions himself as a farmer or herder to Orpheus's artist. Here Ruhl has gone outside of Rilke to draw upon Virgil's depiction of the god Aristaeus. Aristaeus is the would-be rapist of Eurydice who chases her along the river, driving her towards the fatal snakebite. When his bees mysteriously die after the incident, Aristaeus forces Proteus to prescribe a remedy for his bad fortune. Proteus instructs him to sacrifice four bulls and four heifers; out of their rotting carcasses burst clouds of bees. One finds references to a bull, a cow, and bees in the above quotation from the Nasty Interesting Man. Ruhl synthesizes Rilke's depiction of the slim poet with Virgil's portrait of the beekeeper to create a contrast between farmer and artist.

Ruhl's creative use of Eurydice's hair may also be traced back to Rilke. Rilke refers to Eurydice as "that blonde woman, / who'd sometimes echoed in the poet's poems" (stanza 8), and then uses similes of hair and rain to describe her condition after death:

> She was already loosened like long hair,
> and given far and wide like fallen rain,
> and dealt out like a manifold supply [stanza 9].

In Ruhl's opening scene, Orpheus imagines Eurydice's hair as an orchestra that flies her into the sky. Later, after her death, he dreams of her hair becoming water:

> Last night I dreamed that we climbed Mount Olympus and we started to

make love and all the strands of your hair were little faucets and water was streaming out of your head and I said, why is water coming out of your hair? And you said, gravity is very compelling [371–2].

What Rilke employs as two separate similes—those of Eurydice being "loosened like long hair" and "given far and wide like fallen rain"—Ruhl combines into a single image of hair as faucets streaming water. First imagined to serve as an orchestra, hair later becomes the channeling of water (nature) through the art of plumbing.

In Rilke, Eurydice's "deadness" fills her "like fullness." In Ruhl, this fullness comes from her association with her father in the underworld. Rilke's Eurydice "could take nothing in" (stanza 6); at the ending of the play, Ruhl's Eurydice has difficulty recognizing Orpheus. As in Rilke, "her pale hands had grown so disaccustomed / to being a wife." What Ruhl has added is a separating force in the personage of the Father. In Rilke, Eurydice returns to her abundance-filled death, unconcerned with Orpheus's grief. Similarly, in Ruhl, Eurydice shrugs off Orpheus's panicked entreaties with a trite aphorism (398).

Although clearly indebted to Rilke, Ruhl ventures far beyond his influence, freely adapting the myth to suit her needs. She limits the populace of the underworld to only the Lord and the three Stones and adds the character of the Father as a surrogate for her own. Ruhl was motivated to "have one more conversation with" her father ("Turning the World"), who died of cancer at the age of 55 when Ruhl was just 20, and to this purpose employs Eurydice as her alter ego. The play eulogizes her father and provides a powerful study of the process of bereavement within a thematic structure composed of a complex series of interrelated dualities.

Fatal Synthesis

Charles Segal sketches, in *Orpheus: The Myth of the Poet* (1989), a triangular relationship between art, death, and love. The balance between these varies from version to version. For example, in Orpheus's failed attempt to recover Eurydice, art and love prove unable to overcome death. In Ovid, the Maenads' attack on Orpheus is arrested when their spears and stones halt in mid-flight, charmed by the poet's music. In this instant, art triumphs over death, if only momentarily (Segal, 2). In an earlier version dating to the middle of the fifth century B.C., this victory of art, coupled with love, occurs more convincingly, as Orpheus successfully retrieves Eurydice from the underworld (8). The mention in Euripides's *Alcestis* implies success as well, according to Emmet Robbins in "Famous Orpheus" (1982). The title character's husband, Admetus, wishes for Orpheus's musical ability so that he might bring his own wife back from the dead (Robbins, 16). Although art, death, and love certainly figure in Ruhl's version, they are integrated into a complex series of thematic dyads. The concepts of love and art are each split in two—love into that for husband and father, and art into music and language. Traditionally, Orpheus is skilled in music, poetry, and rhetoric as "composite, virtually indistinguishable parts of the power of art" (Segal, 2). Ruhl confines his talent to music.

Ruhl has balanced not only the dualities of life/death, music/language, romantic love/paternal love, but many others as well: lightness/heaviness, overworld/underworld, farmer/artist, memory/forgetfulness, child/adult, father/husband, high/low, internal/external, and perhaps most importantly, art/nature. Art in the last pair refers not to the modern understanding of the fine arts, but rather to the classical Greek concept of art as the totality of human endeavor. Robert E. Wood references Aristotle, in *Placing Aesthetics: Reflections on the Philosophic Tradition* (1999), in distinguishing between nature as the "fundamental framework of our existence" (14), and art as that which arises out of human choice: "The whole of culture is thus arti-ficial [sic] in the literal sense; that is, it is made by art" (15).

Ruhl built the play around the image of Eurydice causing Orpheus to turn around by calling his name; to her, this represented language overcoming music (Svich, 36). The music/language duality is expressed through the pairings of Orpheus and the father, and Orpheus and Eurydice. Orpheus's aptitude for music is offset by a distrust of language, and the father and daughter's love of language by an incapacity for music. Orpheus conceives of language as limited to the expression of ideas that are either right or wrong—another duality—and this ambiguity unsettles him. Eurydice finds stories and language "interesting," and her employment of the word connotes layers of complexity that further unnerve Orpheus. Eurydice reports to her father that Orpheus regretted that "words can mean anything," preferring a concrete thing, such as the human body, which means "only one thing at a time" (385).

Orpheus shows little interest in Eurydice's books and she, in turn, proves incapable of carrying even one of the 12 tunes that Orpheus is orchestrating in his head, or of clapping out a rhythm. Eurydice and her father invite the horror and disgust of the Stones when they vocalize the melody to "I've Got Rhythm." Even the two of them confess their ineptitude (379–80). Love of language is passed down from generation to generation, and music heralds the intrusion of the groom. Father and daughter are only alive to the extent that they are able to associate with the overworld, the language of which they must recuperate in order to reconstruct memory. Music proves useless to this task.

Ruhl illustrates personality as a construct of language by standing her characters upon written materials on three separate occasions. During the first two, Eurydice reacquires language; during the last, Orpheus loses it. Just arrived in the underworld, and freshly dipped in the River of Forgetfulness, Eurydice stands on a letter from Orpheus thinking the melody to "There's No Place Like Home." She associates the object with Orpheus, but is unable to articulate the concept of home. Her father then uses the letter to teach her language, reestablishing the memory of her husband in the process (368–71). Later, Eurydice stands upon the *Collected Works of Shakespeare*. When osmosis fails, she hurls the book in frustrated rage. Her father intervenes and teaches her how to read, and starts with a passage out of *Lear* that expresses the love between father and daughter (377). These events demonstrate the transmission of spoken and written language from parent to child. The first event reconnects Eurydice with her husband, the second with her father. She develops personality and formulates relationships through this (re)acquisition. Having established this visual trope, Ruhl applies it to powerful effect at the close of the play when the amnesiac Orpheus encounters Eurydice's farewell letter. He stands on it, closes his eyes, and hears only by the sound of water followed by silence (411). Lacking a teacher, Orpheus irredeemably loses both memory and self. Water as an agent of oblivion erases individuality as it blurs and dissolves the writing on the letter.

As language draws Eurydice to her father, music pulls her husband away from her. She describes a bittersweet sensation:

Orpheus (David Andrew McMahon) attempts to lead Eurydice (Laura Heisler) out of the Underworld. *Eurydice.* **Madison Repertory Theatre, 2003 (courtesy Brent Nicastro).**

> This is what it is to love an artist: The moon is always rising above your house. The houses of your neighbors look dull and lacking in moonlight. But he is always going away from you. Inside his head there's always something more beautiful [385].

This drift is physically staged when Orpheus moves away from Eurydice as he attempts to lead her out of the underworld. It manifests as early as the opening scene in which, on two occasions, Eurydice is disappointed to learn that Orpheus is thinking about music rather than her.

Ruhl carefully keeps music and words separate, except for the newlywed's rendition of "Don't Sit under the Apple Tree (With Anyone Else but Me)." The lyrics of this upbeat song belie the impression of a romantic, harmonious union of word (Eurydice) and music (Orpheus), suggesting as they do a jealous possessiveness. Significantly, the Father appears onstage during this scene, dancing the jitterbug with an invisible partner. Midway through the song, he checks his watch and rushes off (347–8). Ostensibly the most harmonious point in Orpheus and Eurydice's relationship, the shared song stresses the Father's absence.

Ruhl injects an element of camp with this song. Popularized by the Andrews Sisters, it was one of the biggest hits of World War II (Sforza, 66). It plays on the anxieties of soldiers over the faithfulness of their wives and girlfriends back home while at the same time providing great dance music, no matter who the partner. In "Notes on 'Camp'" (1964), Susan Sontag defines camp as valuing style over substance. The camp sensibility is alert to a double meaning of things: "between the thing as meaning something, anything, and the thing as pure artifice" (281). The lyrics of "Don't Sit under the Apple Tree" certainly would have meant something to soldiers abroad, if they had given them some thought, and yet it was the style and delivery of the Andrews Sisters' rendition, with its high energy and close harmony, that made the song so appealing. Sontag contends that the passing of time is likely to increase an object's camp appeal, as "[t]ime liberates the work of art from moral relevance" (285). Divorced from its wartime context, the social significance of the song recedes and style predominates.

Sontag offers camp as a means of "going beyond straight seriousness," as an alternative to irony and satire, which, to her, "seem feeble today" (288). Although it is highly debatable that irony and satire are played out, camp no doubt counters seriousness. Ruhl uses it, in this instance, to create a moment of lightness. As discussed in the introduction to this study, Ruhl admires Calvino's thoughts on lightness, which involve "the subtraction of weight" (Calvino, 3). Yet even as the song removes weight, its lyrics foreshadow Eurydice's impending departure. The element of camp lightens, but it does not nullify the force of gravity. Noting that "all camp objects, and persons, contain a large element of artifice," Sontag claims that "nothing in nature can be campy" (279). Following this line of reasoning, camp aligns with art in the duality art/nature, as offering a respite from nature's final, inescapable act—that of death. Camp enables one to forget that, ultimately, one must forget.

In all other instances in *Eurydice*, music plays without lyrics. In the first scene, the melody that Orpheus tries to teach Eurydice is wordless. Later, Eurydice and her father sing "I've Got Rhythm" on meaningless syllables, as neither can remember the lyrics. Ruhl mutes Orpheus's lamentation even, having him sing without sound (389). Later, after he has lost Eurydice a second time, he confides to her that he was singing her name over and over again (399). He loses her because music cannot name; her father reclaims her because language can. The first thing the Father says upon Eurydice's arrival in the underworld is her name. He makes a point of explaining that, of all his children, he named only her. The letters of her name, falling in the rain, trigger the return of language and memory (365). The Father stakes the original and irrefutable claim to Eurydice as the one who named her and taught her language.[1]

The duality of high/low may be more precisely layered into the four elements of classical Greek cosmology, ordered from high to low as fire, air, water, and earth. Within *Eurydice*, the elements may be loosely mapped to corresponding concepts:

fire: art or the artistic temperament;
air: life;
water: grieving/forgetting; and
earth: death.

The overall movement of the play follows a downward arc from the highest to the lowest of these. Fire, the element of heavenly bodies, is most often associated with Orpheus. He offers to Eurydice "the sky and the stars" (334) and Eurydice associates him with the moon when weighing the merits of being married to an artist. Eurydice's grandmother, also a musician, is associated with fire as well. According to Eurydice's father, she was "extremely animated" and bore the nickname, "Flaming Sally" (375), which suggests a fiery temperament.

Air occupies the stratum below fire. Within the play it represents life through association with the breath. The language of the dead is a practically silent one, one without breath, as described by the Stones (359–60). Voiced language, as singing and speaking, is associated with life. Orpheus attempts to sing (albeit silently) Eurydice back to life and the Father restores memory through the spoken word. Eurydice's fall to the underworld culminates with "sounds of breathing" (356) in the darkness, an indication that she is not yet completely dead. In the passage from Shakespeare read by the father, Lear compares himself and Cordelia, imprisoned, to birds in a cage. Eurydice and her father, also suffer as trapped creatures of the air.

Next down from air is water. The play overflows with references to this element, in the dialogue, sound effects, and set pieces, which include "rusty exposed pipes," a water pump, and the two rivers of Hades (331). In his design for all three Les Waters productions, Scott Bradley extends the metaphor by pumping the elevator full of 100 gallons of water that flood the stage when the door slides open ("Production Notebook," 36). Bradley gives the set the appearance of the bottom of a Victorian-era swimming pool ("Turning the World Upside Down," 5); water drips down the walls to complete the effect (Hurwitt).

Water is frequently associated with grieving in the play. In Orpheus's dream, the water coming out of Eurydice's hair suggests a torrential outpouring of sorrow, and the salty lake into which they fall, a pool of tears (372). Eurydice is drawn to water: she leaves her wedding twice for the water pump, she asks the Nasty Interesting Man for a glass of water, and she requests a bath when she arrives in the underworld. As water is associated with tears and bereavement, her craving for it manifests a compulsion to attend to the unfinished business of mourning for her father.[2] For all of the sorrowful imagery of water, little actual crying occurs. The Stones weep at the sound of Orpheus's music, but with a seemingly generic sadness. Eurydice comes close to crying on several occasions—for example as she crosses the River Styx and when her father escorts her to her room. It is only after her father has dipped himself in the river, and lies still upon the floor, that finally, like a saturated cloud, she releases her watery load.

Ruhl associates water not only with grieving, but also with forgetfulness. Two rivers figure in the classical Greek underworld: The boatman Charon ferries the deceased into Hades across the River Styx, whereafter a dip in the River Lethe erases memory. Ruhl's stage directions call for the inclusion of the River Lethe as "an abstracted River of Forgetfulness" (331), in which both Eurydice and the Father dip themselves as they seek oblivion. The hand-operated water pump from the First Movement doubled as this river in the Les Waters productions. The raining elevator combines the functionality of both rivers, providing passage and erasing memory. Through its association with both the River Styx and grief, water links the transition from life into death with the process of bereavement.

The act of grieving consists, to a great extent, of a repetitious inventory of past events. In a sense, the grieving individual remembers in order to forget: it is necessary to undertake an "obsessive review" in order to release emotion. Eurydice must first reconstitute her memories before she can review them, which she does with the aid of her father. Her final dip in the River of Forgetfulness signals the completion of the act of grieving. The Father performs obsessive review as he deciphers Eurydice's name in the rain, remembering and grieving simultaneously.

Beneath water lies earth, here associated with death. If the overworld is the realm of breath and life, then clearly the underworld is that of, if not suffocation, at least silence, and death. As the Lord of the Underworld's presence or agent in the overworld, the Nasty Interesting Man associates himself with farming and the earth. In the underworld, the Stones are, by definition, of the earth, and the Big Stone links potatoes to dirt and sleep. The Lord/Child reinforces the association between root vegetables, earth, and death when he brags that he grows downward, "like a turnip" (381).

The action of the play flows in a downward arc through the four elements. The image of Eurydice falling from life, associated with air, into grief, associated with water, or into death, associated with earth, occurs three times. In the opening scene, Orpheus fantastically describes Eurydice's hair as an orchestra that will raise her into the sky. He reassures Eurydice that the clouds will become heavy with water and cushion her fall. In this instance Eurydice passes from air through water, by association with the clouds, and back down to earth. Next, Eurydice's death occurs after she ascends the 600 steps to the Nasty Interesting Man's loft, high in the air, only to fall a much farther distance to the underworld beneath the earth. Finally, Orpheus dreams that he and his lover topple from the summit of Mount Olympus, again high in the air, into a salty lake, in a recapitulation of his fantasy from the first scene, in a minor key. Instead of emitting levitating strains of music, associated with fire as they bring Eurydice closer to the heavens, Eurydice's hair pours forth streams of water, and the clouds cut rather than cushion. Orpheus drowns in his grief; he can only dream of arresting Eurydice's death-plunge in a pool of tears. Down below, the Child promises to snuff out air with earth when he takes Eurydice as his bride. He envisions a silent wedding with "a dirt-filled orchestra" (409). Death, through the medium of the earth, extinguishes music, associated with fire, and displaces air, linked to life.

Another significant duality is that of adult/child. Eurydice longs for her father to give her away at her wedding, defining it as the moment at which a father and daughter "stop being married to each other" (345). The absence of her father prevents the successful completion of the ritual and Eurydice's passage into adulthood. The stage directions describe the lovers as both too young and too in love (332). Her death and passage to the underworld function as a regression in which her father parents her as a young child, looking after her, building shelter for her, and teaching her how to speak and write. When her husband comes to reclaim her, she balks at walking down the aisle with him again to assume the responsibilities of adulthood.

The duality of child/adult dovetails into that of life/death, partly through the agency of the Nasty Interesting Man and the Lord of the Underworld. These two characters, if not representing a single entity, are at least strongly linked. Both are to be played by the same actor, and when the Lord of the Underworld claims Eurydice as his bride, stage directions indicate that he is to sound like the Nasty Interesting Man (408). Furthermore, the Nasty Interesting Man demonstrates an uncanny prescience worthy of his counterpart. For example, he seems to know more than he should about the musician-groom, such as his obsession with the music in his head (354). If not the Lord of the Underworld himself, then certainly the Nasty Interesting Man functions as his agent, for he is the means by which Eurydice meets her death.

In the person of the Nasty Interesting Man, Death woos Eurydice as he does Everyman and Everywoman. She resists him briefly, but her tumble down the stairs only brings her closer to his alter ego. As the Child-Lord on his tricycle, he expresses a prurient interest in her, seductively asks her to whisper in his ear, blows in her face, and announces his intention to be her lover. When he returns, he has grown to ten feet tall, still a child but approaching adulthood. He asserts that he is "ready to be

Eurydice (Laura Heisler), her Father (John Lenertz), and the Nasty Interesting Man (Scot Morton). *Eurydice.* **Madison Repertory Theatre, 2003 (courtesy Brent Nicastro).**

Top: The Lord of the Underworld (Scot Morton) welcomes Eurydice (Laura Heisler) to his realm. *Eurydice.* Madison Repertory Theatre, 2003. *Bottom:* The grown-up Lord of the Underworld (Scot Morton) returns to claim Eurydice (Laura Heisler) as his bride, with the Chorus of Stones (left to right: Karlie Nurse, Polly Noonan, and Judy Reiss) in the foreground. *Eurydice.* Madison Repertory Theatre, 2003 (both photographs courtesy Brent Nicastro).

Polly Noonan as Little Stone. *Eurydice.* **Madison Repertory Theatre, 2003 (courtesy Brent Nicastro).**

a man now" (408) and claims her as his bride. The Lord's maturation signals the approach of Eurydice's ultimate end in stillness and quiet; the consummation of their relationship marks the completion of her life. The maturation process eventually and inevitably culminates in death.

The life/death polarity may be expressed as a continuum, along which Orpheus represents the living, Eurydice the newly-dead, her father the recently dead, and the Stones, the contented and long-dead. Meg Neville's costumes in the Les Waters productions at Berkeley Repertory, Yale Repertory, and Second Stage support this placement of the Stones. *San Francisco Chronicle* critic Robert Hurwitt describes them as "zombie-pale" and clothed in "ghostly Edwardian costumes," Charles Isherwood as "Victorian ghouls." Their pale, ghoulish appearance suggests that they are ghosts of the once-living, as supported by the dialogue. When Eurydice threatens to dip them in the river, the Big Stone deflects her with, "Too late, too late" (410), implying that their memories have previously been erased.[3] They strive for quiescence and advocate the nearly silent language of the dead. A parallel may be drawn to the Angel in Tony Kushner's *Angels in America*. In *Part Two: Perestroika*, she commands Prior, the chosen prophet, to "stop moving" (Kushner, 44). She opposes the forward avalanche of human progress.

The Chorus of Stones (left to right: Ramiz Monsef, Gian-Murray Gianino, and Carla Harting). *Eurydice*. Yale Repertory Theatre, 2006 (courtesy Joan Marcus).

Suffering from AIDS, Prior resists. He explains to the Permanent Emergency Council in Heaven:

> We can't just stop. We're not rocks—progress, migration, motion is ... modernity. It's *animate*, it's what living things do [130].
> ...
> I want more life. I can't help myself. I do [133].

Eurydice and her father as well want more life, and resist the Stones in their effort to claim it.

Another crucial duality is that of art and nature. Ruhl portrays the temporary and ultimately futile domination of nature by art through watery imagery, which is not restricted to the underworld with its two rivers, but occurs frequently in the dialogue of the overworld as well. As early as the second line of the play, Orpheus is offering Eurydice the sea, and by scene's end they are running into it. Water images fall into two categories: natural and channeled. The natural includes the sea, clouds, lakes, and rivers; channeled, the water pump, various sound effects such as a whistling tea kettle and water running through rusty pipes, and Orpheus's shower at his wedding. Natural water represents nature; channeled water, in the form of plumbing, the triumph of art over nature.

As the father traces his steps back to the River of Forgetfulness, place designations follow a progression from art, in the sense of human culture in general, to nature, and also from language to forgetfulness. He leads with the abstract mathematics of numbered highways, then transitions through the ambiguously geometric Middle Road on his way to the definitely pastoral Duck Creek Park, harkening back to his father's hunting exploits and demise in a duck pond, in a farewell nod to his parents. After the bucolic Fernwood Avenue and Forest Road, the streets no longer have names, as the father's capacity for naming diminishes. He passes through a red brick house, presumably his childhood home, and out to the Mississippi River.[4] He observes through a child's eyes a good climbing tree and sleeping catfish, rolls up his jeans, and steps into the river and oblivion. He lies now curled up on the ground, unresponsive to his daughter (402). Man has become child, nature has overcome art, oblivion has washed away memory, and death has taken life.

The raining elevator represents the inseparability of art and nature. The mechanical device carries the deceased to the underworld, which serves as a waystation on the journey to ultimate death. Inside of this device, nature flows as rain that erodes the structures of memory. The elevator follows the general direction of the entire work, which is downwards. It represents the movement from the first to the second term of many dualities: life/death,

I. Navigating Sorrow in Eurydice 31

Father (John Lenertz) and Eurydice (Laura Heisler). *Eurydice.* **Madison Repertory Theatre, 2003 (courtesy Brent Nicastro).**

high/low, lightness/heaviness, and memory/forgetfulness. Other dualities align with that of life/death as well: artist (fire)/farmer (dirt), child/adult, husband/father, and art/nature. Gravity pulls Eurydice down towards death, away from her artist husband and towards the Lord of the Underworld/Nasty Interesting Man who is associated with dirt and farming, and towards her father who is, after all, already dead. A loss of memory accompanies her fall, and the maturation of the Lord of the Underworld associates aging with death. Water, as a force of nature, overcomes the art of plumbing, just as death overcomes the individual personality that has been built up through the art of language.

Not only memory, but time as well depends upon language. Death is a timeless state, and the father only reclaims temporality when he reads Eurydice's name in the rain and reacquires language. Then, he claims, "Time poured into my head. The days of the week. Hours, months..." (365). Later, a temporal compression accompanies the collapse of language as the play concludes. A triangular relationship established by Eurydice in her farewell letter, between herself and Orpheus and his future wife, disappears almost as soon as it arises. After writing, Eurydice dips herself in the river and lies dormant. Almost instantly, Orpheus appears in the elevator, the remainder

At the conclusion of the play, Orpheus (Joseph Parks) arrives in the raining elevator as Eurydice (Maria Dizzia) and Father (Charles Shaw Robinson) lie on their sides. The Chorus of Stones stands to the left. *Eurydice*. Yale Repertory Theatre, 2006 (courtesy Joan Marcus).

of his life compressed into a matter of minutes. The architecture of time rests upon that of language.

Searching the World Over: The Psychology of Loss

Through her firsthand experience, Ruhl has captured many of the psychological aspects of bereavement. In *Bereavement and Health: The Psychological and Physical Consequences of Partner Loss* (1987), Wolfgang Stroebe and Margaret S. Stroebe differentiate between grief, mourning, and bereavement: Grief is "the emotional (and affective) response to loss," mourning is "acts expressive of grief," and bereavement is "the objective situation of an individual who has recently experienced a loss of someone significant through that person's death" (7). Simply put, mourning is the outward expression of grief.

Sigmund Freud pioneered the study of grieving. In "Mourning and Melancholia" (1917), he describes mourning (which would now be referred to as grieving) as the process by which the "libido shall be withdrawn from its attachments to that object" (244), "that object" here referring to the lost love object. John Archer explicates Freud's essay in *The Nature of Grief: The Evolution and Psychology of Reactions to Loss* (1999). Archer reads "libido" as "emotional attachment," and thus interprets the work of mourning as the painful withdrawal of this attachment (16). He asserts that the psychoanalytic framework established by Freud remains influential (17).

Nevertheless, since Freud many advances have been made in the psychology of grief, and numerous models developed. Archer identifies John Bowlby's model, which divides bereavement into four phases, as a widely accepted one. He presents these phases, set forth in Bowlby's *Attachment and Loss, Volume III* (1980), in slightly modified form as:

1. Numbness and Disbelief: A phase of numbness that may be interrupted by outbursts of distress and/or anger.
2. Yearning and Searching: Accompanied by anxiety and intermittent periods of anger....
3. Disorganization and Despair: Feelings of depression and apathy when old patterns have been discarded.
4. Reorganization: Recovery from bereavement [Archer 24].

Bowlby cautions that the phases "are not clear-cut, and any one individual may oscillate for a time back and forth between any two of them" (Bowlby, 85). Archer also describes the non-phasic analytic model, which identifies aspects of grief such as numbness and disbelief; anger and aggression; guilt, self-blame and self-injury; distress and anxiety, yearning and preoccupation; delusions, hallucinations and ghosts; the urge to search; identification with the deceased; changes in self-concept; and hopelessness and depression (see Archer, Chapter 5).

These two models overlap to a great extent. Traditionally, and in accordance with Freud, both attempt a recovery of the bereaved individual through the withdrawal of emotional attachment. More recently, researchers are coming to the conclusion that it is normal for this attachment to persist, and that the process should be one of ongoing adjustment rather than recovery, as reported by Wortman and Silver in "The Myths of Coping with Loss Revisited" (418), published in 2001. Nevertheless, a reorganization of the survivor's psyche is considered essential. The three main characters in *Eurydice* pass through, to varying degrees, the first three of Bowlby's phases, and also exhibit various symptoms from the analytic model. Here, however, death forecloses the possibility of working through the fourth phase. The process of bereavement, termed "grief work" (Archer, 16), fails to result in recovery or adjustment.

Eurydice's wedding triggers the grieving process for both herself and her father. Archer notes that significant events may reawaken feelings associated with bereavement (81). Eurydice notes the importance of her father to the wedding ceremony (345). She enters the first phase of grieving, "numbness and disbelief," upon her arrival in the underworld. Disoriented, she believes she has disembarked at a train station in France. She also exhibits the outbursts of distress and anger typical of this phase. Upon discovering that she is unable to speak, she throws a tantrum that will not be her last (359). During the grieving process, anger is frequently directed at those seen as responsible for the loss or "people who bring home its reality" (Archer, 71) such as, in Eurydice's case, the Stones. Indeed, the first scene of the second movement ends with another outburst, directed at the Stones (366). Her third tantrum occurs when, frustrated at her inability to read the *Collected Works of Shakespeare*, Eurydice hurls the volume at the Stones. Her fourth and final outburst takes place when she returns to the underworld and discovers that her father has dipped himself into the river. She screams at the Stones and strikes at them in vain (407).

Eurydice's time with her father falls under the second stage, "yearning and searching." Preoccupation with the deceased is significant during this phase, which includes "obsessive review" of both happy and unhappy memories. The grieving individual may feel the need to repeatedly talk about past events (Archer, 76–7). The obsessive review shared by father and daughter involves memories from the father's youth, which, although they predate Eurydice's birth, nevertheless reconstruct the family history. Although ostensibly humorous, the father's childhood memories are filled with foreboding. He is shot at with a BB gun and spanked by his mother and a stranger. His father dies and his mother never recovers from the loss. He abandons the piano after his mother humiliates him at a recital for forgetting how to play "I've Got Rhythm" (378).

Although she shares in obsessive review with her father, Eurydice fails to do so with her husband. When Eurydice finally remembers Orpheus to her father, it is in a wistful and ambiguous way. She does not mourn Orpheus, from whom she has been separated not by his death, but by her own. For his part, Orpheus most certainly mourns his bride, demonstrating primarily the second phase, that of yearning and searching. He exhibits characteristic behaviors of this stage, include writing letters to the deceased, the recovery of the lost person in dreams, and the urge to search (Archer, 76–7). Dreams of the deceased, although often happy, typically contain an indication that something is amiss and the dreamer often awakes to an empty feeling (86–7).

I. Navigating Sorrow in Eurydice

In "The Course of Normal Grief" (1993), Shuchter and Zisook report that, in one common dream, the deceased is alive and fulfilling the survivor's ultimate wish (36).

Orpheus's dream of Eurydice follows the patterns described above. It begins happily enough with the deceased quite possibly fulfilling the survivor's ultimate wish, as they begin to make love on Mount Olympus. However, Orpheus quickly notices that something is awry when water begins pouring out of Eurydice's hair. The dream takes a turn for the worse when they fall out of the sky. He awakens disoriented, sorrowful, and frightened. Awake, Orpheus experiences the numbness and sense of unreality characteristic of the first stage. The room begins to float, his blankets assume a menacing aspect, and he questions what people are and who he is (372). In this moment, Orpheus struggles to come to terms with the very notion that Eurydice is no longer living.

However, Orpheus's grieving mostly manifests as the urge to search, or seeking and finding. In "'Seeking' and 'Finding' a Lost Object: Evidence from Recent Studies of the Reaction to Bereavement" (1970), C. Murray Parkes documents a strong desire to find the deceased, in spite of the recognition that the search is futile. This behavior consists of the following:

1. Restless movement about and scanning of the environment.
2. Preoccupation with thoughts of the lost person.
3. Developing a perceptual "set" for the person, namely a disposition to perceive and to pay attention to stimuli which suggest the presence of the person and to ignore those that are not relevant to this aim.
4. Directing attention towards those parts of the environment in which the person is likely to be.
5. Calling for the lost person [189].

Orpheus's behavior coincides with this list. He is certainly preoccupied with Eurydice. He moves about and scans the environment for her, or for a way to reach her. He vows in a letter, "I'm going to find you" (368) and sees her in his dream. He calls for the lost person, literally, over the telephone. When this fails, he immediately turns to the globe and a "scanning of the environment."

As a mythical being, Orpheus takes "seeking and finding" farther than any actual person possibly could. However, his reunion with Eurydice, as staged by Ruhl, does not differ in essence from the experience of the bereaved of Parkes's study. The third item listed above involves "developing a perceptual set for the person," which may predispose the bereaved to hallucinate that person's presence. In a study cited by Parkes, "9/22 widows described actual illusions of the lost person at some time during the first month of bereavement" (191). More commonly, "A comforting sense of the presence of the lost person was experienced by 15/22 widows." A few of the widows in the study were convinced that they perceived the deceased in a state of what Parkes terms "hypnagogic hallucinations" (194). Other studies chronicle sensations and visions of the deceased as common occurrences (Archer, 79). Parkes asserts, "It almost seems that for these people the search has been successful" (194). The myth of Orpheus depicts this archetypal phenomenon.

Although Orpheus finds Eurydice, he is unable to keep her. Like the psychological subjects, Orpheus momentarily reclaims the deceased only to acutely reexperience losing her. Although Orpheus only finds and loses Eurydice once, in actuality "seeking and finding" parallels obsessive review in that the lost object must be repeatedly found and lost.[5] One widow's experience uncannily matches Orpheus's final moment with Eurydice. This woman repeatedly gazed over her right shoulder, claiming, "He [my husband] was always on my right" (qtd. in Parkes, 190). Presumably, when she looked, he "disappeared."

The process of grieving is abruptly cut off at the conclusion of the play. Both the father and Eurydice have symbolically returned to their childhood homes, Eurydice by rejoining her father and the father by revisiting the Mississippi, but in the end they lie silently on the ground. The mourning process detailed above has failed to reach the fourth stage, that of reorganization, which represents recovery from bereavement. None of the characters has detached from the original love-object; the disorganization of phase three has simply lead to disintegration.

A Wistful Desire

As noted above, Charles Isherwood relates *Eurydice*, with its theme of loss, to the events of September 11, 2001. Although such a grandiose claim may seem misdirected against such an intimately personal play, the Western tone to the father's memories suggests a nostalgia not just for him and his daughter, but for the country as a whole. Seen against the wider canvas of post-9/11 America, the invocation of the West suggests a nationalistic remembering. Ruhl did not, however, implant those stories with the destruction of the World Trade Center in mind; indeed, the play was completed before the attacks occurred. Rather, the duck hunting and Western stories derive from her family history. In "Surreal Life: The Plays of Sarah Ruhl" (2008), John Lahr reveals the source of Eurydice's vocabulary lessons: every Saturday, from the time that Ruhl was five years old, her father took her and her sister to breakfast at the Walker Bros. Original Pancake House and "taught them a new word, along with its etymology" (Lahr, "Surreal"). Ruhl confirms that all of the stories told by the Father, even the one in which he swallows a nail, come from her own father's experience. One of the duck hunting stories is taken directly from a transcript recorded by Ruhl before her father passed away (Ruhl, "Re: Eurydice").

The play commemorates not only Ruhl's father but her grandparents as well, through the stories told about them and asynchronous elements dating back to the 1930s. Orpheus and Eurydice first appear in swimming outfits from the 1950s. Orpheus consults "an old-fashioned glow-in-the-dark globe" (321). Eurydice arrives in the underworld in a 1930s suit (359), and her imagined train station suggests the past as does the stage direction that describes her departure from her father, involving as it does a gangplank and steamship (394). These elements suggest three generations of family history. An earlier version included Eurydice's grandmother, who silently crossed the stage from time to time, memory erased. Although her presence had the potential to deepen the sense of family history, Ruhl dropped her when director Les Waters complained that he did not understand the character (*A Conversation*). Eurydice and her father's remembering qualifies as nostalgia, defined as:

> A wistful desire to return in thought or in fact to a former time in one's life, to one's home or homeland, or to one's family and friends; a sentimental yearning for the happiness of a former place or time ["Nostalgia"].

This definition shares, with Archer's description of obsessive review, the desire to revisit memories of happier times. Bereavement may thus be posited as inclusive of a nostalgia for the deceased.

Eurydice belongs to a troika of Ruhl's plays that deal directly with death and bereavement. They are, in chronological order, *Dog Play*, *Eurydice*, and *The Clean House*. Ruhl has subtracted progressively more weight from the latter two. The first depicts the aftermath of a father's death and questions the existence of an afterlife, the second works out a process of bereavement in an imaginary hereafter, and the third exorcises the ghosts of deceased parents and suggests a positive spirit world. The dominant tone of the first is one of loss and despair, that of the second, loving sorrow, and of the third, hopefulness in the face of death. *Melancholy Play* is omitted from this group because it deals with sorrow in a generalized rather than specific sense. *Dead Man's Cell Phone* escapes this category as well, in spite of the inclusion of an afterlife, since the farcical tone and unsavory personality of the deceased obviates any need for bereavement. Whereas Eurydice grieves alone, in *The Clean House* Ruhl provides a community of women to share the burden of caring for, and seeing off, the terminally ill Ana.

II

Joke as Incantation in *The Clean House*

The Fourth Stage of Grieving

Currents of desire shift direction in *The Clean House* as a man leaves his wife for a mistress whose terminal illness he must then confront. Nevertheless, Ruhl approaches death with a somewhat lighter touch in *The Clean House* than in *Eurydice*. She employs magic realist techniques that heighten the sense of whimsy and concludes the latter in hopeful mirth rather than devastating silence. In a world in which jokes can kill, Matilde euthanizes the terminally ill Ana, then recalls the comical circumstances of her own birth and envisions heaven as a place where "everyone is laughing" (109). Currents of compassion draw a nurturing community of women together around the ailing Ana. Although the play contains its share of grief, the final effect is one of lightness and release. As a playwright, Ruhl has advanced from the third phase of bereavement to the fourth, from despair into adjustment and even acceptance.

In *The Clean House*, a young woman, Matilde, has immigrated from Brazil to the United States after her parents die and is working as a live-in housekeeper to married doctors, Lane and Charles. Unfortunately, Matilde hates to clean. Unbeknownst to Lane, her sister, Virginia, comes to Matilde's aid and cleans the house. In the meantime, Charles has fallen in love with a patient, Ana, on whom he has performed a mastectomy. Charles and Ana come to Lane's house, asking for forgiveness while claiming that they are faultless since they have discovered each other as soul mates. At approximately the same time, Lane discovers that her sister has been cleaning her house and threatens to fire Matilde. When Ana hears about this, she offers

Matilde a job; Lane resists, and as a result, Matilde ends up splitting her time between the two households. When Ana's cancer recurs, she refuses further medical treatment. Charles flies off to Alaska in search of a natural, plant-based remedy, leaving the women to nurse Ana.

Matilde's parents continuously amused one another and were, she claims, "the funniest people in Brazil" (13). Indeed, the last joke her father told her mother was so funny that it killed her; he committed suicide soon after. Ruhl stipulates that the actors playing Charles and Ana should double as Matilde's parents, who appear in flashbacks. When Matilde thinks up the perfect and fatal joke, she honors Ana's request to perform euthanasia on her. In the stage directions, Ruhl describes Matilde's journey as one "from the dead to the living and back again" (8). Matilde wears black to signify that she is in mourning (11), and her search for, and implementation of, the perfect, deadly joke, signifies bereavement and succession. Through character doubling, Matilde symbolically rectifies her mother's murder as an act of mercy rather than an accident. Matilde acquires and puts to proper use the power that her father possessed but was unable to control. The perfect joke thus functions as an incantation might in a shamanic ritual, as a means of gathering and focusing otherworldly power.

Ruhl employs a variety of magic realist techniques such as the literalization of metaphor, mirroring, the metaphorization of space, the normalization of the fantastic, and the employment of an impartial narrator-figure. As a literary term, magic realism was first applied in the middle of the 20th century to South American authors who wrote from a presumably magical continent. As a postcolonial strategy, the magical in magic realism challenges European rationalism, offering up an alternative, and equally legitimate, worldview. Like the magic realist, the shaman travels from the ordinary to the fantastic and back again, experiencing both ordinary life and a magical realm of spirits. Shamanism connects the visible to the invisible, the real to the magical, logos to mythos. The magic realist style of the play supports a shamanistic interpretation of Matilde's joke.

Joke theory is relevant to this analysis as well. Philosophers have been contemplating humor at least as far back as Plato. Freud addressed the subject in *Jokes and Their Relation to the Unconscious* (1905), in which he draws parallels between the production of jokes and that of dreams. Since Freud, analysts from various disciplines have advanced numerous theories of jokes and humor. Of particular interest are those of semioticians, who posit that the necessary and sufficient condition for verbal humor is the coexistence of two semiotic frames arising out of a single statement, the juxtaposition of which creates the humorous effect. In *Semantic Mechanisms of Humor* (1985), Victor Raskin characterizes the requisite relationship between the frames as

Matilde (Zilah Mendoza) cleans a lampshade. *The Clean House*. Yale Repertory Theatre, 2004 (courtesy Joan Marcus).

real versus unreal, further breaking this down into actual versus non-actual, normal versus abnormal, and possible versus impossible (111). The witness to a joke must undergo a conceptual shift in order to appreciate its humor. This shift between the real and the unreal resembles that imposed on the reader by magic realism. In *The Clean House*, the joke functions on multiple levels: it generates a frame shift in the semantic sense; and in the shamanistic, metaphysical sense, it initiates an ontological shift, causing the recipient to pass, even, from life into death. Paula Vogel combines themes of humor and death in *The Baltimore Waltz* and indeed the influence of Ruhl's mentor's play may be traced through *The Clean House*, as will be shown below.

Doctors and Housekeepers

An overheard conversation provided the idea for *The Clean House*. Attending a party for doctors with her husband, who is himself a psychiatrist, Ruhl overheard a woman complaining that her Brazilian maid refused to clean,

Left to right: Virginia (Sarah Marshall), Lane (Naomi Jacobson), Charles (Mitchell Hébert), Ana (Franca Barchiesi), and Matilde (Guenia Lemos). *The Clean House*. Woolly Mammoth Theatre Company, 2005 (photograph by Stan Barouh; courtesy Woolly Mammoth).

even after she had had her medicated. The woman's attitude angered Ruhl and the anecdote prompted her to think about social class and cleaning, and the implications of the upper classes being removed from the tasks of everyday living (Weckwerth, 31–2). The story became the opening monologue of the play (Simonson), following Matilde's joke. The shift in Ruhl's concern from the political to the personal manifests in the course taken by the play, which begins with the provocative monologue but then quickly moves into an examination of the relationships between four women. Although they come from varying socioeconomic backgrounds, ultimately their similarities overcome their differences.

Ruhl's family history figures significantly in *The Clean House* as it does in *Eurydice*. Ruhl eulogizes her father in the latter. In the former, Ana's struggle resembles that of Ruhl's father, who succumbed to cancer after a two-year battle ("Playwright Sarah Ruhl"). Breast cancer proved fatal to both of the playwright's grandmothers, as it does to Ana. Ruhl credits the sense of humor in the play to her father (Pressley). In an interview with Pamela Renner, she claims that he cracked jokes up until the end, and this enabled him and his family to distance themselves from the suffering (50). The sibling rivalry between Lane and Virginia may be traced to that between Ruhl and her older sister Kate. The play is dedicated to her husband Tony and her sister, both of whom are doctors, as are uncles and a grandfather (Snyder).

Ruhl was awarded the 2003–2004 Susan Smith Blackburn Prize ($10,000) for *The Clean House* before it was ever produced (Boehm). The award recognizes outstanding playwriting by a woman in the English language (*Susan Smith Blackburn Prize*). Blair Brown, who played the role of Lane in the Lincoln Center production, happened to be one of the Blackburn judges that year. She recounts the unique experience of appraising the play, which prompted her to first laugh, and then cry, and then laugh some more, etc. She later discovered that all of the readers had the same experience. She characterizes the "deceptively simple" play as having the effect of "water running over your hand," one that is both subtle and powerful. She observes that, in performance, she and the other actors never knew when the laughs would come and indeed, at times someone in the audience would be crying while another was laughing. Her observation that the playwright does not cue an expected audience response indicates that surprising shifts take place, changes consistent with magic realism, to which she refers, and to frame shifting as activated by jokes, as will be explored below (*A Conversation*).

The play was also a 2005 Pulitzer Prize finalist (*Pulitzer Prize*). The first act was commissioned by the McCarter Theatre Center in Princeton, New Jersey, in 2000. In its full-length form, it premiered in September 2004 at Yale Repertory Theatre under the direction of Bill Rauch (Ruhl, "Clean House," 4). It has been a regional theater favorite, appearing during the 2005 to 2006 season alone in at least ten venues, including seven productions in the United States, four in Canada, and one in England (Hartman). It finally landed in the Mitzi Newhouse Theatre at Lincoln Center for its New York premiere in October 2006 (Simonson; Ruhl, "Clean House," 6). According to Ruhl, its relatively late appearance in New York was due not to a lack of interest, but rather to insufficient stage height: of the theaters that approached her, only Lincoln Center could accommodate the balcony so crucial to the play's second act, and that venue was booked two years in advance (Cox).

Waltzing and Cleaning

In "*The Baltimore Waltz* and the Plays of My Childhood," included in the collection *The Play That Changed My Life* (2009), Ruhl illuminates her early dramatic influences. As the title of the essay indicates, Paula Vogel's work was primary in this regard. The production to which she refers was a student one at Brown University, which Ruhl saw at the age of 19 during the time that her father was dying of cancer, accompanied by a friend who had lost her own father to AIDS in the 1980s. The performance devastated both of them. Ruhl lists lessons she may have learned unconsciously that evening, brought to consciousness once she became Vogel's student. Foremost among them is the recognition that Vogel "created a modern architecture for grief," a structure that exposed grief while providing distance from it. Furthermore, she employed lightness in the sense of laughing at the horrible. She ignored the fourth wall, and seamlessly transitioned between modes and styles. She demonstrated both the comforting and alienating aspects of language. She conceptualized theater as "a place for memory, and for ghosts," and defamiliarized the familiar, after the Russian Formalist Victor Shklovsky. She provided a ritual response to death within a culture badly in need of one. She taught Ruhl that theater could give the audience a place to mourn (121–3).

Although the effect of these lessons is apparent throughout Ruhl's work, *The Clean House* owes the greatest debt directly to *The Baltimore Waltz*. In Vogel's play, which premiered in 1992, she imagines a trip she might have taken to Europe at her brother Carl's invitation, but which, in real life, she declined, unaware that he was HIV-positive. The invitation came in 1986; Carl passed away in 1988 (Vogel, "Baltimore Waltz," 4). Vogel's play appears to have influenced *The Clean House* not just in sweeping dramaturgical terms, but also in its specific details. Vogel's characters vacation in an imaginary Europe (Vogel, "Baltimore Waltz," 4); Ruhl's inhabit a "metaphysical Connecticut" (Ruhl, "Clean House," 7). Vogel has christened her alter ego Anna after the love interest in *The Third Man*, a film that her play spoofs. Ruhl utilizes the same name, with a Latinized spelling, for her Argentinian Ana.[1] In both works, siblings with a two-year age difference engage in moments of intense rivalry (Vogel, "Baltimore Waltz," 17; Ruhl, "Clean House," 30). Both playwrights overlap locations: in Ruhl, Ana's balcony overlooks Lane's living room; in Vogel, Carl dispassionately analyzes a painting in the Louvre as his sister makes love to a French waiter in their hotel room (Vogel, "Baltimore Waltz," 22–3).

Both plays include references to foreign language, film, and dancing. Ruhl opens with a joke in Portuguese, and Matilde and Ana converse in a mélange of Portuguese, Spanish, and English as they sort apples on the balcony. Linguistic and cultural markers isolate Matilde from the American characters while binding her with the other Latina, Ana. In Vogel, Anna attempts basic travel phrases whereas Carl speaks six European languages fluently (7). In terms of film, Vogel spoofs *The Third Man* (1949) while basing her imaginary Europe upon Hollywood cliché (6), and signaling Carl's homosexuality through a furtive exchange of stuffed rabbits with the mysterious Third Man. In *The Clean House*, when her husband invites her to go apple picking with him and his lover, a distraught Lane lambastes him by referring to an *arrangement* in a foreign film (68). She perhaps alludes to the West German film *The Perfect Arrangement*, released in 1971 with the tagline, "The Triangle That Worked out ... Almost" ("The Perfect Arrangement")! As with film, dance assumes greater significance in Vogel than in Ruhl. It serves as the primary metaphor in *The Baltimore Waltz*, as the siblings' trip is framed as an imaginary waltz through Europe. The grotesque dance between Anna and a stiff Carl is followed by an elegant and graceful reprise of loving remembrance. In *The Clean House*, Matilde's parents dance ineptly, inebriated with laughter.

Both works exhibit a distrust of modern medicine. Vogel infects Anna with ATD, or Acquired Toilet Disease, a fictional ailment contracted by sharing the toilet with elementary school students (11). Her doctor's admission that there is no cure and his ridiculous suggestions to avoid spreading the disease lampoon the medical profession's helplessness in the face of AIDS at the time, as well as superstitious fears about its transmission. Modern medicine also proves insufficient in Ruhl. Distrustful of doctors and hospitals in general, Ana declines treatment when her cancer recurs.

Both plays confront death with humor. In the "Playwright's Note" to *The Baltimore Waltz*, Vogel has published a letter from Carl in which he details his last wishes, laced with black humor. A similar sense of humor colors *The Baltimore Waltz*. It lightens the pathos as the brother's health declines, and takes the form of the grotesque when the quack doctor guzzles Anna's urine (51–4) and when Anna waltzes with a stiff, corpse-like Carl (55–6). Ruhl's father's jokes, like Carl's, benefited everyone concerned. Ruhl relates that they put the people around him at ease and demonstrated a heroism and selflessness ("Playwright Sarah Ruhl"), qualities also to be found in Ruhl's Ana. Although the influence of Vogel's play on *The Clean House* runs deep, Ruhl's work nevertheless stands independently as the unique expression of her own creative voice. Ruhl has fully absorbed her mentor's teachings and made them her own.

"Like Water Running Over Your Hand"

In addition to death and humor, significant themes of *The Clean House* include cleaning, community, and rationality versus emotion. Ruhl intends cleaning to assume a spiritual, cleansing dimension as the play advances into

Matilde (Guenia Lemos, left) and Lane (Naomi Jacobson, right). *The Clean House.* Woolly Mammoth Theatre Company, 2005 (photograph by Stan Barouh; courtesy Woolly Mammoth).

the second act (Wren, 146). In an interview with Pamela Renner, Ruhl remembers a workshop at Brown University with a member of the theater collective DAH from Belgrade, during which it was considered essential to mop the stage beforehand. Ruhl attributes the act of cleaning with the power to imbue both sacred and secular spaces with a spiritual quality. She includes theatrical space in this discussion as both sacred and profane (Renner, 50). Through cleaning, Ruhl also explores class issues and what it means "to be alienated from your own dirt" (qtd. in Weckwerth, 32).

The immigrant Matilde hates her job, and this presents a problem for Lane, who wants her house to be cleaned with minimal supervision on her part. She balks at giving orders to her unmotivated employee; early in the play, she practically begs her to clean the bathroom. Eventually, seeing that Lane is on the verge of tears, Matilde coaches her to order her as if she were a nurse (12). When Lane finally does, Matilde starts polishing silver, a task that she abandons the instant Lane leaves the room (14). Later, when Lane comes home from work to find Matilde sitting in the dark, Matilde insinuates that she has disturbed her concentration and caused her to forget the joke that she was thinking up. Matilde brings their discussion to a close by pretending that she will clean up before she goes to bed, but then turns out the light to sit in the dark (32–3). Matilde throws away her antidepressants (23). She plays the comic, high-status servant rather than the obedient domestic. However, her genuine compassion belies the role, and she comforts Lane when she has trouble supervising her, and again when her husband leaves her.

Lane prefers to maintain class barriers, essentially telling Matilde and Virginia that she would rather not get to know the help too well (13, 45). Lane overlooks Matilde's dislike of cleaning and discounts her emotional life. When Matilde confesses that she is mourning her parents, Lane stresses that cleaning supersedes personal concerns (13). She expresses surprise when Virginia reveals that Matilde, rather than being depressed, simply does not like to clean (42). The intimate nature of their economic relationship only intensifies Lane's discomfort—after all, Matilde literally handles her dirty laundry. Lane attempts to keep Matilde at arm's length even as she grants her access to her underwear drawer.

As much as Matilde hates to clean, Virginia loves to. She enjoys cleaning her own home because, she claims, it both clears her head and makes her feel clean (18–9). She offers to clean her sister's house because it gives her purpose. Another theme of the play is the attainment of a sense of purpose through appropriate employment. As opposed to Matilde, who would much rather be creating jokes, Virginia derives great pleasure and a sense of accomplishment from cleaning, exulting in the satisfaction of transforming a toilet from a dirty to a clean state (23). Virginia's obsession with cleanliness stems from an impulse to impose order on the world. Her rationalization for not wanting children belies a great fear of losing control: she imagines beautiful children growing up in an ugly world, ultimately left naked in the road, raped and dying, while indifferent strangers pass by (21–2). Her household belongings function as surrogate children, ones that rest safely in their place as she tucks in the silverware (21). She finishes cleaning her own house by mid-afternoon, and this ritual gives meaning to her life. She half-jokingly credits cleaning with preventing suicide, which might tempt her if her days were free (10). Cleaning grants her a shred of meaning in a life that has "gone downhill" since she reached the age of 22 (22). Unlike Matilde, for whom cleaning is a necessary burden, through it Virginia escapes the curse of abundant leisure time.

In the second act, cleaning assumes a spiritual dimension that is not, however, manifested on the physical plane. On the contrary, the pristine, white living room that contains Lane's ordered, controlled life is incrementally sullied by apple cores, exploding yellow spice, potting soil, and finally Ana's wasted body. Lane only realizes compassion for Ana once she has surrendered to filth. She shouts her newfound affinity for dirt at her sister, wishing her house to be filled with "shitty" cows and dirty, unmatched socks (82). Lane only humbles herself to pay a house call on Ana once her environment reflects her inner turmoil. Through externalizing her pain, she is eventually able to release it and arrive at a state of compassion.

Virginia exuberantly lets go as she contributes to the mess in her sister's living room. After Lane vehemently prohibits her from cleaning anymore, she creates a gigantic mess (84). Making a mess purges pent-up emotion and frees Virginia from her compulsion to clean. Ultimately, the acceptance of chaos and disorder leads to the acceptance of Ana's death. Early in the play, Virginia envisions hospitals as places for storing the waste of dead bodies (10). When Ana's body finally comes to rest in Lane's living room, the ambiance is that of a temple rather than a hospital. The women close Ana's eyes, wash her body, and say a prayer (106–9). Virginia herself weeps her farewell (105). Her acceptance of her own lack of control has facilitated a profound attitudinal shift.

The characters gather around Ana's body as a community. In the first act, Ruhl establishes the isolation of each of the characters. Lane rarely sees her husband and imagines him tied up in surgery all day. She explains to Matilde that they used to keep in touch throughout the day with their beepers, a practice they abandoned as they began to take their relationship for granted (32–3). They have become so disconnected that she is oblivious to his affair, which is a price she pays for not doing her own laundry—she has missed Ana's brightly colored panties cohabiting with her husband's socks. Matilde is isolated in a foreign country, both of her parents recently deceased. More than Matilde, even, Virginia expresses the loneliness and isolation of modern existence. Without employment or community, her life lacks purpose. She considers her husband on par with a piece of furniture, one that should be functional but not too beautiful (25). Although Virginia meets with her sister over coffee, Lane forestalls an attempt to get together for dinner (31). Virginia's relationship with her sister fails to satisfy her social needs.

Only with Matilde is Virginia able to create some sort of meaningful bond. They spend time together as Virginia cleans. Desperate for anyone to talk to, Virginia immediately shares intimate details about her personal life. They chat about the structure of jokes and imagine the details of Charles's suspected affair. Faced with having Matilde hired away from Lane in the second act, Virginia imagines her as a sister during an older time when women gathered in the square to chat and wash clothes. She laments, "Now we are all alone in our separate houses and it is terrible" (65). Lane longs for a simpler, more communal lifestyle.

Another theme is that of head versus heart, or rationality versus emotion and intuition. This theme plays out in the love triangle between Charles, Lane,

Virginia (Sarah Marshall, left) and Matilde (Guenia Lemos, right). *The Clean House.* **Woolly Mammoth Theatre Company, 2005 (photograph by Stan Barouh; courtesy Woolly Mammoth).**

and Ana. Charles and Lane describe their marriage as built on rationality. They fall in love in anatomy class under distinctly unromantic circumstances, over a cadaver (93). Although Charles and Ana also meet within the medical establishment, their relationship quickly takes an emotional, even irrational turn. They fall in love and "kiss wildly" within a few lines of setting a date for surgery (55), and conceive of themselves as *basherts*, or soulmates. Curiously, Charles expresses this metaphysical dimension in a tone of scientific objectivity, as if it were genetically predetermined (61–2). Charles justifies the disruption of his marriage by ascribing the certainty of the empirical to that which is intangible.

Charles delineates a particular kind of logical justice that brought him and Lane together, as a sort of reward for good behavior (53). For her part, Lane is able to quantify the reasons that Charles should be in love with her as though on a resume (40). Theirs is a marriage based on intellect and respect; in contrast, Charles's affair with Ana stems from a passion rooted in the metaphysical. The whirlwind affair of the heart destroys the respectable marriage of minds. Ultimately, however, with Ana's passing, Lane implicitly reclaims her husband. Ana predicts that she will take care of him because she still loves him (104–5), and Lane tenderly kisses Charles on the forehead when he delivers the tree (108). Rather than a reuniting of minds, however, this plays as an act of compassion and forgiveness. Not only humor, then, but compassion as well tempers the impact of Ana's death, one that the cold logic of medical science is unable to prevent.

The title of the play suggests the term "clean room," which is an environment in which dust and other airborne contaminants are reduced to a minimum to facilitate the production of delicate equipment or the "manipulation of biological materials" ("Clean Room"). A synonym for "clean room" is "white room," and this term seems to have inspired the color scheme of Lane's living room as indicated by the stage directions (8). The sterile setting represents an extreme attempt to maintain control over both the physical and emotional environment at the expense of comfort. The title also suggests that a house is not necessarily a home; only after the whiteness of Charles and Lane's dwelling is sullied does it become one.

Magic Realism

German art critic and historian Franz Roh introduced the term magic realism in 1925 to characterize a Post-Expressionistic style of painting (Zamora and Faris, 15). In 1949, Cuban novelist Alejo Carpentier referred to Roh as he formulated his concept of *lo real maravilloso americano* or "marvelous American reality" (75). Carpentier argues that Latin America is a land of the marvelous, with its dramatic terrain of jungles and mountains, and the miraculous, supported by the people's faith in the supernatural. He accuses the European surrealists of artificially manufacturing the marvelous, claiming that the American artist may draw inspiration directly from his environment (Carpentier, 85–7).[2] The term magic realism first achieved common usage during the 1960s boom in Latin American literature, but has since been applied to fiction from across the globe, particularly within postcolonial contexts.[3]

Within a colonial or postcolonial context, the "realism" in magic realism refers to the world as perceived through a European, rationalist perspective; the "magic" refers to the local, indigenous way of seeing things, inclusive of the miraculous. The magic intrudes upon or intermingles with the European rationalism, in the process subverting it and demonstrating alternative modes of perception. Various scholars, including Anne C. Hegerfeldt, argue that the designation of magic realism should not be limited to postcolonial contexts. Superstition and magical thinking exist in virtually every culture and can be set against rationalistic, mainstream perspectives (31–2). Hegerfeldt urges a modal rather than generic application of the term in order to open it up to a wider application not limited by geographic or temporal constraints (Hegerfeldt, 1–6).

Although critical work in the area of magic realism has primarily focused on literature, film and theatre have been broached as well. Not infrequently, the label will be applied to theatrical works, as may be found in reviews of *The Clean House* (Blanchard; Rizzo, "The Clean House"; Robertson, "The Virtues"; Rooney). However, differences in the functionality of magic realism in the theater as opposed to fiction have not yet been delineated. Obviously, the phenomenology of theater differs significantly from that of literature. Basically, the reader of fiction creates the world of the book with his or her mind's eye, without the benefit or distraction of a staged reality.

New York Times critic Campbell Robertson identifies a new aesthetic that he calls "whimsical realism," placing *The Clean House* within this category without specifying any other dramatic works that may also qualify. This nomenclature suits Ruhl particularly well, since her plays abound with whimsy. Her employment of magic realism is subtler than, for example, that of José Rivera, as seen in *Cloud Tectonics*, with its temporal displacements, or *The Winged Man*, which is true to its title. However, as the following analysis will show, the difference between whimsical and magical realism is one of degree rather than kind.

Matter-of-Factness

Both Hegerfeldt and Wendy B. Faris, in *Lies That Tell the Truth: Magic Realism Seen through Contemporary Fiction from Britain* and "Scheherazade's Children: Magical Realism and Postmodern Fiction," respectively, provide lists of magic realist techniques that will be drawn upon in the following discussion. One of these techniques concerns the role of the narrator. Magic realism differs from fantasy in that it is based in the style of realism. The fantastic and realistic coexist and both are conveyed in a matter-of-fact tone (Hegerfeldt, 53). In literature, the narrator relates all events equally without marking the magical as extraordinary. Within the theater, the same effect is achieved through the characters' acceptance of the fantastic. For example, Matilde calmly witnesses Lane's fantasy of her husband with his lover (47), and the deadly efficacy of Matilde and her father's jokes are accepted without question. Similarly, Lane acknowledges objects tossed impossibly from Ana's balcony into her living room.

In magic realist literature, the narrator typically observes from a fresh, childlike perspective, one that accommodates the miraculous. Although Matilde is not a narrator per se, she nevertheless fulfills this function. For one thing, she stands apart from and comments on the action. On two separate occasions she distances herself by comparing the proceedings to a soap opera, first during the initial encounter between Charles, Lane, and Ana (68), and next in describing fights between Charles and Ana (76). Ruhl establishes a special relationship between Matilde and the audience by bookending the play between her joke in Portuguese and the story of her birth, and by positioning her as narrator of her parental flashbacks.

Matilde exhibits a childlike directness and guilelessness. Although duplicitous with Lane around work issues, she deals with her directly and compassionately in other ways. Matilde responds supportively when she sees that Lane is frustrated to tears (13–4), and when Virginia comes to the door and asks Matilde if she is the maid, Matilde unabashedly asks, in turn, if Virginia is "the sister" (15). She openly reveals her feelings about cleaning when it is safe to do so, as in speaking to Virginia (19). She also plays surrogate child to the parental triangle of Charles, Lane, and Ana. At their initial meeting, the women fight over her as if in a custody battle. Later, Lane interrogates her about Charles and Ana as a mother might question her child about her estranged husband and his new partner. Matilde thus fully occupies the role of childlike narrator.

Double-Casting, Mirroring, Metamorphosis

That the same actors play both Matilde's surrogate and actual parents demonstrates a particularly theatrical form of the magic realist technique of mirroring. As Faris states, "Repetition as a narrative principle, in conjunction with mirrors or their analogues used symbolically or structurally, creates a magic of shifting references" (177). Matilde herself recognizes the similarity, telling Ana at their first meeting that she looks like her mother (57), in a moment that metatheatrically acknowledges the audience's suspicion of double-casting. Ana reacts in kind, immediately embracing Matilde as a daughter and inviting her to come live with her. Although Matilde's instantaneous rapport with Ana owes something to cultural commonalities, it also conveys Matilde's connection with her mother.

Matilde's parents take on almost mythic significance as they appear in flashbacks in which they laugh relentlessly, even superhumanly. Charles and

Ana also find themselves drawn together by an invisible force, in their case an overwhelming sense of love and destiny rather than humor. Both Matilde's father and Charles demonstrate the gap between intention and result. The father spends a year concocting a joke to surprise his wife on their anniversary; the fatally hilarious joke succeeds only too well (11). Charles seeks a cancer cure in the wilds of Alaska, but his journey only separates him from his beloved during her time of greatest need. Both men have good intentions, but bungle the result. It is left to the women, ultimately, to take care of each other. In each of these examples, the mirroring produced by double casting highlights the similarities between the two couples.

The couples also demonstrate the magic realist technique of metamorphosis. Faris cites examples from various works of literature: a pair of characters transmogrifies into a "sinister twin fetus," a hellish location becomes "a kind of paradise of earthly delights," and a character is made invisible by a witch. She asserts that these transformations "embody in the realm of organisms a collision of two different worlds" (178–9). In Ruhl, the two different worlds that collide are those of Matilde's parents and Charles and Ana, when the latter, through an onstage costume change, revert to the former. With Charles slumped over Ana's dead body, Matilde opens the final scene by cueing their resurrection as her parents. This magic realist convention manifests in a distinctly, and transparently, theatrical manner: the actors simply shed a layer of costuming. This tightens the correspondence between Charles and Ana and Matilde's parents, and enables Ana's death to flow into Matilde's birth scene. As Faris notes, a meta-fictional dimension is often present in contemporary magic realist literature (175). The meta-theatrical costume change reminds the audience member to think metaphorically rather than literally.

Ghosts

Matilde's parents appear three times in the play, twice before the tenth scene in the first act, and at the conclusion of the play as a whole. Each time Matilde introduces them with, "This is how I imagine my parents." Although presented as imaginal rather than spectral, her mother and father fulfill functions typically assigned to ghosts in magic realist literature. In "Magical Romance/Magical Realism: Ghosts in U.S. and Latin American Fiction" (1995), Lois Parkinson Zamora details some of these:

> [G]hosts carry the burden of tradition and collective memory: ancestral apparitions often act as correctives to the insularities of individuality, as links to lost families and communities, or as reminders of communal crimes, crises,

cruelties. They may suggest displacement and alienation or, alternatively, reunion and communion [497].

The appearances of her parents concretize Matilde's longing for, and desire to be reunited with, them, and her cultural displacement in general. Further, they remind her of the crisis that terminated her mother's life.

In their introductory scene, the parents dance poorly, laugh until they kiss and kiss until they laugh. They are drunk on laughter that spills over into sexuality and back again. Matilde notes their poor dancing ability, and their clumsiness conveys their inebriated state. Her father explains that he is inseparable from his wife because he is always waiting for the next joke. Their passion for humor both exceeds the human and, as described by Matilde, passes over into the animalistic as they avoid eye contact and laugh like hyenas even when making love (11). Their obsession with laughter and the humorous, mingled with sexuality, approaches a Dionysian ecstasy, and the tragic consequence of their overindulgence takes on mythic significance.

If these ghosts, haunting their daughter, belong to a sort of ecstatic cult of laughter, then they are also the holders of its initiation mysteries. In their second appearance, her mother defers explaining a dirty joke to Matilde until she turns 30. Matilde laments that, as she approaches the age of 30, she will never know the joke (24). Her sorrow underscores her isolation and grief. However, the stage directions indicate that her parents both look at her at this juncture before exiting, and this pregnant glance may indicate an expectation that is fulfilled when Matilde puts to rest her mother's double, Ana, with the perfect joke. Matilde enforces a peculiar sort of justice to right her father's wrong, reenacting the killing as one of mercy rather than mishap. The ghosts manifest long enough to see Matilde attain and even surpass their level of comic mastery, after which they share with her "a moment of completion" (109). Matilde's recounting of her birth marks the culmination of her apprenticeship.

Literalization of Metaphor

Another characteristic of magic realism is the literalization of metaphor, demonstrated in that Matilde's mother "dies laughing." Matilde rejects the doctors' tenuous explanation that she asphyxiated on her own saliva (11). Although Ruhl's own father did not literally die laughing, he faced his illness with a courageous humor and made jokes until the very end, as did Vogel's brother. One could metaphorize them as people who died laughing. This metaphor is then made literal within the play. On several occasions, Ruhl pairs laughter with weeping. Shortly after learning of her husband's infidelity, Lane expresses uncertainty as to how to react to a joke told in Portuguese, and then alternates between laughing and crying (48–9). In a moment archetypically theatrical, Lane's face alternates between the conventional masks of comedy and tragedy. Ruhl thus establishes an affinity between laughter and tears that will reemerge in Matilde's final monologue, in which she describes laughing and then crying at her own birth (109). The laughter associated with the deaths of Ana and Matilde's mother is tinged with sorrow. As Matilde enters the world, crying follows laughter. Ruhl characteristically blends pathos and humor.

Overlapping Space as Metaphor

Hegerfeldt expands the role of literalization in magic realism beyond that of metaphor and positions it as an umbrella concept (56–9). For example, ghosts represent the literalization of the influence of the past, in the case of Matilde, her longing for her parents and the oppressive effect of their tragic deaths. In her discussion of literalization, Hegerfeldt notes techniques that deconstruct "traditional dichotomies such as abstract/concrete, word/thing, past/present" (57). The mirroring that occurs between Matilde's parents and Charles and Ana concretizes an analogy; whereas a realist text might draw comparisons between two different couples, a magic realist one utilizes the technique of mirroring, reinforced onstage by techniques such as double casting and onstage metamorphosis through costume change.

Ruhl also makes the abstract concrete through her manipulation of space. She theatrically metaphorizes space by overlapping locations. In placing Ana's balcony over Lane's living room, the playwright allows the messiness of the affair to overflow into Lane's neatly ordered world. The presentational and representational coexist, and the "metaphysical Connecticut" becomes metaphorical as well. The state of internal chaos and disorder imposed upon Lane through the disintegration of her marriage manifests externally through this inventive use of space. The discomfort with which she imagines Charles and Ana together towards the end of the first act is intensified by their physical proximity.

Alaskan snow falls on the balcony and the living room as Charles seeks a yew tree. The first instance occurs after Lane has forgiven Ana, and Charles appears in the distance, trudging across the stage dressed in a parka and bearing a pickax (93).[4] The snow falls equally on both women and represents their reconciliation and mutual concern for Charles. The snow collapses the distance between the women and Charles, and thus manifests a psychic

Matilde (Zilah Mendoza) on balcony; Lane (Elizabeth Norment) on her couch. *The Clean House.* **Yale Repertory Theatre, 2004 (courtesy Joan Marcus).**

proximity as a physical one. The snow recurs when Charles explains, by telegram, that he must learn to fly a plane in order to bring home the tree. The snow suggests both psychic closeness and physical remoteness. Ana longs for the warmth of his presence. Snow also suggests Ana's passage through life's final season and functions effectively as stage spectacle. Here once again Ruhl employs magic realism in a distinctly theatrical manner.

Mythos and Logos

Hegerfeldt convincingly argues that "the magic realist mode is used to explore and question ways of knowing the world" (157) along cultural lines. Western empiricism is examined and found somewhat lacking. Alternative modalities provide a different means of knowledge production, often drawing on oral traditions. These two paradigms may be expressed as logos, corresponding to Western empiricism, and mythos, or narrative knowledge. The magic realist attempt to reclaim rejected forms of knowledge is consistent with efforts made by both postmodernism and postcolonialism. Hegerfeldt supports her argument with quotations from Jean-François Lyotard's *The Postmodern Condition*, with its critique of the rationalist worldview.

Ruhl sustains a tension between mythos and logos throughout *The Clean House*. The two doctors practice the empirical science of modern medicine; Matilde counterbalances them with narrative in the form of stories about her parents and joke-telling. Alternative modes of healing trouble modern medicine at various points in *The Clean House*. During the surgery, Charles and Ana break out into "an ethereal medieval love song in Latin about being medically cured by love" (51). Ana admits avoiding doctors her entire life and she falls in love with Charles in spite of herself. She resists the standard doctor-patient relationship and refuses to give herself over to a scientific approach to healing that she mistrusts. She accepts her cancer diagnosis stoically and takes charge by demanding an immediate mastectomy and refusing less radical alternatives. Later, when her cancer recurs, she declines further treatment altogether. She explains that people develop a relationship with cancer as they talk about it in medical terms, sacrificing their own language in the process. She characterizes this relationship as a "bourgeois invention," preferring to establish a relationship with death rather than the disease (96). She approaches medicine through mythos rather than logos, expressing her dislike as a problem of language rather than procedure, of relationship rather than diagnosis. She prefers to die at home, or at least in Lane's home, rather than in the hospital, and refuses even painkillers. She crosses over into the next world with the assistance of the shamanic figure Matilde, who ministers to her with the perfect joke, rather than passing away in a hospital room attached to a machine.

Community

Magic realist texts tend to value community over individual achievement. Faris notes that, "the Jungian rather than Freudian perspective is common in magical realist texts; that is, the magic may be attributed to a mysterious sense of collective relatedness rather than to individual memories or dreams or visions" (183). Ana's illness draws together the initially isolated Lane, Virginia, Matilde, and ultimately Charles. The women achieve their fullest sense of community as they gather around Virginia's homemade chocolate ice cream, eating out of the same container. The sharing of food bonds them and while they eat, Ana relates the story of the captain who attempted to transport ice from Europe to South America; by the time he arrived, the ice had melted (100). This anecdote refers to Charles's quixotic journey, from which he does eventually return with a supposed cure; he is too late, however, as Ana has passed away.

Magical, Not Absurd

Ruhl's magic realism may superficially resemble absurdism, as both genres are to a great extent defined by their seemingly irrational departures from realism and a strong reliance on the staging of metaphor. However, magic realism differs from absurdism in a number of crucial ways, and Ruhl's work is clearly aligned with the former. Martin Esslin introduced the latter term in his definitive *The Theatre of the Absurd*, initially published in 1961 and revised in a third edition in 1980. In it, Esslin describes a theatrical movement that emerged after the Second World War, one based in the philosophy of existentialism. Esslin differentiates between existentialist and absurdist playwrights. Whereas the former employ language and logic to argue their case for the irrational, inexplicable nature of the human condition, the latter prefer to demonstrate the uselessness of language and its inadequacy to address the illogical nature of existence. Engaged in "a radical devaluation of language," they attempt "a poetry that is to emerge from the concrete and objectified images of the stage itself" (Esslin, 26).

Esslin centers the theatre of the absurd in Paris, highlighting the works of Samuel Beckett, Arthur Adamov, Eugene Ionesco, and Jean Genet. In *The French Theater of the Absurd* (1991), Deborah B. Gaensbauer roughly dates

Left to right: Charles (Mitchell Hébert), Virginia (Sarah Marshall), Ana (Franca Barchiesi), and Matilde (Guenia Lemos). *The Clean House*. Woolly Mammoth Theatre Company, 2005 (photograph by Stan Barouh; courtesy Woolly Mammoth).

the movement to 1948 through 1968 (xv). However, just as the term magic realism need not apply only to works of literature from the 1960s Latin American boom, the term "theatre of the absurd" does not need to be confined to two decades in France. Esslin addresses non–Parisian playwrights as well, and in a later edition devotes an entire chapter to Harold Pinter; indeed, playwrights such as Edward Albee continue to write in this mode. Albee's recent *The Goat, or Who Is Sylvia?*, in which an architect conducts an affair with a barnyard animal, serves as just one example. In it, the brutal poetry of the absurdist stage is powerfully realized when the philandering husband's wife brings home the carcass of her husband's paramour, whom she has slaughtered, and heaves it onto the carpet.

Nevertheless, the movement is moored in the postwar decades, influenced in France by the development of nuclear weapons, "the return to a smug bourgeois complacency," and distrust of the United States along with disillusion with the Soviet Union. It expresses "a very personal but widely shared anguish and seemingly incurable ennui" (Gaensbauer, xvii) and reflects suspicion "of a language that had been worn out in slogans, propaganda, and jargon" (xix). Ruhl grew up some decades after this, during a time with its share of dire problems, but without an immediate memory of the Second World War and in a society grown accustomed to, albeit uneasily, the threat of nuclear weapons. Although Ruhl clearly has experienced grief and melancholy, these emotions are not equivalent to postwar anguish and ennui.

Ruhl's characters do not inhabit an absurd world, but rather one rich with meaning. Ruhl has stated that two of her major preoccupations are the themes of love and death, and her characters find meaning in the face of the latter through the former, namely through relationship and community. The encounters between Eurydice and her father in the underworld do not project an existentialist viewpoint; rather, they are imbued with a loving tenderness that is sufficient unto itself. In *Melancholy Play*, Frances's friends join rather than abandon her when sadness turns her into an almond. Matilde's joke kills, but out of compassion, and the deceased Ana joins a community that extends beyond that of the living. As with Albee's goat, the absurdist image frequently demonstrates the brutality and senselessness of life. Ruhl's images usually convey, on the contrary, interconnectedness. She could perhaps be best qualified as a humanist. Her short play about global warming, *Snowless*, serves as an example. In it, she expresses a faith in human ingenuity as capable of solving the current climate situation. This worldview is congruent with the values typically present in magic realism, but at odds with those of absurdism.

Furthermore, as a former poet, Ruhl cherishes, rather than devalues, language. As noted elsewhere, she economically constructs each line to "sing." In *The Clean House*, she imbues language with the power to both kill and redeem. This approach is fully consistent with the practices of magic realism, in which "[t]he reader may experience a particular kind of verbal magic—a closing of the gap between words and the world, or a demonstration of what we might call the linguistic nature of experience" (Faris, 176). Absurdists are, on the contrary, interested in demonstrating the gap between words and the world and the utter inadequacy of language.

Tonal Frequencies

The shifts of tone in *The Clean House* may be, to a large extent, attributed to its magic realist modality. In the first act, living room realism alternates with Matilde's parental fantasies. These shifts reinforce the mirroring between Matilde's parents and Charles and Ana, since the latter are first introduced through a fantasy of Lane's. Matilde imagines her parents; Lane introduces her husband and his lover. Matilde's parents have only been seen laughing manically thus far. Charles and Ana shift the tonality as they kiss each other on different body parts in what Lane describes as "a sacred ritual" (46). These two visions of sexuality and love are complementary rather than oppositional, particularly in light of the metaphysical significance accorded to humor in the second act. The earthly humor of her parents, with their sharing of dirty jokes, supplements the otherworldly attraction between Charles and Ana.

The second act opens fantastically as Charles operates on Ana. Unlike the previous magical scenes, this one is not framed as emanating from any character's imagination. Ruhl utilizes the magic realist technique of literalization to express the characters' emotions in song, thereby transforming the normally clinical act of surgery into a love duet. The surgery/duet concludes with a kiss as Charles removes the sheet to reveal Ana's "lovely dress" (52). Later in the second act, the boundary between realism and magic blurs, as seen in the overlapping of essentially realistic scenes in balcony and living room. This softening allows for the externalization of internal states, particularly through the dishevelment of Lane's living room. This entry into a liminal space helps Ruhl to achieve her stated aim of dealing with cleaning on a more spiritual level. She introduces a third tone in the second act, that of soap opera melodrama. It first occurs in the flashback to Ana's diagnosis, during which she and Charles instantaneously fall in love. Ruhl satirizes this style, as in Charles's proclamation, "Ana, Ana, Ana, Ana ... your name goes backwards and forwards ... I love you" (56). This scene provides a strong contrast to the surgery, described by David Rooney in the Lincoln Center production as "a scene of unsettling beauty and sadness" (Rooney).

Ruhl breaks the fourth wall in order to allow her characters to transmit their thoughts directly to the audience. She opens the play with monologues from Lane, Virginia, and Matilde, allows Matilde to introduce her parents' scenes and discuss jokes, and also gives her a closing monologue. Ana and Charles also deliver monologues near the opening of the second act in which they describe their mutual attraction. Brecht used direct address to contribute to the alienation effect, and indeed it does work against a realist style. However, a magic realist script by definition obviates strict realism. As Hegerfeldt argues, the reader or audience member may come to question both the realist and magical elements, suggesting that a sort of alienation is already taking place.

Humor Theory: Jokes That Kill

Jokes in *The Clean House* take on shamanic significance, and through that relate to magic realism, as will be demonstrated through the application of humor theory. Philosophers as far back as Plato and Aristotle have contributed to this area; more recently, psychologists and linguists have conducted pertinent research. In *The Philosophy of Laughter and Humor* (1987), John Morreall suggests three encompassing theories: those of superiority, relief, and incongruity (3–6). According to superiority theory, "laughter is always directed at someone as a kind of scorn" (3), and a joke elevates the status of the teller at the target's expense. Its supporters include Plato, Aristotle, and Hobbes. Relief theory treats laughter as "the venting of excess nervous energy" (6) or the preservation of psychic energy, according to Freud. Incongruity theory, however, appears to be more comprehensive than the other two. It holds that "what amuses us is some object of perception or thought that clashes with what we would have expected in a particular set of circumstances" (6), and can be found in Kant, Schopenhauer, and Kierkegaard.

Semantic theories originating in the mid 1980s fall into this latter category. In *Semantic Mechanisms of Humor* (1985), Victor Raskin proposes a set of two requirements as the "necessary and sufficient conditions for a text to be funny" (99). His definition relies on the notion of a "script" associated with every word in a statement, a script consisting of a lexicon of associated words and ideas representing "the native speaker's knowledge of a small part of the world" (81). His two conditions are:

(i) The text is compatible, fully or in part, with two different scripts
(ii) The two scripts with which the text is compatible are opposite in a special sense [99].

The "special sense" is an oppositional one—that between "real" and "unreal" situations. He breaks this opposition down into three subcategories, actual versus non-actual, normal versus abnormal, and possible versus impossible. He further stipulates that, "in each of the jokes [used as examples] ... there is an element which renders the unreal situation less unreal than it looks" (111).

David Ritchie updates Raskin's theory in "Frame-Shifting in Humor and Irony" (2005). Ritchie refers to frames rather than scripts. He posits that jokes initially set up a socially acceptable frame. The punchline introduces a second frame that subverts the first "in the sense that it contradicts the polite fictions or 'stipulated' realities by which we ordinarily conduct our everyday social interactions." He lists some of these stipulated realities as "the constraints of physical reality ... as well as a pretense that political, religious, and social leaders always behave in a role-appropriate manner and that bodily functions are always under control" (281). He analyzes the following joke as an example: "By the time Mary had her fourteenth child, she'd finally run out of names to call her husband" (276). A "strong pronatalist sentiment" in the United States will incline the typical hearer to consider a new addition to Mary's family to be a positive event, despite the large size of her family. The initial frame sets up the expectation that Mary is having difficulty naming her new baby. The "culturally licensed ending" would be the "sharing of a moment of affectionate mirth" over this difficulty. The substitution of the word "husband" for "baby" at the end of the joke subverts this frame. The alternate scenario takes into account "the pain and discomfort of pregnancy and childbirth and the inconvenience and expense of child-rearing" (281).

Although more comprehensive, the newer semantic theories of humor do not invalidate the historic ones. For example, aggression theory sheds light on the three jokes told in Portuguese by Matilde. According to this theory, a joke's attack on a particular social group will strengthen the bond between the teller and the listener. This effect is commonly achieved through ethnic jokes in which one group is portrayed as inferior. Matilde's jokes highlight gender rather than ethnicity, attacking men specifically. In doing so, they create the potential for bonding between women. Two of the jokes ridicule male sexuality and the third attacks Argentinian men.[5]

Matilde opens the play by telling a "dirty" joke in Portuguese to the audience. The joke concerns a virginal young man who consults a doctor about his wedding night. The doctor first tells him to put a $10 bill in his right pocket and practice saying "10! 10! 10!" while moving his hips to the right. After a week, he tells him to put a $20 bill in his left pocket, and alternate between saying "10!" and "20!" while moving his hips from side to side. Finally, he instructs him to place a $100 bill in front, and say, "10! 20! 100!" while moving his hips correspondingly. When finally in bed with his wife, he is unable to maintain the pattern and exclaims, "Oh, fuck the change: 100! 100! 100!" (112–3). This joke contains several elements common to sexual humor which, according to Raskin, is usually categorized under "suppression/release-based theories" included under the umbrella of release theory. Sexual language replaces sexual behavior that is "normally suppressed and repressed," providing a socially acceptable outlet; the pleasure derived from this type of humor is nevertheless "of a sexual nature" (148). The sexual pleasure is enhanced in the telling of the joke by Matilde's hip movements in accordance with the doctor's instructions. The joke provides a social context that safely contains this movement. The physicality also alerts audience members, who may not understand Portuguese, that a joke is being told.

The joke also evokes "the binary script of sexual ignorance or inexperience," which is quite common in sexual jokes. The young man's inexperience justifies his willingness to follow the doctor's somewhat unusual instructions.

The joke also includes a sexually obscene trigger in the utterance of the word "fuck" in the punchline. In certain primitive jokes the inclusion of such a trigger is adequate in itself to provoke laughter with, as Raskin puts it, "certain audiences" (152), presumably unsophisticated ones. Ultimately, however, the joke points out the sexual selfishness of the young man, who abandons a technique presumably designed to maximize his wife's pleasure to focus on his own. The placement of the most valuable bill at the front indicates a degree of complicity on the doctor's part. The joke potentially bonds women together by attacking sexual selfishness in men.

The second joke told by Matilde in Portuguese falls into the same category. She riddles an uncomprehending Lane, "Why are men in bed like microwave food? They're done in thirty seconds" (113). This much shorter joke compares two quite disparate types of objects, men and microwave food, to posit a general inadequacy in men, again having to do with sexual selfishness and lack of staying power. The reference to microwave food implies a product of inferior quality. In both of these jokes, the woman's pleasure is sacrificed. The microwave joke also references a woman's traditional role as food-preparer, hinting at male ingratitude for responding to home-cooked meals with a substandard offering in bed. Thus it criticizes male sexual ineptitude while subtly reinforcing traditional gender roles. The last joke told by Matilde targets gender and ethnicity rather than sexuality. She attacks Ana's countrymen: "The best investment ever is to buy an Argentinian for what he is really worth and later sell him for what he thinks he is worth" (113). The joke casts Argentinian men as conceited, a stereotype that Ana seems to appreciate. It strengthens the bond between the newly-acquainted Matilde and Ana since the latter immediately offers to hire and house the former. Traditionally, sexual humor has been made by men at the expense of women. Since such humor tends to objectify the target of the joke, the "dirty" joke has had the effect of solidifying male power in a patriarchal society while marginalizing women. By turning the tables, Matilde reclaims female sexuality in an empowering manner.

In the ninth scene of the first act, Matilde shares her musings on humor with the audience. She describes the perfect joke as one that causes the hearer to both forget and remember his or her life, and one that looks stupid when written down. Furthermore, "the perfect joke was not made up by one person. It passed through the air and you caught it. A perfect joke is somewhere between an angel and a fart" (24). In spite of the last statement, which suggests oppositional frames, Matilde clearly does not subscribe to any of the three major theories of humor. She endows the perfect joke with metaphysical significance and credits jokes with a cleansing capability (26). This purgative quality exceeds the release offered by humor theory.

Furthermore, Matilde believes that, as a joke-writer, "Sometimes you have to suffer for the really good ones" (71) and that:

> The perfect joke happens by accident. Like a boil on your backside that you pop. The perfect joke is the perfect music. You want to hear it only once in your life, and then, never again [74].

She again mixes images of the sacred and profane in her description of the perfect joke, which serves as a parable for death. The recipient undergoes a singular experience that is both intensely physical and metaphysically freeing. Death functions as the final joke, an abrupt frameshift that subverts physical existence and earthly consciousness.

Shamanism and Frame Shifts

In *The Clean House*, then, a joke may serve as metaphor even for the passage from life to death. At the level of utterance, the perfect joke functions as a curse or incantation, capable of initiating the final journey. Matilde's father's anniversary joke inadvertently lands as a fatal curse. Matilde whispers the appropriate words in the correct order, as one would a magic spell, in order to speed Ana on her way. Both Matilde and her father function as shamans do in non-industrial societies. The shaman officiates at rites of passage, such as births and deaths, and mediates between the worlds of the living and the dead. As Matilde does with her parents, the shaman communicates with the spirits of the deceased. Frequently the role is passed on along familial lines through a process of initiation (Smith 14). In Matilde's case, this consists of both receiving and withstanding the perfect joke. Her task is metaphysical and communal. She expresses doubt that she will survive the transmission: "I'm looking for the perfect joke, but I'm afraid if I found it, it would kill me" (35).

Matilde's belief in the purgative action of jokes conforms more closely to the ideology of shamanistic healing than it does to the joke theory of release. Shamans frequently function as healers in their communities. They commonly attribute illness to the intrusion of malevolent spirits into the patient's body, or to the introduction of foreign objects sent by adversaries, which they attempt to expel through ritual. In "Dark Side of the Shaman" (1989), American anthropologist Michael F. Brown offers an example from the Peruvian Amazon. The Aguaruna believe that sorcerers "introduce spirit darts" into their victims. A shaman must remove the dart or the victim will die. The dart is perceived "as a piece of bone, a tiny thorn, a spider, or a blade of grass" (252). An anthropologist who became initiated into shamanism in the course of her research, Barbara Tedlock authored *The Woman in the Shaman's Body: Reclaiming the Feminine in Religion and Medicine* (2005). She quotes a Native American healer, Essie Parrish, who envisions these intrusions as a form of uncleanliness:

> When I take it out you can't see it with your bare eyes. But I can see it. The disease inside a person is dirty. I suppose that's what white doctors call "germs," but we Indian doctors call it "dirty" [18].[6]

Matilde envisions jokes as shamanic rituals that sweep away the "rottenness" festering inside of a person's body.

The shaman travels from ordinary to extraordinary worlds and back again, and thus easily inhabits the magic realist landscape. Carpentier identifies a popular belief in the supernatural as an essential feature of *lo real maravilloso*. Although relatively little has been written about the connection between shamanism and magic realism, Renato Oliva broaches the subject in his analysis of a Nigerian poet and novelist in "Re-Dreaming the World: Ben Okri's Shamanic Realism" (1999). Oliva situates both on the threshold:

> If, as we have already noted, one of the characteristics of the shaman is his ability to shift his level of consciousness, thus moving between conscious and unconscious, reality and dream, natural and supernatural, this is equally true of magical realism. One of the typical elements of magical realism is, in fact, the constant crossing of thresholds and frontiers [177].

One frequently crossed boundary in magic realism is that between the living and the dead, manifested through various hauntings. The shaman as well passes freely into the domain of the deceased to communicate with spirits, and officiates at important transitional events such as births and deaths.

Excepting the lack of malevolent intent, Matilde's father's verbal killing of his wife would be accepted as quite probable within the worldview of shamanism. Danish anthropologist Peter Skafte interviews a Nepalese shaman, Ashok, who believed that he fatally cursed his three business partners in "Interview with a Killing Shaman" (1992). He directed "a deadly mantra" against them, and one became ill and died within a few weeks. He wished to take back the curse, but nevertheless both of the remaining two died within the month, one from dysentery, one hit by a car. He believes that the gods retaliated for his misuse of power, as shortly thereafter his two children took ill and died (Ashok and Skafte, 236). Once spoken, the curse could not be recalled. From this perspective, Matilde's father's utterance could easily prove as fatal as a loosened arrow or the spirit darts described by Brown.

The above accounts come from such diverse regions as the Peruvian Amazon, North America, and Nepal. In 1951, Romanian religious historian

Mircea Eliade published the seminal *Shamanism: Archaic Techniques of Ecstasy*, documenting similarities in shamanic practices in hundreds of societies across the globe (Narby and Huxley, 4). Although it was previously believed that shamanism began in North Asia more than 40,000 years ago and later spread into the Americas, newer studies indicate that it was "independently reinvented over and over in many places," and that the similarities occur because shamanic practices "are based on an understanding of the human immunological system and psychobiology rather than on a narrow set of culture-historical traits or patterns" (Tedlock, 14–5). Even though the details vary from location to location, the general principles are remarkably similar. The five tenets of shamanism as presented by Tedlock may be summarized as: (a) all entities are imbued with a holistic life force, (b) all things are interconnected, (c) the world consists of interconnected cosmic levels between which the shaman is able to move, (d) societies designate shamans who are able to change events in the ordinary world, and (e) actions taken in an alternative reality affect normal reality, and vice versa (20–1).

Frustrated at Ana's refusal of further treatment, Charles abandons the hospital and allies himself with the shamanic healer in his search for a plant-based remedy. His exact intentions remain unclear, as Matilde reports both that he hopes to derive a new medicine from the tree, and that he simply wants to plant it in Ana's courtyard as aromatherapy (86–7). Lane notes that the anti-cancer drug Taxol was made out of the bark of the yew tree in 1967 (86). As Jordan Goodman and Vivien Walsh report in *The Story of Taxol: Nature and Politics in the Pursuit of an Anti-Cancer Drug* (2001), Taxol is now synthetically produced (2). The synthetic product continues to be used in the treatment of, among other cancers, those of the ovary and breast, and qualifies as the "best-selling anti-cancer drug ever" (1). Charles returns to the source, so to speak, either to derive a better treatment from it or to apply it to Ana in its raw form.

Up to a point, Charles's quest follows that traced by Joseph Campbell in *The Hero with a Thousand Faces* (1949). Campbell has extracted the archetypical heroic journey:

> The hero ventures forth from the world of common day into a region of supernatural wonder: fabulous forces are there encountered and a decisive victory is won: the hero comes back from this mysterious adventure with the power to bestow boons on his fellow man [30].

Charles ventures forth into the harsh conditions of Alaskan snow, trudging through a blizzard with his pickax, teaches himself how to fly a plane, and returns with his boon intending to bestow it on his beloved. His tardy return, however, is less than triumphant. Earlier, he is unable to even complete a joke about breasts and breast surgeons, forgetting the punchline (53). Given the significance accorded jokes in this work, this failure marks Charles as not only inept, but impotent.

Ultimately, Charles contributes a significant object to the final tableau. In shamanic cosmology, the healer scales a great tree or mountain to arrive at various levels of existence (Tedlock, 21). In providing what the stage directions describe as "an enormous tree" (107), Charles supplies a metaphorical and metaphysical ladder to convey Ana to the afterlife. Rather than serving to sustain life as Charles had hoped, the tree reaffirms the continuity between life and death, the interconnectedness of the realms of the living and the dead. The yew itself symbolizes sorrow, death, and resurrection ("Yew"). Its foliage served as a symbol of mourning in ancient Egypt, a practice sustained by the Greeks and Romans. In Great Britain, it is commonly found in church graveyards (Partridge). The tree may live to be 1000 years old or older (McKillop), and early Christians presumably adopted the yew as a symbol of the resurrection due to its evergreen foliage and long life span. The tree regenerates itself by extending shoots down from its branches into the ground, which then become new trunks as the inner core decays with age, so it may be said to resurrect itself (Partridge). Beneath Charles's yew tree, Matilde's recounting the story of her birth symbolizes both her own rebirth, as she assumes her father's role as joke teller, and Ana's passing. Between the two of them, Matilde and her father "officiate" at two deaths and a birth: Matilde's joke facilitates Ana's passing, and jokes told by her father induce Matilde's birth and her mother's demise. Matilde is born under a tree, and the onstage yew suggests a soul's journey from a pre-nascent realm into an infant's body.

Shamans typically inhabit rural, agrarian societies, and so are highly in tune with the cycles of nature. The ending of *The Clean House* suggests early Orphic myths discussed in connection with *Eurydice* in which Orpheus's destruction and rebirth parallels the diurnal cycle. Matilde symbolically murders her mother in the person of Ana and then relates her own birth, which functions as the resurrection following the destruction of the mother. The new replaces the old as it does in nature. In contrast to the dripping stillness of *Eurydice*, Ruhl offers a vision of death flowing back into life, of a current that cycles rather than plummets, marked by laughter instead of silence. A community of both men and women gathers in support of one of their members in *Melancholy Play*. They perform a ritual in order to assist Frances, who has turned, out of melancholy, into an almond. Tilly fulfills the role of shaman, weeping an elixir of tears that reunites the entire group in the almond state. Ruhl invokes Jacobean drama and European cinema, and employs a multilingual thesaurus in order to convey sorrowful humor, in the process bringing humor to her *Melancholy Play*.

III

Melancholy Plague

Farcical Melancholy

As in *Eurydice*, water imagery in *Melancholy Play: a contemporary farce* is frequently associated with sadness or, more precisely, the feeling of melancholy. A sudden rainfall prompts Tilly, the protagonist, to mourn the impermanence of flowers, and she later likens herself to a river of sorrow; characters longingly smell the ocean all the way from Illinois and dream of sea voyages; and drinking from a vial of tears transforms each of them into an almond. The object of loss here, however, is concealed and the cause of Tilly's melancholy remains uncertain; she seems to enjoy the emotion for its own sake. In spite of this apparent vagueness, *Melancholy Play* may be read as a continued expression of the playwright's grief as manifested in the other two works just discussed, both through its celebration of melancholy and through explicit and implicit references to death. Indeed, the central crisis of the work, that of being transformed into an almond, serves as a metaphor for death, and the ever-present Julian, the cellist, functions as a death figure providing accompaniment as the ensemble partakes in a sort of Dance of Death as they progress towards the terminal "almond state."

Ruhl draws on Jacobean literature for inspiration, both in terms of dramatic presentation and style and for a definition of melancholy. She both directly quotes and paraphrases Richard Burton's *The Anatomy of Melancholy*, a treatise that delves into the causes and cures of the malady in great detail. She insists that "melancholy in this play is Bold, Outward, Sassy, Sexy and Unashamed. It is not introverted. It uses, instead, the language of Jacobean direct address" (Ruhl, "Melancholy," 231). Ruhl further defines Elizabethan and Jacobean melancholy as "an outward, yearning, active thing," rather than "a depressive, internal, shaggy, filmic state" (qtd. in Weckwerth, 32). The Black Death was a terrifying threat before, during, and after the reign of James I, and Ruhl has implanted references to this as well that collectively equate melancholy with the plague.

Jessica Thebus directed the premiere of *Melancholy Play*, produced by the Piven Theatre in Evanston, Illinois, in June 2002. As Ken Prestininzi, who directed a later production at Brown University in November 2007, points out, the word "play" in the title refers both to a theatrical work and an enjoyable engagement with something (Gray). Thus the title in conjunction with the subtitle, *a contemporary farce,* presents the dual contradictions of playing with melancholy and a melancholic farce. Ruhl plays with melancholy as she draws upon the term's historical usage and contrasts it to the modern American notion of depression as an ailment that is best treated, and eradicated, through the application of pharmaceuticals. Each of the other characters falls in love, in turn, with Tilly because they find her sorrowful mood irresistible; the currents of desire flow towards her. She herself relishes the feeling and creates rich associations with the word "melancholy" through her invocation of foreign words that denote different types of sadness. The work is a contemporary, as opposed to traditional, farce for a number of reasons. The dictionary defines farce as "a light, humorous play in which the plot depends upon a skillfully exploited situation rather than upon the development of character" ("Farce"). Ruhl certainly exploits the situation of Tilly's emotional state in a humorous fashion, but adds weight by giving serious consideration to that state. For example, the dolorous musical score performed on the cello lends a certain aura of gravitas. The subgenre to which the work most closely belongs would be the bedroom farce, which derives much of its situational humor from acts of infidelity. In Ruhl's play, although Tilly changes sexual partners several times, since none of the relationships are bounded by marriage these shifts fail to evoke the standard sense of moral transgression. As a result, *Melancholy Play* is devoid of the subterfuge and evasion that provides the foundation for much of the comedy in a traditional bedroom farce.

The farcical plot can best be traced through Tilly's changing partnerships or, more generally, the attractive pull that her melancholy exerts on those she encounters. Her psychiatrist, Lorenzo the Unfeeling, falls for her first; she resists his advances, finding him altogether too cheerful. She develops a closer affinity for her tailor Frank, who is somewhat melancholic himself. Next, a haircut leads to an intimate encounter with her stylist Frances. However, that too is short-lived, as she becomes involved with an offstage character, a woman who writes obituaries. Along the way, Frances's live-in girlfriend Joan, a nurse, also develops a crush on Tilly, although her love is not consummated. Midway through the play, the protagonist suddenly becomes inexplicably and relentlessly happy and the rest of the characters, who had fallen in love with her due to her exquisite sadness, now find her intolerable. Frances meanwhile seems to have caught Tilly's melancholy and begins to change into an almond, completing the transformation when she downs a vial of Tilly's tears. Unable to change her back, the rest of the ensemble joins her in the "almond state" by partaking in a tear-drinking ceremony. To complete the farce, Frank and Frances discover that they are long-lost twins, separated at birth.

As the plot develops, so does the definition of melancholy. Ruhl differentiates it from the American notion of depression and links it to its Jacobean sense while also associating it with a particular vision of European culture. As a practitioner of American psychiatry, Lorenzo offers to medicate away Tilly's malady; she refuses, preferring to cling to her sadness. Indeed, she is only undergoing treatment at the behest of her employer. Whereas Lorenzo regards her condition as a clinical one, she prefers to express it in romantic terms, as a sexy state that strangers find irresistible (275–6). Hers is a nostalgic melancholy that refers to two different pasts. One is an idealized, cinematic Europe, the other, Jacobean England. In the former, life moves at an unhurried pace and one may spend long afternoons gazing out the window at the rain. Children are raised in sweet-shops, as was Lorenzo (235); reservations are made at restaurants in grand hotels (241); and old Italian men play cards in the piazza while drinking out of small cups (251–2). Ruhl's set directions suggest a hotel lobby or drawing room out of this idealized Europe, with a chaise, red velvet chairs, chandeliers or lamps, and perhaps a Victrola (226). Her costuming instructions reinforce this impression by clothing Joan in "an old-fashioned nurse's uniform," and she instructs that the Illinois of the play be both "iconic and cinematic" (228). Joan herself evokes the cinematic when she tells her lover Frances, after first meeting Tilly, that she has a "sexy sad feeling" as if "in a European city before the war" (279). The inhabitants of this imaginary Europe have the leisure time at their disposal to fully experience an erotic melancholy, as does Tilly.[1]

Cult of Melancholy

In addition to this past, which resembles a cinematic Europe, Ruhl points to Jacobean England through her references to *Anatomy of Melancholy* and her appropriation of Jacobean stage techniques. Her selection of this time period is apt, since a so-called cult of melancholy can be traced through the literature of Early Modern England during a span of years inclusive of the reign of James, which extended from 1603 until his death in 1625, as described by Lawrence Babb in *The Elizabethan Malady: A Study of Melancholia in English Literature from 1580 to 1642* (1951). Babb references Burton and cites examples from, among many other works, Shakespeare's *Hamlet* and Webster's *The White Devil* and *The Duchess of Malfi* (106–14). The composer John Dowland, whose motto was *Semper Dowland, semper dolens* ("Always Dowland, always mourning"), is associated with the cult as well. Melancholy itself was simply fashionable during this period, although the causes of it were hard to pin down. According to Peter Holman in his *Dowland: Lachramie (1604)* (1999), contemporaries suggested causes such as "social change, political uncertainty, challenges to religious and intellectual certainties, frustrated ambition, or just *fin-de-siècle* malaise" (50).

Robert Burton likewise fails to identify any clear, single cause; rather he extensively catalogs each and every conceivable possibility. *The Anatomy of Melancholy* was published in five editions, the first in 1621 and the last in 1638 (Jackson, viii). Ruhl quotes from Burton's subtitle in an epigraph: "What Melancholy is, with all the kinds, causes, symptomes, prognostickes, and severall cures of it" (Ruhl, "Melancholy," 223). His methodology consists of literary quotation, and he has assembled an exhaustive collection of citations. His list of causes and cures is so vast as to be practically meaningless, an expansiveness that Ruhl spoofs. For example, Frank delineates melancholy's causes as stars, love, death, morning, afternoon, evening, and "odd times in between morning afternoon and evening" (234). Joan's list of the cures for and causes of melancholy turn out to be identical, consisting as they do of food, music, and love (313). A list is set to music in Scene 7 in "A Song from the Company." It cites various types of junk food in reference to Burton's implication of bad diet (Burton, 1:216–25); Ruhl's snacks include Cheetos, Doritos, and cheddar Goldfish (305). The song also conflates the two pasts of the play, those of Burton's England and a cinematic Europe, listing stars, love, and death as causes, and remembering the slow, sweet, idealized European life replete with "rain-drenched cobbled streets" (305). Melancholy is thus positioned as a romantic longing for a more leisurely time. It is without discernible cause and must be allowed to run its course, and is as incurable as the bubonic plague once was.

Melancholy is one of the four humors of early modern thought, the theory of which derives from the writings of Galen (c. 130–200 A.D.). Each humor is associated with one of the four elements and its attributes, melancholy with earth as being cold and dry (Evans, 324–7). Sir John Harington's translation from Latin of *The Englishmans Doctor, or the School of Salerne* (1608) lists the predominant qualities of the melancholic personality as a desire for solitude, studiousness and pensiveness, and extremeness in love (Evans, 328). Tilly's personality matches the type in a general sense. She is somewhat solitary, excusing herself from company on occasion; she is apt to sink into thought for long stretches, as when she considers the "lost Art/ of the Handkerchief" for three hours (Ruhl, "Melancholy," 269); and she tends to be extreme in love, for example becoming so overwhelmed at having all of her friends gathered together to celebrate her birthday that she must excuse herself to go lie down (286).

Multilingual Melancholies

Ruhl does not confine herself to a Jacobean definition of melancholy. Tilly expands the definition through references to foreign words. Ruhl encourages her casts to seek out these words that, unsurprisingly, are culturally significant. In the first instance, Tilly struggles to remember not just a word, but rather the phrase *mono no aware*: "There's a word in Japanese for being sad in the springtime—a whole word just for being sad—about how pretty the flowers are and how soon they're going to die" (240). The 18th-century literary scholar Motoori Norinaga popularized the phrase to advance a Japanese aesthetic distinct from the Chinese (Varley, 216–8); it has since become a defining concept of Japanese culture. It means roughly an appreciation of the beauty of things as dependent upon an awareness of their impermanence. The concept is emblematized by the cherry blossom due to its fragile beauty and short life (Linhart, 228)—hence Tilly's reference to dying flowers.

Kazumitsu Kato analyzes the term epistemologically in "Some Notes on *Mono no Aware*" (1962). *Mono* means, generally, "things." *Aware* is a qualitative term that occurs spontaneously as in an exclamation and "expresses serious and profound feelings towards *mono*." *No* is a connecting particle between the two other terms. The phrase may thus be understood as signifying a flash of insight about the nature of things involving "an identification by the perceiver with the object" (559), which object may be either human or non-human. In order to truly experience *mono no aware*, one must have a deep understanding of the world inclusive of both the phenomenal and the noumenal. The experience originates in the mind of the beholder and occurs spontaneously through an immediate identification (Kato, 558–9). Ruhl again references this concept when Tilly becomes overwhelmed at the beauty of her guests, whose faces appeared to her as flowers, as they play duck duck goose (286). Tilly is able to appreciate this beauty because the slow, melancholic pace at which she lives invites the state of *mono no aware*.

The next foreign word that Tilly evokes is in Portuguese, and means a "longing for someone who is far away" (248). The word is *saudade* and it assumes differing shades of meaning in the Portuguese and Brazilian idioms. It has been adopted by the Portuguese as indicative of their national character and includes the meaning of "a melancholic longing for an idealized past, whether in one's own home place or in the Portugal of some vanished golden age," a meaning that was cultivated by 19th-century Portuguese writers. More specifically, it refers to the sense of loss that the Portuguese colonizers of and settlers in Brazil felt for their home country (Ortiz-Griffin and Griffin, 177). This meaning is paralleled in *Melancholy Play* through the nostalgia for a Europe of the past as viewed from the state of Illinois, situated as it is in a country that was formerly a British colony. Ironically, Tilly looks back not to a golden age of wealth and glory, but to one in which the suffering was richer.

In *Death without Weeping: The Violence of Everyday Life in Brazil* (1992), Nancy Scheper-Hughes discusses the Brazilian meaning of the word at some length. As with the Portuguese, the national identity incorporates *saudade*, conceptualized as a "Brazilian sadness." Scheper-Hughes admits that the concept cannot be fully comprehended without a deep understanding of Portuguese and Brazilian poetry, a knowledge that she confesses that she herself lacks (434–6). It is not comparable to the American concept of depression, bearing a richer meaning inclusive of

> complex associations between pleasure and regret, desire and pain, attachment and loss. It is not to be confused ... with the biomedical concept of depression, which has medicalized and reduced the associations among painful longing, burning desire, and unbearable loss to a psychiatric symptom [436].

One may certainly feel *saudade* for a deceased loved one although not for a dead infant, since the latter lacks a personal history (437).[2] The painful memory of the deceased is preferable to no memory at all so that one could even exclaim, as Tilly might if she spoke Portuguese, "*Ai, que saudades de saudades que eu não tenho!* Oh, what sad longings for the longings that I don't have" (435).

The sense of *saudade* as a longing for someone who is not present informs the speech that Tilly gives shortly before she alludes to the Portuguese word, in which she grieves over the departure of her customers from the bank, while she is forced to stay there all day (247–8). The depth of feeling for her customers exceeds what might normally be expected of a bank teller. As Kato explains, one who truly understands *mono no aware* is one who possesses a "broad and profoundly human feeling" (558). In the context of these non–English words, Tilly's melancholy assumes a humanizing function in that her feeling, and the expression of it, connects her more closely to those around her.

The Russian word for melancholy serves a similar function. Tilly describes its meaning as "to love someone but also to pity them" (260). The word *zhalost'* is typically translated as *pity*, although according to David S. Danaher in "The Semantics of *Pity* and *Zhalost'* in a Literary Context" (2002), the meanings of the two words differ considerably. The Russian word may be used in either a negative or positive sense, but the latter dominates in contemporary usage. Whereas the English word *pity* implies a superiority of subject over object, *zhalost'* assumes an affinity between the two. The subject empathizes with, and perhaps even shares in, the pain of the object. Contained in the usage of *pity* is the assumption that the sufferer is responsible for his or her situation, whereas with *zhalost'* no such assumption is made; rather, misfortune or other circumstances beyond control are seen as the cause. A desire on the part of the subject to alleviate the object's suffering may also be implied. The instinctive love of a parent for a child qualifies as *zhalost'*. Danaher reports that Virginia Woolf, whose *Orlando* Ruhl has adapted for the stage, "saw the suffering-*zhalost'* relationship as one of the key themes of Russian literature and one of the most difficult for a Western reader to comprehend" (Danaher, 1–6).

Once again the foreign, forgotten word suggests a humanistic suffering based on awareness and compassion. Tilly alludes to it upon learning that Frances lives with a nurse named Joan who "kind of" takes care of her. Exactly what Tilly means is unclear, though perhaps she is implying that Joan both pities and loves Frances, which certainly becomes the case after Frances turns into an almond. Through allusions to *mono no aware*, *saudade*, and *zhalost'*, Ruhl enriches the sense of the word *melancholy* and thereby elaborates on the nature of Tilly's suffering as well as its cultural framing. Although audience members may find themselves unable to identify these words during performance, they will nonetheless benefit from the richness they contribute to the work as Ruhl has layered their meanings into the text of the play.[3]

Melancholy a Cause

Death is included in various lists of the causes of melancholy, but within the logic of the play the inverse is true as well: melancholy is a cause of death. The characters catch the condition from Tilly one at a time and, as it runs its course, it ultimately terminates in the almond state (a metaphor for death) for all of them. Melancholy spreads like the plague, a much-feared disease of the Jacobean era, and both its cause and cure remain a mystery, as did those of the plague prior to the 19th century. Ruhl's personal history supports this interpretation, as she lost not only her father but also both grandmothers to cancer, which emulates the plague of the past in the sense that its causes are unknown and its remedies uncertain. Just as the plague has decimated families, cancer has robbed Ruhl of three close relatives. Also operational within the work is the phase of grieving referred to as "seeking and finding" as described in the chapter on *Eurydice*. The rest of the characters search for and find Frances in the sense that they discover a way to join her in the almond state, much as Orpheus succeeds in following Eurydice to the underworld.

Before examining the deadly spread of melancholy, other references to death will be discussed. The foreign words offer an entry point. *Saudade* may be experienced as a longing for someone deceased, as is mentioned above. *Mono no aware* encompasses an awareness of the transitory nature of life and an appreciation of beauty based on the knowledge that neither life nor beauty can last. Even in contemporary English, melancholy is by definition inclusive of a sense of mourning: "Affected with, characterized by, or showing melancholy; mournful; depressed" ("Melancholy"). Another death-related element in the play is the recurring theme of the loss of parents, which takes the form of abandonment but is presented in a way that hints at a more permanent disassociation. Lorenzo describes being orphaned on the doorstep of a candy shop and then being rejected once again by his mother when she comes to visit him. She wears black as if in a state of mourning (235–6). Frank describes himself and his sister as being abandoned by a mother who "sailed the fjords and never came back," followed by their father who "longed" to join his wife (315). The trope of death as a voyage across a body of water dates back at least to the Greek myth of the River Styx and the boatman Charon, who ferried souls to the underworld. Frank and Frances's parents have thus metaphorically passed away rather than just moved on.

Ruhl invokes this watery trope on other occasions as well. Rejected by Tilly, Lorenzo fantasizes riding in an almond-shaped boat through the afternoon and into the evening, with the passing of the diurnal cycle into darkness reinforcing the death motif. The fantasy manifests a death-wish on the part of Lorenzo, one which is, however, frustrated as he finds himself stalled in the afternoon. He is unable to visualize the piazza with its old men playing cards, men that "know [his] family name" (250–1). The failure of his imagination demonstrates his inability to conjure the idealized, cinematic Europe so integral to Tilly's sense of melancholy. Possessed more of an American than European sensibility, Lorenzo is unable to mourn and therefore unable to visualize death in all of its fullness. Possessed as she is with a sense of *mono no aware*, Tilly enriches her experience of life with a melancholy that acknowledges the inevitability of death. She longs to "go on a ship for three years" so that she can write "a long letter to Frank by candlelight" (281). Her feeling at the moment she imagines this could be best described as *saudade* in the sense of longing for someone who is not present. She longs to increase her longing for him by expanding the distance between them to the greatest distance possible, that between the living and the dead across a body of water. At this moment, Frank enters to wish her a happy birthday and draws her back from her reverie. She abruptly recovers from her melancholy and becomes as happy as someone rescued from the brink of death.

The almond is clearly linked to death and melancholy, and not just through Frances's transformation. Two of Ruhl's three epigraphs refer to almonds. In the first, A. Jaruwat, M.D., describes a part of the brain called the *amygdala*. Named after the Greek word for almond, it is the center of emotion in the brain and is susceptible to "seizures [and] uncontrolled electrical storms within the brain" that can cause "feelings of sadness or fear" or even the "smell of bitter almonds" (qtd. in Ruhl, "Melancholy," 231). Ruhl references this passage when Frank apprehends Tilly's happiness as an approaching storm (290). To credit Tilly's sudden mood change to a storm in her brain fails to adequately explain it, since the source of the storm itself remains a mystery. Through its association with this portion of the brain, the almond is linked to inexplicable emotions such as melancholy. The second epigraph is uncredited and probably written by Ruhl. It concerns the ancient symbol of the *mandorla,* which consists of two overlapping circles that form an almond shape when circumscribed; its name is from the Italian word for almond (290). The *mandorla* is used in medieval art to enclose an ascending religious figure suspended between earth and heaven or life and death (although the shape used in these cases is that formed by the intersection of the circles). The *mandorla* encloses saintly figures that are suspended between earth and heaven or life and death ("Mandorla"). Through this symbol, the almond is directly linked, not only to death, but also to transfiguration, that is, a change in outward form or appearance such as that undergone by Frances.

The Black Death

Ruhl's work abounds with oblique references to the plague. The bubonic plague, or Black Death, appears to have first arrived in Europe from India via

Asia Minor in the 14th century, arriving in Sicily in 1347. Within a year it had spread across the continent and reached England, eventually earning the status of the "most feared of all the diseases that afflicted late medieval and early modern Europe" (Porter 1). It advanced with great speed, was highly contagious, resulted in a high mortality rate and afflicted a large percentage of the population (1). Within a relatively brief time period inclusive of James's reign, London experienced five major outbreaks, in 1593, 1603, 1625, 1636, and 1665 (Moote and Moote, 10). As the bacterial cause would not be identified until after the advent of microbiology in the 19th century, along with the discovery of its means of transmission from rats to humans through fleas (275–8), earlier societies were forced to arrive at methods of treatment and containment through trial and error.

The most overt references to the plague occur in the scene in which Joan and Tilly are trying to decide what to do with Frances, now an almond. Tilly first advises against notifying the authorities (311). In *The Great Plague* (1999), Stephen Porter reports that it was common for communities to conceal outbreaks in order to avert almost certain social and financial disruption. However, Tilly's warning comes too late; a letter slipped under the door warns of a general epidemic of melancholy and advises quarantine (312). The letter references the plague in a number of ways. Quarantine was a standard means of attempting to contain its spread: Most of those infected in England were shut up in their own homes for a time period lasting 40 days after the household's last fatality (Moote and Moote, 14). As turning into almonds is equivalent to dying within the play, the letter suggests that people have been dropping dead in the streets. Lorenzo reinforces this image when he exclaims that it is an epidemic (313). The letter recommends a means of dealing with the "deceased" which suggests mass burial. The almond is to be placed in a "zip-lock bag," which is somewhat akin to the modern body bag, and deposited in a mailbox. Presumably the mailbox will fill up with almonds as a burial pit would with corpses. Mass burials were standard during plague epidemics as the only practical means of disposing of the great number of corpses.

A nursery rhyme memorializes the Black Death:

> Ring around a Rosie
> A pocket full of Posy
> Atchoo! Atchoo!
> We all fall down!

In *The Great Plague: The Story of London's Most Deadly Year* (2004), Moote and Moote explicate the rhyme:

"Ring around the Rosie" characterized the red tokens of plague that appeared on the chest. The "pocket full of Posy" was a satchel of herbs worn as protection against infectious air. "Atchoo" was the sound of sneezing that spread the plague from person to person. "All fall down" was the sadness of sudden death, as people were known to collapse on the streets, sometimes with few symptoms of the sickness [7–8].

Ruhl substitutes the children's game duck duck goose for the nursery rhyme. The person who is "it" walks around the participants, who sit in a circle, and touches each on the head as she says either "duck" or "goose." The person designated "goose" becomes "it" and must, in turn, tag the person who was "it" before that person runs around the circle and takes the seat of the "goose." In the Midwestern variation of the game represented in the play, a person who is tagged out sits in the "mush-pot" in the center of the circle. Once there are too few people left in the circle, the game is started over ("Duck Duck Goose"). The game mimics the spread of the plague. Although person-to-person transmission only occurred in the relatively rare pneumatic version of the disease, the Jacobeans were not aware of this, hence the practice of quarantine. The plague struck apparently at random with no indication of who would be designated "goose" next, and those afflicted most often did not survive and were consigned to the burial pit, matched in the game by the mush-pot. The population of active players is depleted to the point at which it is not possible to continue playing, symbolizing that the disease has run its course.

The term "mush-pot" bears a similarity to the word "mushroom," and Tilly employs a peculiar image involving the latter and the release of spores in warm and slightly damp weather as she describes her melancholy to Lorenzo (237). The fleas that transmitted the plague from rats to humans required warmth and humidity in order to increase their population to plague-inducing and sustaining levels (Scott and Duncan, 59). The rat flea, which transmitted the plague from rats to humans, thrives at temperatures of 64°–74° F with high humidity (Barroll, 95). Tilly's mushroom propagates by releasing spores "now and again." The plague bacteria spread when fleas were "released" from a rat to find a new host, either rodent or human. Tilly metaphorically spreads her melancholy through the release of her infectious spores.

As recited in the play, the lists of causes and cures for melancholy, which are so numerous as to be impractical, not only refer to the breadth of Burton's attempts but also to the confusion evident in historical efforts to understand the plague. The four causes most often proposed were: "(1) God's punishment for a wicked people; (2) corrupt air; (3) certain conjunctions of the stars and planetary aspects; (4) the individual's natural bodily constitution" (Evans, 333). In regard to the last of these, an excess of any of the four bodily humors, including melancholy, was considered a possible cause, with the appropriate treatment consisting of measures taken to reduce the level of the offending humor (Wilson, 6–7). As included in Ruhl's lists and considered by Burton, "stars a cause" certainly applied to the plague as well since astrological factors were given wide credibility. The first cause, that of God's retribution, does not figure at all in Ruhl's play, but the second, that of corrupt air, does so to a significant extent.

Miasmatic air was widely considered to be a cause and/or carrier of the plague, and could be produced by divergent causes such as "contaminated soil, the motion of the planets, or even earthquakes" (Moote and Moote, 70). An urban center such as London would have abounded in sources of noisome emissions such as garbage and sewage, and even heavy fog was considered a factor. Burton recognizes "bad air" of all types to be a cause of melancholy as well (1.237–41) and devotes quite a few pages to how to improve air, including a discussion of when it is prudent to open a window, and which window one should open (2.65–6). Ruhl specifies that her set should include "many windows" and, "if possible, a real balcony, opening into the night air" (326). Although her characters fail to list air as either a cure or a cause, the windows provide a visual representation of the need for fresh air in the treatment of both melancholy and the plague.

Of all the characters, Lorenzo is the most resistant to melancholy, and he is also the only one to adopt measures consistent with those taken to ward off the harmful effects of miasma. Some felt that pleasant odors would ward off bad air, and so would protect themselves by carrying "nosegays, sprigs of rosemary, rue, or other sweet-smelling herbs, and ... by puffing a pipe of tobacco" (Porter, 18). Raised in a sweet shop, Lorenzo seems to have built up a resistance to melancholy. He eats marzipan while seeing patients and, while doing so, laughs at Frank as the patient discusses his melancholy (300). Eventually Lorenzo succumbs to the "almond state," but only by drinking from the vial of tears, which visually serves as the agent of infection. Lorenzo links it to death when he tells Frank that the Romans buried vials of tears with the dead (299). Frances finalizes her transformation when she quaffs Tilly's tears, and her friends join her as in a suicide pact when they partake of the toxic elixir. Through its association with the plague, melancholy kills them all.

Dance of Death

Julian's cello playing accompanies the action from start to finish, "scoring melancholy inside the head" like "an organ at a silent movie." Ruhl stipulates that he should remain onstage the entire time (227–8), but that the rest of the characters do not notice him or hear his playing until the end (322). She requests that he be "handsome, and brooding," and preferably from outside the United States (228). As a foreigner, then, he would possess an innate sense of melancholy that the Americans in the play, other than Tilly, lack. He can reasonably be envisioned as an inhabitant of Tilly's slow, sorrowful, and cinematic Europe. Although the characters do not acknowledge Julian or his music, Ruhl instructs the actors to "respond to the music as actors, rhythmically and tonally" (227). Julian, then, is setting the pace and tone of the performance without the characters being aware of him doing so. He plays the role of the musician Death to whose melodies the characters respond in a Dance of Death.

As defined by James M. Clark in "The Dance of Death in the Middle Ages and the Renaissance" (1950), the Dance of Death consists of representations of a dance or procession including both the living and dead. Either a single or multiple figures represent death, and the living are arranged according to social position (1). The representation of the dance emerged during the Middle Ages and reached its apex in a series of woodcuts by Hans Holbein produced during the 16th century. Its depictions served as a reminder of the impermanence of earthly life and of the leveling power of death, which brought down both high and low. The death figures are frequently shown playing musical instruments. The plague functioned as a major inspiration for the Dance of Death ("Dance of Death").

Julian serves as a single death figure, playing a musical instrument to which the characters, unbeknownst to themselves, "dance." Although they are not arranged in order of precedence, a variety of professions is represented including, if the former careers of Frank and Frances are counted: psychiatrist, bank teller, nurse, physicist, accountant, tailor, and hairdresser. They are only able to perceive Julian and hear his music once they have passed into the almond state, at which point he joins with them in a waltz, expressing the dance as such and bringing the play to a close. Just as the final scene represents the demise of the ensemble, it concludes the grieving process of seeking and finding. As Orpheus follows Eurydice to the underworld, Joan and her companions pursue Frances into the afterlife. The joyful celebration brings to mind the gentle confusion implied in Matilde's vision of heaven, in which everyone is laughing without comprehending the joke. Equally befuddled, Frances and friends are unable to determine where they are but nevertheless take pleasure in each other's company. Before joining Frances, and after drinking the tears, they hold a ceremony that is somewhat like a memorial, vocalizing something "between a madrigal and a liturgical chant" (319). They commemorate lost, broken objects, and passageways (320).

They also invoke measures against miasma, such as onions, which were thought to absorb the infection from bad air (Porter, 17), and the wind blowing through an open window, believed to have a cleansing effect. They are all permanently cured of both melancholy and the plague as they are blown into another world.

Sadness and Lightness

As discussed in the introduction, Ruhl admires Italo Calvino's *Six Memos for the Next Millennium*, particularly his essay on "Lightness." Citing *Saturn and Melancholy* (1964) by Raymond Klibansky, Erwin Panofsky, and Fritz Saxl, Calvino defines melancholy as "sadness that has taken on lightness," and humor as "comedy that has lost its bodily weight." Humor lacks "a dimension of human carnality" present in comedy. The "weightless gravity" of the Jacobean period derives from "melancholy and humor, inextricably intermingled," as may be found in Hamlet (or in one of his many "avatars" in Shakespeare, such as Jacques in *As You like It* [Calvino, 19–20]), who himself characterizes melancholy as "humorous sadness" (qtd. in Calvino, 20). The humorous complement to the sadness in *Melancholy Play* is easily discernible. The formulation of melancholy as a combination of sadness and lightness deserves closer scrutiny.

The cinematic references in the play conjure up an elegant yet sorrowful Europe that encompasses both of these qualities. One film that captures this melancholic mood is *The Third Man* (1949), set in Vienna after the Second World War.[4] The film is an example of British *film noir*. Its interior settings convey a sense of old-fashioned grandeur, whereas many of the exterior shots depict the ruins of a war-ravaged Vienna. Holly Martins, a hack writer of cowboy novels, arrives in the city at the behest of his friend, Harry Lime, only to discover that Harry is presumed dead in an automobile accident. Holly suspects foul play and sets about investigating the incident. In doing so, he meets and befriends Harry's girlfriend, Anna. The characters are desperate: Holly arrives from America broke; Anna is a struggling actress with a fake passport, in danger of being deported to Czechoslovakia; and Harry, who it turns out is still alive, is hiding from the police. In the midst of this misery, several characters express the sentiment that it would be better to be dead than alive. And yet, the mood of the film is surprisingly cheerful.

The distinctive zither score contributes significantly to this mood. Although at times doleful, it is more frequently cheerful and often even exuberant. The music lightens various scenes, such as the one in which Holly is waiting for Harry by the Ferris wheel, or the one in which Holly is mistakenly accused of murdering the porter who works in Harry's apartment building. Certain performances lighten the mood as well. Harry Lime has profited from the deaths of children by selling watered-down penicillin on the black market. Orson Welles plays him as a charming, likable, and remorseless villain. Even when threatening to throw his old friend off of the top of the Ferris wheel, his tone remains light and collegial. The young boy who mistakenly accuses Holly of murdering the porter does so gleefully, laughing as he chases the panicked Holly and Anna down the street as the zither music strikes up. Director Carol Reed handles his heavy subject matter with a light touch throughout, demonstrating the European melancholy alluded to in the play.

In Ruhl's work, Tilly's melancholy may be gauged by the extent to which sadness or lightness predominates. The terms take on gravitational significance when Tilly equates happiness with floating and sadness with falling (275). Later, when her mood consists almost entirely of lightness, she tells Frank that she is trying, in vain, to become heavier. When overcome by joy at her birthday party while playing duck duck goose, she insists on counteracting the sensation by going into the other room to lie down (286). After her party, a lightness predominates which isolates her from the other characters in contrast to her irresistible sadness, with which her sense of empathy was associated through the state of *mono no aware*.

Tilly assumes responsibility for Frances's transformation, implicating her own state of self-absorption brought about by an excess of happiness. Frances turns into an almond because her melancholy lacks lightness. Whereas Tilly wears her melancholy with grace and beauty, Frances "unravels" (295). Tilly's melancholy opens her up; Frances's sadness shuts her down. Lorenzo's mood consists of lightness without sadness, which is framed as a sort of American happiness induced by anti-depressant drugs. Lorenzo's happiness, like Frances's sadness, cuts him off from the world. He is an unsympathetic psychiatrist, unaware of his own emotions. The almond epidemic could symbolize both a wave of sadness and its opposite: a societal overabundance of happiness. Both extremes have the same isolating effect. The events of the play suggest that both sadness and lightness are essential for a balanced emotional state.

Ruhl favors lightness in *Dead Man's Cell Phone*, in which the currents of desire once more transport characters across the boundary between life and death. Unlike Tilly, the protagonist, Jean, is a person who strives for invisibility; she has a kind heart but lacks Tilly's irresistible aura of melancholy. Only Dwight falls in love with her; a kindred spirit, he has been dominated all of his life by his mother and brother. Jean experiences a moment of *mono no aware* early in the play, gazing on the face of Gordon, who is Dwight's brother, and at that moment falls in love with him. His face *"is transfigured, as though he was just looking at something/ he found eminently beautiful"* (10). He appears to have experienced *mono no aware* as well, gazing at Jean. As he remembers later, "I look over at her, and she looks like an angel" (57). The transient nature of life is readily apparent to both of them, since their moments of revelation occur immediately before and after his death.

IV

Falling in Love with Long Distance: *Dead Man's Cell Phone*

Beyond Grieving

As in *Eurydice* and *The Clean House*, Ruhl explores the themes of memory and death in *Dead Man's Cell Phone*. In *Eurydice*, memory serves as the very fabric of relationship and personality; in *The Clean House*, as the connective tissue binding the individual to the family of origin; and in *Dead Man's Cell Phone*, as a malleable, imaginal construct. The father revives Eurydice's personality by restoring language and memory, and Matilde conjures the ghosts of her parents through the act of remembering them. In *Dead Man's Cell Phone*, Jean fabricates stories about the deceased Gordon that recast him in a better light; in doing so, she constructs a fulfilled image of him for the benefit of his family and loved ones. Rebecca Bayla Taichman directed the premiere at Woolly Mammoth Theatre Company in Washington, D.C., in June 2007. Ruhl made slight revisions for productions in New York and Chicago in March 2008. The New York premiere occurred at Playwrights Horizons, featured Mary-Louise Parker as Jean, and was directed by Anne Bogart.

The currents of desire flow as airwaves, as the plot revolves around Gordon's cell phone, which Jean acquires after discovering him dead of a heart attack in a café. Although a stranger to him, as the first to find him she feels compelled to notify his callers that he has passed away. In doing so, she becomes involved with the primary figures in his life, which include his mother, his wife, his brother, and his mistress. Jean, a lonely yet kind person, constructs a romantic image of Gordon with which she falls in love, but which is at odds with what she learns about him from his family and mistress. She ameliorates the suffering of Gordon's survivors by misleading each into believing they were foremost in his final thoughts. Jean travels to South Africa to handle some of Gordon's unfinished business, and she is seemingly killed there and then transported to a peculiar hell in which souls are condemned to spend the rest of eternity with the person that they loved the most. This person turns out to be Gordon, who quickly disillusions her. As the plot speeds towards its conclusion, she returns to the land of the living where she is reunited with Gordon's brother Dwight, with whom she realizes, in a reversal of current, she has fallen in love. Upon learning of the nature of the afterlife from Jean, Gordon's mother throws herself on the barbecue and self-incinerates in order to be reunited with her eldest son. The play closes with Jean and Dwight pledging to love each other with "the strongest love in the world" (98).[1]

As Ruhl progresses in her plays, further and further from the point of loss, the characterization of the deceased male resembles her own father less and less. The father in *Eurydice* is closely based on Ruhl's own; Matilde's father in *The Clean House* shares a strong sense of humor with Ruhl's, but this characteristic is taken to a magic realist extreme; in *Dead Man's Cell Phone*, Gordon does not even fill the role of father, but rather that of a love interest, albeit older. His selfishness and ruthlessness contrast sharply with the caring and concern displayed by Eurydice's and, by extension, Ruhl's own, father. As the personality of the deceased changes, so does the relationship between the female protagonist and the deceased,

Jean (Polly Noonan) encounters Gordon (Rich Foucheux) in the afterlife. *Dead Man's Cell Phone.* **Woolly Mammoth Theatre Company, 2007 (photograph by Stan Barouh; courtesy Woolly Mammoth).**

which is nevertheless always marked by longing. This longing finds temporary fulfillment in Eurydice's reunion with her father, is manifested and eventually released by Matilde through the visions of her parents, but is repudiated in Jean's encounter with Gordon. The afterworld that he inhabits bears no resemblance to the joyous heaven described by Matilde, and is potentially even more unpleasant than the Greek-inspired underworld of *Eurydice* which, although flat and gray, is also peaceful and quiet. The afterworld of *Dead Man's Cell Phone* traps one for eternity with the person that one loved most, with all of the potential for psychological distress that that entails. Jean quickly finds Gordon to be intolerable; it is her good fortune that she is able to return to the land of the living.

Power Phone

The cell phone both connects and isolates; as such, it is an emblematic device of the information age. Like the Internet, it closes distances of thousands of miles while virtually removing the user from his or her immediate environs. The cell phone is the portable electronic device par excellence as it gains more and more functionality to operate as web browser, e-mail station, camera, and global positioning device. Ever increasing computational power enables it to assume more and more of the tasks previously possible only on larger machines.

In Foucault's terms, knowledge is power, a truism especially relevant in the information age. In *Dead Man's Cell Phone*, the titular device functions as a power object. It serves as the matrix of all of Gordon's business and social communication and houses valuable data in the form of his associates' contact information. Jean assumes Gordon's power when she appropriates his cell phone, and with it the license to shape knowledge to suit her needs. As the possessor of his phone, Gordon's family bestows Jean with privileged status that enables her to rehabilitate Gordon's image by concocting fantasies about his last moments on earth. Jean both desires and is repulsed by the device that puts her, so to speak, on the power grid. Described as someone who *"doesn't want to take up space"* (7), she rescinds even virtual space as she rejects the cell phone, retaining the right to disappear (52). To her way of thinking, unavailability equals invisibility.

Alternately, she desires the cell phone in the sense that it connects her to her fantasy of the other in the image that she has constructed of Gordon. She imagines that his ringing phone is somehow keeping him alive, that the "molecules" of sound will mingle with his essence in the air (53). Retaining the cell phone not only preserves a connection with Gordon, it enmeshes Jean in his social network as it causes her to appear on the "grid." This makes her visible to the Other Woman, among others, who covets the cell phone's data and is willing to inflict bodily harm in order to obtain it. Once Jean loses the power object, she is unable to maintain her fantasy of Gordon, which is disproved in their underworld encounter.

Disillusioned and fallen off the grid, Jean retreats to Dwight, who offers, in the back of the stationery store, a pre-technological sanctuary. Within the supply closet, the couple has previously shared an appreciation of embossed paper, explored through the sense of touch, which led to Dwight (ineptly) braiding Jean's hair and even greater intimacy. This scene, which closes the first part of the play, was beautifully realized in the premiere production mounted by Woolly Mammoth Theatre in Washington, D.C. In accordance with the stage directions, bits of paper fell from the sky like snow, followed by the lowering of paper lanterns shaped as houses as Jean and Dwight embraced in the closet; the elements harmonized in a peaceful, heavenly stage picture. Just as Eurydice and her father love written language, Jean and Dwight cherish the embossed words that can be felt on the page, as opposed to digital, ephemeral cell phone transmissions that zip through the air. Dwight even dreams of romance alphabetically: "Two lines—us—connected by a diagonal. Z" (62). He envisions a grid of only two nodes, invisible to the rest of the network.

This paper-based sanctuary is a nostalgic one. From his vantage point in the afterlife, Gordon observes that the pace of modern life violates the integrity of body and soul. Souls lag behind bodies in transit, so that people are most vulnerable to catastrophes such as bombings in airports and subway stations, which he envisions as types of hell (58). The set of the Woolly Mammoth production resembled a tiled subway station in chrome and off-white, in keeping with this passage. The semi-circular back wall towered over the actors and a thrust stage. In contrast to the back wall, the stationery store closet was finished in the appearance of a fine wood such as oak and was rolled on with the back, to which a few large-sized letters of the alphabet were affixed, facing the audience. Stagehands spun it around to reveal an interior lined with shelves and books, resembling an old library. The closet evoked a feeling of sepia warmth and cocooned Jean and Dwight from the cold sterility of the set at large. Theirs was a sanctuary of warm touch, in contrast to the subway station hell in which Gordon tormented Jean by attempting to rip his organs out of his body. Through the setting, Ruhl expresses nostalgia for a time when life moved at a slower pace and when human relationships could develop more directly, with less reliance on technological devices.

Ruhl revised the play for productions in New York and Chicago in March

2008. The New York premiere occurred at Playwrights Horizons, featured Mary-Louise Parker as Jean, and was directed by Anne Bogart (Isherwood, "A Nagging Call"). Steppenwolf Theatre Company mounted the Chicago production (Ruhl, *Dead*, 2–3). Theatre Communications Group has published the new version. Changes include Mrs. Gottlieb reading from *A Tale of Two Cities* at the memorial service (15), Gordon appearing onstage just before the intermission and opening his mouth as if about to speak while Jean and Dwight kiss in the stationery closet (56), and Jean and Dwight agreeing that the letter Z will be their secret password (63). In the rewritten version, the stage directions suggest an alternative to Woolly Mammoth's subway design: when Jean and Gordon meet in the underworld, it is in a café and they repeat the gestures from the first scene *"over and over again"* (80).

Ruhl has expanded the scene between Jean and the Stranger in the airport, which was brief in the Woolly Mammoth version, enhancing the mood of *film noir*. Jean's transition back to life has been reworked as well. In the Woolly Mammoth version, Jean calls out just a few lines to Dwight before reappearing at the airport. In the newer version, she tries unsuccessfully to call him on the cell phone and then repeats their agreed-upon secret password, "Z," two times, upon which she is whisked into his arms. Jean's exhortation to love in the final scene now includes an acceptance of Dwight's potential shortcomings, which include tendencies to burn toast, wear bad shoes, and say the wrong thing (98). This addition reinforces the impression that Jean has abandoned idealized love in favor of a practical, if no less romantic, attachment.

These changes only strengthen the script. Mrs. Gottlieb's reading of the Dickens passage at the memorial service reinforces the theme of isolation. Gordon's silent appearance at the end of Part One foreshadows his disruption of Jean and Dwight's nascent romance and anticipates the opening monologue of Part Two. The endless repetition of the first scene in the afterlife traps Jean and Gordon in the moment of their initial encounter, during which Jean first started to idealize Gordon. The campy, *film noir-ish* struggle in the airport sets the zany tone for the final sequence, and Jean's attempt to call Dwight on the cell phone from the afterlife succinctly demonstrates both the promise and limitations of technological communication. Finally, Jean's recognition of Dwight's flaws only strengthens their bond.

A Taste for Flesh

Gordon preys upon the misfortune of his donors, and a social Darwinism is at work in which the aggressive characters take advantage of those who are less so. Hermia tells a story that illustrates the exploitive nature of Gordon's business. According to her, her husband purchased a kidney from a man in Brazil for $5,000 cash to sell to a woman in Israel, making a profit of ten times that amount from the transaction. After his money was stolen on the return voyage, the Brazilian man mailed pictures to Gordon's home of his lost kidney, which "looked like a broken heart" (74). With the proceeds from the sale, Gordon bought his wife a rare and expensive yellow diamond.

Gordon preys on those weaker than him. His position in the food chain as the top predator is expressed both in his appetite for flesh and in his opportunistic behavior. He blackmails a former business associate who has become a sushi chef into giving him the choicest cuts of *hamachi*. He perceives humans as collections of body parts. During his last morning alive, he notes the implacable curve of his wife's "back" and decides against giving her a kiss on the "cheek" that might soften her "face" (57–8). On the way to the subway, he notes that one umbrella covers "three bodies." The subway is "a tomb for people's eyes" (58). The man behind the counter in the café is a "giant" with "really huge knuckles" (60). Lentil soup fails to satisfy his carnivorous appetite. When informed the café is out of lobster bisque, Gordon is too late to purchase Jean's portion as she has almost finished it, having beaten him to the kill. Gordon's inability to scavenge off of Jean signals a weakening that foreshadows his impending collapse. Moments later, his heart starts giving out and, once it does, Jean appropriates his cell phone and with it, his power.

Gordon's mother shares his aggressive personality and his taste for meat. Inviting Jean to dinner, she explains that the menu will consist of " large quantities of meat," since she is anemic and steak "just goes right through" her (32). Indeed, Jean and Dwight discover later that she has served a meal consisting entirely of meat dishes (43). These two are more passive than the other characters. Dwight recalls that his brother had dominated him since childhood, in one instance wrapping him up in a blanket and pushing him down the stairs (54). Mrs. Gottlieb makes no attempt to conceal her preference for Gordon. As Gordon explains, he realized early on that he was more charismatic than his brother and felt no qualms about taking advantage of him (85). As a vegetarian, Jean feeds lower on the food chain and, like a grazing animal, lacks the fighting instinct of a Gordon or a Mrs. Gottlieb. Only after she returns from hell does she request a steak, and a rare one at that (94–5). As a plot device, this fires up the barbecue upon which Mrs. Gottlieb will throw herself. Jean's desire for meat also signifies a rise in her status in relationship to Gordon; she quits her self-assumed, subservient position as his receptionist and takes her place among the other top-tier

Left to right: Hermia (Naomi Jacobson), Jean (Polly Noonan), and Mrs. Gottlieb (Sarah Marshall) at dinner. *Dead Man's Cell Phone*. Woolly Mammoth Theatre Company, 2007 (photograph by Stan Barouh; courtesy Woolly Mammoth).

carnivores. Released from the clutches of the alpha male, she is free to mate with the less-dominant Dwight.

The Unknowable Other

Hermia laments the impossibility of true human connection, and refers to the Dickens passage from *A Tale of Two Cities* included as an epigraph in the script. In it, Dickens describes the impenetrability of the human soul through the metaphor of a horse-drawn coach that isolates and cloaks the individual traveler (Ruhl, *Dead*, 5). This point is borne out by relationships in the play: Gordon and Hermia's marriage is a sham, Gordon is uncertain of his mother's love, Mrs. Gottlieb has played favorites with her sons, and Jean has lived in isolation. Jean has invented Gordon's final moments. Gordon actually does think of each of them in turn, as he recounts from the afterlife, but refrains from calling any of them for the selfish reason that what he wants to hear last is an "indescribably tender" female voice (61). Due to his past

Left to right: Mrs. Gottlieb (Sarah Marshall), Dwight (Bruce Nelson), and Jean (Polly Noonan), after Jean returns from the afterlife. *Dead Man's Cell Phone*. Woolly Mammoth Theatre Company, 2007 (photograph by Stan Barouh; courtesy Woolly Mammoth).

conduct, he recognizes that the possibility of eliciting that tone from any female is quite slim. Indeed, the woman most inclined to think of him in tender terms is the one who is a stranger.

Ruhl posits relationship as perceptual. Jean loves Gordon only as long as she can sustain her fantasy of him, and Hermia imagines herself to be someone else in order to tolerate making love to him. Gordon's unethical line of business has contaminated his personal life and impaired his capacity for intimacy. He conceptually dissects others into fragmented physicalities that he evaluates to determine whether or not they will satisfy his mercantile appetites. Obsessed with his own needs and wants, he finds himself unable to undertake even the conciliatory act of kissing his wife goodbye in the morning. In contrast, Jean acts kindly and looks for the best in everyone. She finds the goodness she is looking for even in Gordon.

The dismal state of Gordon and Hermia's marriage may be partially attributed to incompatibility. Hermia confesses to Jean that she felt that she had married "the wrong man" (71). She was repulsed by his business: "Sexual revulsion can be caused by moral revulsion" (73). And yet she acknowledges complicity in his livelihood through her enjoyment of the concomitant financial

Hermia (Naomi Jacobson, left) and Jean (Polly Noonan, right) share a drink. *Dead Man's Cell Phone.* **Woolly Mammoth Theatre Company, 2007 (photograph by Stan Barouh; courtesy Woolly Mammoth).**

rewards. Their lovemaking was like a fun house of mirrors, in which she would pretend to be another woman with whom he was having an affair, and then imagine what he was imagining her to be (69). She imagines herself and Gordon as two mirrors infinitely reflecting one another, never settling on a foundational image.

The future happiness of Jean and Dwight remains somewhat uncertain. With the cell phone removed and Jean rid of her obsession with Gordon, they are free to pursue their relationship. Jean proposes that they love each other with "the strongest love in the world" (98). However, the closing lines of the play trouble this proposition as Dwight suggests that they "love each other better than the worthies did" (98). Ruhl provides as an epigraph the concluding stanza from John Donne's sonnet "The Undertaking" to which Dwight is referring:

> ... you have done a braver thing
> Than all the *Worthies* did;
> And a braver thence will spring,
> Which is, to keepe that hid [qtd. in Ruhl, *Dead*, 6].

The poem has alternately been titled "Platonic Love" (Redpath, 290), and in it the speaker brags of attaining a nonsexual love. The Worthies were generally considered to be nine historical figures generally not recognized for their capacity for spiritual love (Redpath, 290). The humor in the poem derives from a number of factors. For one, the speaker brags about not bragging about his accomplishment. Moreover, he claims both to have loved a virtuous woman and that no such woman exists (Pinka, 67). In reference to the sonnet, then, Dwight is suggesting that he and Jean undertake a platonic love that they keep a secret from others.

Dwight's reference must be considered, however, within the context of character and scene. Dwight is a quirky bumbler. His cure for the hiccups is to drink a glass of bourbon upside down (36); one of his talents as a child, as remembered by his mother, was to "grow stiff as a board" while his friends would carry him around at his mother's parties (38); and he has difficulty completing even such a simple task as braiding Jean's hair, weaving two strands rather than the usual three (55). His reference to a John Donne sonnet reinforces his shared love of the written word with Jean; the inappropriateness of the citation is consistent with his character. Within the context of the play, by the "Worthies," Dwight could be referring to those characters who have achieved greater material success than he and Jean, particularly Gordon and Hermia, who have not loved particularly well. As a reference to his brother's marriage, then, Dwight's citation of Donne supports Jean's entreaty to absolute love, even as the actual content of the poem somewhat dims his endorsement. Ruhl intends the ending to be "an actual hymn to love" (Ruhl qtd. in Lahr, "Surreal"). The ending as revised for the New York premiere reinforces this interpretation as Jean promises to love Dwight in spite of, or perhaps even because of, his faults, rather than blindly vowing to establish "the strongest love in the world."

A Comic Dead Man

Although *Eurydice* and to a greater extent *The Clean House* both contain a good dose of humor, this humor is leavened with pathos. The dominant mood of *Dead Man's Cell Phone* is, however, definitely comic. The memorial scene, set in a church, is no exception. Mrs. Gottlieb praises the church ceiling, which she considers high enough to contain her grief, as she begins her eulogy, which was delivered to great comic effect by Sarah Marshall in the Woolly Mammoth production. When the ringing of Gordon's phone, in Jean's possession, interrupts the service, Mrs. Gottlieb launches into a vulgar diatribe against cell phones in general. This in turn derails the entire service, which concludes with a campy rendition of "You'll Never Walk Alone," a song from Rodgers and Hammerstein's *Carousel* (1945). In the musical, it is sung after Billy's death and reprised later at his daughter's high school graduation. Significantly, the song alludes to the dead guiding the living, as Billy is allowed to return to earth in order to assist his daughter. Billy, who commits suicide after a foiled robbery, redeems himself through this intervention and wins entry into heaven. Similarly, Jean attempts to redeem the deceased Gordon, albeit unsuccessfully. Sarah Marshall's enthusiastic rendition of the song elicited much laughter from the audience.

Ruhl's work played as a comic *tour de force* at Woolly Mammoth. Highlights included Marshall's performance and Rick Foucheux's deft handling of Gordon's soliloquies. The tone becomes highly farcical as Jean returns to the world of the living and is whisked away by Dwight, who suddenly appears in South Africa, back to his mother's house. Mrs. Gottlieb reveals that Hermia, in a random plot twist, has returned to the ice follies as a professional skater. Jean abandons her vegetarianism and Mrs. Gottlieb self-incinerates while reprising "You'll Never Walk Alone," to which Dwight shrugs that she always loved his brother best. Finally, Jean and Dwight vow everlasting love. All of this takes place within a seven-page scene. The Woolly Mammoth production recaptured some of the tenderness of the stationery closet scene by once again lowering the paper-house lanterns as the lights went down.

Postmodern Ruhl

As Ruhl is writing during the postmodern era, it can rightly be expected that a postmodern sensibility will inform her work. The term resists easy definition. In *The Theater of Transformation: Postmodernism in American Drama* (2005), Kerstin Schmidt provides useful guidelines specific to the theater. She posits a theater of transformation as a model, rather than a norm, of postmodern drama. Given the sprawling nature of any definition of postmodernism, her model provides a convenient basis for discussion. A useful starting point is to consider the ways in which postmodern drama departs from traditional drama. A postmodern drama troubles "most of the features that have traditionally defined it, such as character, plot, and agon" (13).

Ruhl's work in general, however, honors these three traditional features. As noted in the introduction to this study, Ruhl has expressed an interest in drama that proceeds by way of small transformations rather than building to a big climax. Although her plots do not drive relentlessly forward in the style of, say, Greek tragedy, events are nevertheless linked by cause and effect. Her characters are traditional as well, which is to say they are constructed as cohesive rather than fragmented entities. And certainly agon, or conflict, figures in her work. Ruhl's *oeuvre* resists categorization with those of the postmodern playwrights highlighted by Schmidt, who include Jean-Claude van Itallie, Megan Terry, Rochelle Owens, and Suzan-Lori Parks. Parks may serve as an example, most markedly in her earlier plays: She frequently replaces linear plot development with a strategy of repetition and revision inspired by jazz improvisation, she represents identity as fragmented and shifting rather than cohesive and stable, and she avoids staging conflict within the standard protagonist/antagonist binary. Ruhl's treatment of these three traditional elements is, compared to Parks, conservative.

Schmidt identifies three issues that are critical to her definition of a postmodern theater:

> [T]he postmodern sense of self[;] a problematization of the dramatic text, performance and authorship in postmodernism[;] and aspects of the theatrical space and its relationship to postmodern mediatized culture [13].

As demonstrated in comparison to Parks, Ruhl's characters fail to meet the first criterion. In regards to the second issue, Schmidt notes that postmodernism is associated with the "death of the author." As a collaborative art, the theater subjects a writer's efforts to interpretation in the very act of staging the dramatic text, and thus the writer's autonomy is challenged from the outset. Under postmodernism, a playwright's position may be destabilized to an even greater extent; for example, scripts might be developed collaboratively in a workshop environment. Language itself might be devalued, and the emphasis placed on creating images rather than stories (59). Ruhl stages powerful images, but they are placed in the service of narrative and there is no doubt that, in her case, the author is alive and well as evidenced by the great care she takes in selecting every word of dialogue, and even in carefully crafting stage directions. She thus fails to align, in many respects, with Schmidt's first two issues. However, one aspect of Schmidt's second issue, that of intertextuality, merits examination in regard to Ruhl's work. For the sake of convenience, this will be discussed in relation to Schmidt's third issue.

Her third issue is "aspects of the theatrical space and its relationship to postmodern mediatized culture." Schmidt here relates time to space. She contends that "postmodern drama ... aims at deconstructing time as a continuum and a linear progressive movement" (76). This may be achieved by presenting events and objects asynchronously, as Ruhl does in *Eurydice* and *Melancholy Play*. In *Late*, Ruhl compresses time during the holiday sequence in order to represent the pressure that Mary feels to conform to a middle-class, heteronormal, family-oriented existence. Schmidt's third issue also addresses the influence of the media upon contemporary life. Although Ruhl does not deploy video images or other media on the stage, she does draw on film for inspiration. However, she does so more to inform her narrative structure than her theatrical space, and so her appropriation of specific films may more aptly be framed as an example of intertextuality than a reflection of mediatized culture.

Intertextuality occurs in *Dead Man's Cell Phone* in the referencing of *film noir*. Gordon's lack of ethics bring to mind the antihero Harry Lime from *The Third Man*, as discussed in conjunction with *The Clean House*. Lime is engaged in an illegal penicillin trade that is harming children and, like Gordon, sacrifices morality for the sake of profit. The Other Woman of *Dead Man's Cell Phone* is based upon the *femme fatale*, with her foreign accent, world-weariness, and a concern with beauty and glamour that references classical movie stars. Two scenes in particular spoof *film noir*; these are the clandestine meetings between Jean and the Other Woman at a café and at the Johannesburg airport.

During their first encounter, the Other Woman assumes that Jean was also having an affair with Gordon. They are thus positioned as rivals, which in a sense they are, since the Other Woman was Gordon's mistress and Jean imagines herself to be in love with him. The humor in the scene derives from a stylistic clash: the Other Woman behaves as though a *femme fatale* from the 1940s or 1950s, in contrast to Jean who behaves like an ordinary, modern woman. For example, Jean simply fails to register the accusation that she was Gordon's lover. The Other Woman admits that she arranged the meeting in order to find out if Gordon mentioned her before he died. Even so, she claims to "hate sentiment" (21), as would a hard-boiled *femme fatale*.

The *film noir* influence is even more pronounced in the encounter at the Johannesburg airport. The Other Woman has disguised herself in a raincoat and sunglasses as a stranger with "*an Eastern European accent*" and the stage directions call for "*film noir music*" (76), with which she is associated elsewhere as well. Choreographed violence breaks out when Jean reneges on the organ sale: the Other Woman pulls a gun and Jean crumples her with an expert kick to the leg, which the Other Woman counters with a blow to the head. As in the café scene, Jean deviates from the *film noir* scenario, offering here a speech about the importance of love, and a lamp in the shape of a kidney. Both scenes play as spoofs of *film noir* in which a bumbling incompetent is thrown into situations that are outside of her frame of reference.[2]

Although Ruhl spoofs *film noir*, that is clearly not her primary purpose in writing this play. Rather, the referencing of *film noir* subtracts weight. The slipping in and out of *film noir* parody is consistent with the tonal inconsistency of postmodern intertextuality as noted by Schmidt (37). Other genres incorporated into *Dead Man's Cell Phone* include character-based comedy, fantasy, and farce. The journey to the underworld is best categorized as fantasy. As discussed in conjunction with *The Clean House*, Ruhl's work does not qualify as absurdism. Nor does this particular play establish the foundational sense of realism required for magic realism. Up until the last scene, much of the humor is character-based; after that, the plot accelerates and the play becomes farcical. The work as a whole may best be classified as a postmodern comic fantasy.

It is worth noting a connection between Schmidt's paradigm of transformation and Ruhl's theater training through the person of Viola Spolin, the renowned teacher of theater improvisation. Schmidt adopts this paradigm from an acting technique that was practiced in Joseph Chaikin's Open Theater. In this context, transformation "meant the abrupt taking on and dropping of different roles without any accompanying changes in setting, costume, or lighting" (12). Schmidt credits Spolin with originating the exercise. The Piven Workshop, where Ruhl received her early theater training, was established in order to continue Spolin's teachings. Certainly Ruhl was exposed to the spirit of this exercise, if not the exercise itself, as evinced by her expressed preference for small transformations over big climaxes. Nevertheless, a proclivity for fragmented or shifting characterizations can only be found, in Ruhl's plays, in the onstage transformation of Charles and Ana into Matilde's parents in the final scene of *The Clean House*. Elsewhere, Spolin's influence manifests as a fondness for minimalistic settings that allow for quick scene changes.

Magic realism is generally understood to be a component of postmodernism (Dawson, 171). In "Scheherazade's Children: Magical Realism in Postmodern Fiction" (1995), Wendy B. Faris analogizes the relationship between modernism and postmodernism. She situates Scheherazade of *The Thousand and One Nights* as "a popular paradigm of the high modernist narrator—exhausted and threatened by death, but still inventing" (164). Magic realism corresponds to Scheherazade's children as a generative force that replenishes fiction. Faris associates modernism with epistemology, or questions of knowledge, versus postmodernism's concern with ontology, or questions of being. Whereas a modernist will be inclined to remember and reconstruct, a postmodernist invents (166). Faris notes that Jean-François Lyotard characterizes postmodernism as a search for new forms that attempt to present the unpresentable, and suggests that magic realism does just that (185).

Faris's argument appears to fly in the face of Schmidt's definition of postmodernism. According to the latter's guidelines, magic realism does not qualify as postmodern at all. For one thing, magic realism typically does not trouble character, plot, and agon to an appreciable degree. Indeed, Faris observes that magic realist fictions "often (though not always) cater with unidirectional storylines to our basic desire to hear what happens next" (163). In terms of character, although metamorphosis may occur in the sense of drastic transformation, and therefore indicate an unstable identity, the type of fragmentation that might be found, for example, in a Parks play is not typical of magic realism. Conflict tends to play a traditional role within the unidirectional storylines. However, this discrepancy may be attributed to the wide scope of postmodernism rather than to a faulty analysis on the part of either scholar. Indeed, Faris lists aspects of magic realism that are congruent with Schmidt's larger definition of postmodernism. These include metafictional (or meta-theatrical) dimensions, intertextuality, defamiliarization, the employment of "repetition as a narrative principle," and a tendency to oppose the established social order (Faris, 175–80).

In addition to magic realist tendencies, Ruhl may be classified as postmodern in her employment of intertextuality and her playful sense of time; she qualifies as a traditionalist in her adherence to more-or-less-standard constructs of plot, character, and agon. In general, she demonstrates a postmodern rather than modern attitude: she affirms a playful disposition rather than seeking the truth and origin of things, and expresses a greater interest in ontology than epistemology. Ruhl's postmodern tendencies are readily apparent in the asynchronicity and intertextuality of *Late: a cowboy song*. Ruhl deals directly with American archetypes, such as those of the cowboy and the American family, brushing up against the American dream in the process. She also raises questions about art and life by invoking the modernist American painter Mark Rothko and draws a parallel between the act of cooking and the creative process. She interrogates sexual orientation and gender, questioning traditional definitions of family as well as blurring the lines that delineate male and female. This play, and the issues it raises, will be examined in the following chapter.

V

A Cowboy Stew

Swirling Broth: The Ruhl Recipe

Tony Kushner has famously compared a good play to a good lasagna. Both should be overstuffed to the point of collapse, and just barely held together by "culinary engineering magic" ("On Pretentiousness," 61–2). A Ruhl play, however, is more like a clear soup than an overstuffed lasagna. In *Late: a cowboy song*, Mary appreciates a broth in which "bright and clear" vegetables are separately suspended (141). Rather than overloading her play to the point of collapse, Ruhl selects a relatively few choice ingredients and suspends them, in a balanced manner, in a delicious broth, as in Mary's soup. The juices of her thematic materials simmer and mingle as she brings the concoction to a rolling boil. Her dialogue is sparer than that of Kushner; she strives for poetic economy. Although Kushner's writing is certainly elegant he does not shy away from playful verbosity, one example being the entire first act of *Homebody/Kabul*, which consists of a monologue delivered by the Homebody, who delights in obscure, multisyllabic words. A Kushner play requires some digesting, and although one by Ruhl certainly serves up food for thought, it tends also perhaps to clear the head, as Mary's soup does. The analysis of *Late* offered here will be broadened to identify ingredients present in much of Ruhl's work. In this instance, her thematic material includes sexual and gender identity as well as the myths of the cowboy and the American family. As usual, she crafts lean dialogue and delights in the crisp, poetic turn of phrase and in whimsical juxtaposition.

Ruhl has jokingly described her own writing process as "hell" (Kaplan), so Mary's trying attempt to prepare soup easily reads as a metaphor for the playwright's own creative process. In consulting the broth recipe in *The Joy of Cooking*, Mary is appalled by the violent instructions that call for bones to be "disjointed and crushed," a scummy crust to be pushed to the side, and the addition of "uncooked fowl carcasses" (152).[1] Although a Ruhl play is surely more nutritious than a consommé, the process of writing one may be as violent as that of preparing the soup, as Ruhl draws on her sometimes painful memories as raw material, disjointing and crushing the bones of her own experience to cook up a work of art. In rewriting, the scummy foam must continually be scooped to the side and discarded in order to achieve clarity.

It's a Not-So-Wonderful Life

Late: a cowboy song premiered at the Ohio Theatre in New York City, produced by Clubbed Thumb, in April 2003 under the direction of Debbie Saivetz. Ruhl draws inspiration from a wide range of sources. She built *The Clean House* around an overheard anecdote, *Eurydice* on Greek myth. In *Late* she looks to *It's a Wonderful Life* (1946), a film in which everyman George Bailey, played by Jimmy Stewart, sacrifices his dreams for the greater good. He abandons his plans to attend college, travel, and then "build things," instead rescuing his deceased father's savings and loan, marrying, and starting a family. The film was released in a postwar America that valorized personal sacrifice and was entering a period of unprecedented prosperity. Citizens were eager to resume life as normal, the baby boom was just beginning, and gender roles were clearly defined. The movie idealizes the American family as exemplified by that of George and Mary, whose family survives George's crisis of confidence stronger than ever.

George hits rock bottom when his absent-minded uncle loses an $8,000 deposit on Christmas Eve, jeopardizing their business and exposing George to charges of embezzlement. As a stressed George returns home later that day, he loses his temper, yells at the children, knocks over a model of a bridge representative of his dream to someday build something, and throws objects against the wall. He collects himself and apologizes when he notes the horrified looks on his children's faces, only to once again fly into a rage and storm out the door. Donna Reed as Mary plays the supportive wife throughout, protective of the children but also solicitous towards her husband. As the evening progresses, George's guardian angel preempts a suicide attempt by throwing himself first into the icy river, thereby compelling his ward to rescue him. In a sequence reminiscent of *Christmas Carol*, the angel reveals how poorly the town would have fared had George never been born. Chastised and renewed, he returns home to his loving family and the grateful townspeople, who pass the plate to replenish the missing funds.

Ruhl isolates the pattern of domestic abuse to be found in the film. In *The Domestic Violence Sourcebook* (1998), Dawn Bradley Berry outlines the three stages of domestic violence: (1) tension builds as the man becomes "edgy, critical, [and] irritable" while the woman appeases him; (2) the violent outburst; (3) loving contrition, during which the man might apologize and ask for forgiveness, swearing to reform himself. The woman, grateful for her partner's positive behavior, willingly forgives the abuse and the couple reconciles. The violence is liable to become more severe with each repetition (35–7), and the abuse may be physical, psychological, or both (1–2). In the film, the first stage occurs when George returns home and behaves irritably towards his family. He passes into the second stage when he knocks over and throws objects against the wall, moves into the third stage as he expresses contrition, and then retreats once more into the second stage, storming out of the house in a fit of rage. At the film's conclusion, he fully enters into the third stage as he reconciles with his wife and children.

Ruhl bases Crick and Mary on the film couple. Crick is given to outbursts of anger and threatening behavior, which ultimately escalate to the point of physical violence. He throws a pot (184), a loaf of bread (186), and a Christmas present (208) against the wall, makes his hand into a fist while arguing (170), and waits at home with baseball bat in hand (215). During their final encounter, he "puts his hands on the back of her neck, hard" (217). They typically reconcile through physical affection. In both works, the couples have been acquainted since childhood and experience financial difficulties. Unlike George, however, Crick is unable to provide any semblance of economic stability. Crick is a version of George stripped of his redeeming social conscience. Reduced in this way, his domestic profile comes to the forefront.

Tellingly, Crick enjoys *It's a Wonderful Life* and views it on three separate occasions. The first is on New Year's Eve; he watches as the townspeople celebrate George with a rendition of "Auld Lang Syne." Absorbed in the movie, Crick deflects Mary's suggestion that they visit her mother, who is "all alone." Ironically, Crick's fascination with the ideal cinematic family forecloses the possibility of a holiday get-together and he even interferes with Mary's phone conversation by turning up the volume. The next viewing occurs on Thanksgiving. After a fight, he finds himself alone with their baby, Blue. In the film, George fumes what is essentially his marriage proposal as an angry diatribe in which he vows never to marry and to pursue instead his own best interests. The conflicted George grabs Mary by the shoulders with great vehemence as he delivers the speech; they kiss passionately and wed shortly thereafter. She has taken a romantic interest in him since childhood, much as Crick has loved his Mary since their eighth birthday party, at which he was too lovestruck to blow out his birthday candles. Crick watches the movie for a third time on Christmas. Structured as a flashback, the movie opens as George considers suicide, and Crick views the opening sequence in which various characters pray for the protagonist. Ironically, the last line from the movie heard during the play is, "Please, God, something is the matter with Daddy" (Ruhl, *Late*, 203), a sentiment that Ruhl's Mary takes to heart as she finally abandons Crick for good.[2]

The love triangle is a common thematic ingredient in Ruhl's work, such as: father, daughter, and her lover in *Eurydice*; husband, wife, and other woman in *The Clean House*; a lesbian couple and another woman in *Melancholy Play*; a woman and two brothers in *Dead Man's Cell Phone*; and two men and a woman in *Passion Play*. In *Late*, she adapts and intensifies the triangle from the film. In an early scene, Mary and Violet flirt with the young George as soda jerk. The coquettish Violet never poses a serious threat to the more proper, and hence more suitable, Mary. In the play, Red supplants Violet, and Mary, rather than George, occupies the apex of the triangle. Unlike Violet, Red successfully disrupts the couple.

Holiday Fatigue

Holidays bring out the best and worst of family life. In the movie, George traverses emotional peaks and valleys on Christmas Eve, an appropriate choice of holiday as divine intervention returns him to the fold. The first of many holidays to occur in *Late* is also Christmas, during which Mary and Crick enact their dysfunction in mild form. Crick, an aficionado of modern art, presents Mary with an abstract painting. She smoothes over her initial dismay to grant a kiss of half-hearted approval. A stronger note of discord is sounded on New Years Eve. Mary calls first her mother and then Red as an isolated Crick cries over the movie (157).

On Veteran's Day, Crick loses his job and comes home early, forcing Mary to conceal that she has been horseback riding with Red. On Thanksgiving, the couple reconciles after a fight. In Part 3, a sequence of holidays passes with accelerating velocity to culminate in an outburst from Mary. In the next scene, she calls her mother to complain that every day seems like a holiday. Trapped in the holiday sequence, Mary desperately emulates the ideal American family, which has been linked to Christmas Eve in particular, and holidays in general, through *It's a Wonderful Life*. The holidays come full circle, from Christmas to Christmas Eve. Unlike the cinematic Mary, who is reunited with her husband on the latter, the stage version abandons her abusive spouse for the other woman.

Two of the American playwrights that will be linked to Ruhl in a later chapter have written one-acts in which holidays mark the passage of time; these are Wilder's *The Long Christmas Dinner* (1931) and Guare's *In Fireworks Lie Secret Codes* (1981). Wilder tracks a family through 90 years of Christmas dinners. At intervals, nurses wheel in newborns through a portal stage left, which symbolizes birth, and characters teeter out another stage right that signifies death. The holiday dinner serves as an occasion for reminiscing and is the conduit through which generations pass. The conversation tends towards the banal as Wilder sets the everyday and ordinary against the flux of birth and death. In this regard the work is thematically similar to *Pullman Car Hiawatha*, with which it was published in 1931, and the later *Our Town*. Unlike Ruhl's, Wilder's characters cherish their holiday time together, but as in Ruhl, time passes too quickly. The family is an archetypal American one, more or less free from conflict, and not tested as is George and Mary's or Mary and Crick's. The curtain falls as the sole remaining occupant, the aged spinster cousin, exits through the death portal. Even her exit, however, alludes to the continuing cycle of life, as she mutters the names of the newest additions to the family, christened after the ancestral couple who established the Christmas tradition 90 years before.

Guare's play takes place on the Fourth of July as five well-to-do friends watch the fireworks from a New York City penthouse and remember past holidays. One recounts ringing the bells during a hectic service at the Church of the Nativity in Bethlehem on Christmas day; another tells a story of a man wrongly accused of sexual harassment on the New York subway on Memorial Day. The characters compare the "hysterical" nature of holidays to the poetry of ordinary days, in keeping with which the host's partner shocks him with the announcement that he is returning to England after 12 years in the United States. One guest contends that Tennessee Williams's dramatic poetry sprang from the everyday language of New Orleans, another that Harold Pinter was just writing about the "neighborhood on an ordinary day" (257). Here, holidays mark time differently than they do in Wilder or Ruhl. The English host especially remembers the Fourth of July in 1976 for the tall ships sailing up the Hudson, which sets him to counting his years in New York (258). In spite of this, holiday remembrance primarily invokes anecdote. The British expatriate complains that he cannot fully understand America, hence the title of the play. Nevertheless, this play lacks the hysteric energy of Ruhl's holiday sequence, as the observations are couched in witty repartee and even the expatriate's startling revelation is met with a measured, well-reasoned response from his partner (258).

Guare and Ruhl both incorporate the song "I'm Dreaming of a White Christmas," an Irving Berlin melody from the movie *Holiday Inn* (1942). One of Guare's characters saw the movie as a child: "Bing Crosby and Fred Astaire opened a nightclub that was only opened holidays and Irving Berlin wrote a song for each holiday." When asked what they did between holidays, she admits that they "never delved that deep" (252). The two men vie for the affection of the singer/dancer played by Marjorie Reynolds. The Crosby character discovers that farming, taken up as an escape from a grueling performance schedule, is more difficult than he had hoped, and cooks up the Holiday Inn scheme to ease his workload. Mary and Crick sing a verse of "I'm Dreaming of a White Christmas" during the holiday sequence, for which sequence Ruhl may well have drawn inspiration from the movie.

"She's No Cowgirl, She's a Cowboy"

Ruhl sets the myth of the American cowboy against that of the American family. Red personifies the rugged individual in opposition to the self-sacrificing family man. In *The Cowboy Hero: His Image in American History and Culture* (1979), William W. Savage, Jr., examines the myth of the cowboy as established through entertainment and the media. Characteristics include a folksy sort of wisdom and an ignorance of current events (20–3), a knowledge of the ways of nature (24), and a courteous manner towards ladies (97). Additionally, skillful horsemanship is on display in countless Western films. Ruhl has bestowed all these characteristics on Red to gently satirize the archetype. For example, she and Mary share a moment of cowboy wisdom in the café as they ponder how the proprietors of Vietnamese and Korean restaurants must feel about making food for Americans, considering U.S. military interventions in those countries. They conclude that they do not understand how wars begin and end, and Red simply expresses her appreciation for simple food. When Mary expresses befuddlement and an incapacity for making simple decisions, such as whether to eat a potato chip or take a walk, Red laconically asserts that she simply does what she feels like doing. Red demonstrates her knowledge of the ways of nature through her skill with horses. Mary reports that Red "sings horse lullabies for a job" (130). She works outside the city limits (148) and knows how to break horses (179–81). Not only is she courteous to ladies, she defines Mary as one for knowing how to accept a compliment (210). Red acts the gentleman cowboy to Mary's lady.

Red's songs punctuate the action of the play. She establishes the improvisational nature of her lyrics as she concludes her first song with the nonsensical rhyme "crayon" for "man" (133). Red upholds the cowboy tradition of singing to soothe animals; music was used to calm cattle to keep them from stampeding at night (Savage, 79). She also personifies the commercial image of the singing cowboy. Country music performers first adopted the "strong, masculine image of the cowboy" beginning in the 1930s because it outsold that of the "yokel" or "barefooted clodhopper" (Savage, 80–1). Red soothes horses and Mary's baby with lullabies, and expresses her inner thoughts and feelings in song, as in a love song for Mary (148), a celebration of the carefree life (158), a lamentation over a broken heart (175), and an exhortation for Mary to leave Crick (188). She thus loosely chronicles the transference of Mary's affection from Crick onto herself. Ruhl uses song elsewhere to reinforce thematic ideas, as in the "Song from the Company" in *Melancholy Play*, which laments the passing of Tilly's sorrow (305–6), and in the "Spring Song" in the first part of *Passion Play* (which was cut, however, from later versions).

Another mythical quality of the cowboy is "unadorned masculinity" as reinforced through cigarette advertising (Savage, 4). Ruhl calls for the Marlboro Man to hover in the distance in her set design. The Marlboro Man was fashioned to sell a product previously intended for women; the ad campaign started in the 1950s, appeared in television commercials through 1970, and later continued in print ads. The campaign was finally discontinued when two of the ad models died of lung cancer (Schalch). Visual artist Richard Prince began exhibiting rephotographed Marlboro ads, cropped and with text erased, in 1983 (Heartney). This effort has been situated within the first wave of postmodernist photography, which "pillaged the mass media and advertising for its 'subject'" and challenged assumptions about authorship (Solomon-Godeau, 204). In "Living with Contradictions: Critical Practices in the Age of Supply-Side Aesthetics" (1989), Abigail Solomon-Godeau observes that the release of Prince's cowboy images coincided with the beginning of the Reagan presidency, and that this series "pointedly addressed the new conservative agenda and its ritual invocations of a heroic past.... Prince made visible the connections among cultural nostalgia, the mythos of the masculine, and political reaction" (204).

Although Ruhl's appropriation of the Marlboro Man does not reference the Reagan administration, it does evoke connections between cultural nostalgia and the mythos of the masculine. Ruhl troubles the gender of this mythos, stressing, in her character description of Red, "She's no cowgirl, she's a cowboy" (121). In *Gender Trouble* (1999), Judith Butler calls on drag to posit gender as performative rather than ontological (171–80). She discerns three strands of corporeality that figure in drag: "anatomical sex, gender identity, and gender performance" (175). Red is presumably anatomically female, although sexual ambiguity is not ruled out. Blue's androgyny and Red's masculinity challenge the heteronormal relationship between Crick and Mary, and by extension the idealized American family as depicted in *It's a Wonderful Life*.

Blue is born with both male and female sexual features. Ruhl gives special thanks to Anne Fausto-Sterling and her *Sexing the Body*, published in 2000 (Ruhl, *Late*, 122). Fausto-Sterling is a professor of biology and gender studies at Brown University and is also Paula Vogel's spouse ("Paula Vogel, Anne Fausto-Sterling"). She opposes the prevalent medical practice of surgically altering sexually ambiguous newborns, advocating for greater acceptance of the intersexual individual (95–109). Mary's beliefs coincide with Fausto-Sterling's, and she expresses concern at least, if not outright opposition, about the procedure performed on her child (164). Crick and Mary's tussle over the baby's name extends the battle over her identity. Crick prefers Jill because "things are going to be weird enough, without her having a weird name" (167). Mary favors Blue both to honor Red (147) and to express a unique individuality (167). Ruhl stipulates an invisible Blue, a child as blank as the two fortunes that Mary unwraps in the Chinese restaurant, ones that invite strange and beautiful futures (213). Ruhl advances Blue's androgyny as a state of creative opportunity rather than confusion.

Shades of Rothko

Ruhl frequently evokes painters in her work, such as Edward Hopper in *Dead Man's Cell Phone*, René Magritte in *Melancholy Play*, and Mark Rothko in *Late*. Hopper appears in two stage directions in the first of these, both describing Jean alone on the stage (33, 62). An American realist, Hopper often depicted a loneliness that was "quiet, passive, [and] stark" (Sweet), as befits Jean's isolation. Mark Strand's epigraph bolsters Ruhl's choice, in that it describes the trapped space of his paintings, and the figures within them that "must keep themselves company" (qtd. in Ruhl, *Dead Man's Cell Phone*, 3, 2008 version). In *Melancholy Play*, "A Song from the Company" references Magritte in connection with a nostalgic, slow, sweet, and balconied life (306). Much of the Belgian surrealist's art conveys an early 20th-century European sensibility, as seen in the clothing and furniture in his paintings. This sensibility complements that of the cinematic Europe referenced in the play.

Rothko figures more prominently in *Late* than the artists do in the two other works. Ruhl specifies a backdrop that is a cross between one of his paintings, with his palette of reds, blues, and greens, and the cowboy's open sky (121–2). The names Red and Blue reference that palette. Many of Rothko's paintings do indeed suggest landscapes, with two panels of color separated by a horizontal dividing line. The painting Crick is fired for touching matches the pattern of a Rothko, with "red on top and white on the bottom" (177). The painting evokes his tears, as one by Rothko might; the modernist's work has been known to elicit a religious, mystical, or spiritual response (Chave, 1).

Ruhl links Crick's response to modern art with clearing the head and altering temporal perception. A scene is devoted to Crick examining his painting from different perspectives (151), and he later claims that this act of contemplation slows down time (207). For Mary, time speeds inexorably forward as manifested by the holiday sequence. A dance with Red finally applies the brakes, two-stepping them into sync and "horse time" (214–5). Mary here explicates the title of the play: the cowboy song simply abolishes the concept of lateness. In tune with nature, Red escapes the frenetic pace of modern life and entices Mary to join her. Mary and Red are able to "experience time at the exact same speed" (213), a synchronicity missing with Crick. He invites Mary to contemplate his painting, but it simply does not affect her (207).

The blurring of the boundary between high and low culture, an aspect of intertextuality (Schmidt, 40–1), may be found in Ruhl's setting for *Late*, combining, as it does, the palette of Rothko with the image of the Marlboro Man. The set is to suggest a landscape, and the experience of the landscape, and by extension nature, as mediated by the high culture of modernist painting and the low culture of cigarette advertising. A state of transcendent peace may be arrived at either through an experience of modern art, in the case of Crick, or through the cowboy lifestyle, as exemplified by Red. The American transcendentalists extolled serenity achieved through the direct experience of nature; Ruhl's characters approach bliss through high art that suggests nature, and a mediatized apprehension of the cowboy experience. In both cases, a copy of nature has replaced the original, or more precisely a simulacrum of a nature that never existed. Yet Ruhl does not mourn the absence of nature but rather deploys the simulacra with playfully postmodern verve.

In the closing scene Mary and Red, in cowboy hats, stand over a stroller and croon a lullaby that curiously references a girl "who rides like a man—/ With a mask" (219). This conclusion references gender as performance. Ruhl frequently defends against sentimentality through humor, for example in the fast-paced conclusion of *Dead Man's Cell Phone*, which ironizes Jean and Dwight's coupling. In this case she alternatively counters sentimentality by drawing attention to the themes of gender and sexual identity. Furthermore, the godlike presence of the Marlboro Man, looking down as from an invisible billboard, ironizes the image of the cowboy as situated in a transcendent space outside of hectic, modern life.

The employment of contemporary media may be regarded as a form of intertextuality, since "texts" in the postmodern sense are not limited to written works. Ruhl's quotations of *It's a Wonderful Life* and the Marlboro Man draw on popular, mediatized culture. Ruhl's appropriation of the abusive patterns from the 1946 film may be read as a feminist act in the sense that Ruhl draws attention to and champions the abused spouse, who is positioned as ancillary to the male protagonist in the film. In the play, she empowers her as the protagonist who frees herself from a destructive marriage. The reworking of an appropriated text is consistent with the political efforts of various postmodern feminist playwrights as listed by Kerstin Schmidt, author of *The Theater of Transformation: Postmodernism in American Drama* (2005), including Suzan-Lori Parks, Ntozake Shange, Adrienne Kennedy, and others (39).

Schmidt differentiates between modernism and postmodernism in a number of ways. She paraphrases Jacques Derrida to posit two different modes of interpretation, the first associated with modernism, the second with postmodernism: One "seeks to discover the truth and the origin of things, whereas the other affirms a playful disposition" (Schmidt, 20). Under modernism, a disassociation from nature would perhaps be cause for anxiety and alienation, whereas under postmodernism it would most likely be seized upon as an opportunity for play. Ruhl utilizes the latter approach as she employs the Marlboro Man to expose the constructedness of the cowboy image and to counter and augment it with her own interpretation of the female cowboy. The characters seek not the origin of things, but an experience of stillness, and the path to that stillness is presented as multiple rather than singular, accessible through both high and low culture. Ruhl appropriates images in a playful, postmodern manner in her one-act, *Snowless*, as well. In it, she quotes at length from Maurice Maeterlinck's *The Life of the Bee*, a work that she clearly admires as she thanks the author, in her stage directions, for his "beauty" (Ruhl, *Snowless*, 10). The graceful prose extracted from Maeterlinck's nonfiction study serves to educate the audience about the plight of the bee in the face of global warming; in this case Ruhl draws on the external text for didactic purposes. The tactic of filling up dialogue with direct quotation, from a nonfiction work at that, demonstrates a postmodern intertextuality.

Additional Ingredients

It has been seen that the Ruhl recipe calls for heaping quantities of mythology and archetype. Nostalgia is also an essential ingredient, indicative of a longing for a simpler, slower time; perhaps this represents a desire on the part of the playwright to revisit her own intact childhood family. Although death and bereavement do not dominate in *Late* as they do in other works, they are nevertheless included in small measure. Mary reveals her fear of death in a journal entry in which she imagines instantaneous surcease by heart attack, a falling window, and spontaneous combustion (158). Her obsession with death manifests a generalized anxiety about her life and marriage. Crick compares weddings to funerals in a passage that equates love with death as things best cloaked in pretty ceremonies.

Ruhl frequently incorporates food and drink in her plays. On several occasions, Crick expresses a preference for meat and specifically (and ironically) beef, a cowboy favorite (124); Mary and Red reacquaint over a bowl of soup (141). Sometimes food reinforces community, as when the women gather over homemade chocolate ice cream in *The Clean House* (98–100), or in the conciliatory meeting over tea between Joan, Frances, and Tilly at which, appropriately enough, the hostess serves sandwiches in the shape of triangles (269). Elsewhere, an excellent cup of coffee enables Virginia to culturally situate Matilde (20). Food and drink sometimes isolate characters as when, at another triangular meeting, the jilted wife, Lane, eschews a warm beverage for hard alcohol on ice (59). In *Dead Man's Cell Phone*, the vegetarian Jean goes hungry at a table set entirely with meat (33). Apples (71) and spice (76) spill over from Ana's balcony to clutter her rival's living room in *The Clean House*. In *Eurydice*, the thirsty protagonist abandons her wedding party for the water pump, where she fatefully encounters the Nasty Interesting Man (349–50). Ruhl serves up food and drink with her customary wit, as when Mrs. Gottlieb condescends to Jean that she is as comforting as "a very small casserole" (26).

The playwright's wit is certainly a hallmark of her style and, as it is evident throughout her work, one example from *Late* should suffice. In the museum, an invitation to see a painting induces labor:

> CRICK: Or we could head over to contemporary art. You could see my favorite painting in the entire world.
> MARY: What's it called?
> CRICK: Untitled.
> *She doubles over in pain* [162–3].

Ruhl's quirkiness is evident in this play as well, as in Red's job, which is to sing horses to sleep. Her style has been discussed elsewhere, but her postmodern proclivity for mixing high and low art bears repeating. Frequently, past and present coexist. As Ruhl has stated, "I tend to like the ancient and the modern up against each other" (qtd. in Pressley). She also prefers a happy ending, as in Matilde's vision of heaven in *The Clean House*, the reunion at the conclusion of *Melancholy Play*, the coupling of Jean and Dwight in *Dead Man's Cell Phone*, the formation of a new family in *Late*, and Pontius's airborne departure in *Passion Play*. Ruhl is an optimist; her heroes and heroines resolve their difficulties and attain happiness — with the obvious exception of *Eurydice*.

In *Passion Play*, Ruhl brings the modern and, if not the ancient, at least the early modern up against each other. If *Late* is a soup, then *Passion Play* is a buffet. Shifts in Ruhl's style and concerns can be traced through the three-part cycle, the writing of which spanned 12 years. The first part resembles *Eurydice* in its dense imagery and tragic, watery ending. Although less imagistic, the second part is no less tragic, concluding with a little girl fated to a concentration camp. In the third part, a Vietnam veteran puzzles over his shattered life, and ultimately assembles something new from the pieces. The cowboy appears here as well in the persona of Ronald Reagan, who liked to portray himself as a rugged, American outdoorsman. The play journeys from Elizabethan England, to Nazi Germany, and finally to South Dakota and Washington, D.C., starting in the year 1575 and ending in the present day. Queen Elizabeth, Adolf Hitler, and Reagan make appearances, and Elizabethan sailing ships and big, beautiful fish puppets navigate currents of air and water.

VI

Apocalypse Deferred: *Passion Play*

Passionate Beginnings

Passion Play is Ruhl's most ambitious work to date. Each of its three parts depicts the staging of a historical passion play, and the totality spans from Elizabethan England to the present day and runs some three-and-a-half hours. Ruhl began writing the first part, which served as her undergraduate thesis at Brown University under the auspices of Paula Vogel (Wren, 31), 12 years prior to the premiere of the revised cycle at the Goodman Theatre in Chicago in the fall of 2007 (Ruhl, "Playwright's Note," ix). The first part premiered at Trinity Repertory Company in Providence, Rhode Island, in 1997. Ruhl's mother drove her to see it, and they had an accident on the way in which the playwright was momentarily knocked unconscious. Nevertheless, they made it to the play (Lahr, "Surreal"). A prized children's book, *Betsy and the Great World*, alerted Ruhl to the passion play staged at Oberammergau, Bavaria. The actors met by the story's protagonist are as holy as the parts that they play. The play germinated as Ruhl pondered the relationship between actor and part, and imagined a Pontius Pilate who coveted the role of Christ, an impure Virgin Mary, and a megalomaniacal Christ. She wrote the Elizabethan part first, and determined to write the second when she learned that Hitler's visit to the Oberammergau passion in 1934 was greeted with great enthusiasm, and that almost all of the residents of the village, including most of the cast, had joined the Nazi party by the end of the war (Svich, 37).

As follows from Ruhl's early musings, in the first part of the cycle the character who plays Pilate envies his cousin the role of Christ; in the second,

Crucifixion scene from Part 2 with Joaquín Torres portraying Jesus. *Passion Play.* **Goodman Theatre, 2007 (courtesy Liz Lauren).**

Hitler visits Oberammergau; and in the third, the actor who plays Jesus narcissistically advances his career. Ruhl began the second part while still an undergraduate at Brown University (Vogel, "Sarah Ruhl," 58). The first part was awarded the Fourth Freedom Forum Playwriting Award through the Kennedy Center American College Theatre Festival and thus qualified for a reading at the Sundance Theater Laboratory in 2000 (Wren, 31–2). The Sundance reading caught the attention of director Mark Wing-Davey, who was there working on Naomi Iizuka's *36 Views*. Wing-Davey was struck by Ruhl's voice, by her language and approach. In July 2002, he staged the first two parts of *Passion Play* at the Tristan Bates Theatre in London on a budget of £100. The one-week run was extended, and replacements found for those with prior commitments, when "the actors all fell in love with the play" (Wing-Davey, qtd. in "Directing *Passion Play*," 10). Artistic Director Molly Smith staged the entire cycle in 2005 at Arena Stage in Washington, D.C., which commissioned the third part (Isherwood, "The Life and Times"). Ruhl revised the third part for the Goodman production, which she had not had time to complete to her satisfaction for Arena Stage ("A Passion for Theater," 4).

Top: Ascension scene from Part 3. *Passion Play*. Goodman Theatre, 2007. *Bottom:* Nicole Wiesner (left) as Mary 2 and Joaquín Torres (center) as John the Fisherman portraying Jesus tied to chair in Part 1. *Passion Play*. Goodman Theatre, 2007 (both photographs courtesy Liz Lauren).

Each part depicts the staging of a passion play from a different historical period: Elizabethan England in 1575; Oberammergau, Germany, in 1934; and Spearfish, South Dakota, from 1969 through the present day. According to Ruhl, about 100 villages would have been presenting the passion in 1575; during that year, Queen Elizabeth banned all religious plays due to their Catholic associations. Hitler attended the Oberammergau passion twice in 1934, and praised its anti–Semitism (Ruhl, "Playwright's Note," x). The Bavarian production fulfills a pledge made to God in 1633 that, in exchange for protection from the plague, the townspeople would mount a passion play every ten years (Creamer, 7). The tradition continues to this day ("Oberammergau"), as does that of the Spearfish, South Dakota, production (*Black Hills*). Known as the *Black Hills Passion Play*, it was established in 1939 by Josef Meier, a German immigrant who had led a touring version in the United States starting in 1932 (Sponsler, 142–3). As Tom Creamer notes in "Queen, Fuehrer, President: Politics, Passion and Play," Ruhl has chosen the settings with "great care" at periods of "great political charge" that were "each dominated by figures able to imprint their personalities on history" (6). Ruhl stages Queen Elizabeth, Adolf Hitler, and Ronald Reagan as leaders who effectively utilized theater in the political arena and to explore "the relationship of community to political icons" (Ruhl, "Playwright's Note," 4).

Three Passions

Characters play the same biblical character throughout the cycle, and conform to or diverge from their role to varying degrees from part to part. Currents of desire manifest as various passions, both religious and secular. In part one, Mary 1 fails to safeguard her chastity and remain true to her virginal namesake. She lusts after the actor playing Jesus and wanders outside at night in search of male companionship. Impregnated by the actor playing Pilate, and in despair over her unworthiness in the eyes of God, she drowns herself. That actor, appropriately enough named Pontius, conforms to his part in that he hates his good-looking and virtuous cousin John, who plays Jesus.

The second part highlights the anti–Semitic bias evident in the Oberammergau passion. The Village Idiot of the first part has become Violet, an orphaned Jewish girl. The soldier Eric, who plays Jesus, captures her for internment in a concentration camp. The actress playing the Virgin Mary, here named Elsa, submits to a German officer's advances. The Footsoldier, playing Pontius, flirts with Eric; the German officer witnesses this and threatens them. Thus both Jewishness and homosexuality are identified as targets of Hitler's regime.

In the third part, the actors playing Pilate, called P, and Jesus, called J, are now brothers competing for the love of the former's wife. P returns from Vietnam a broken man. Meanwhile, his brother J has achieved celebrity as a soap opera star. While P is overseas, J sleeps with his wife, Mary 1, obscuring the paternity of her daughter, Violet. J pushes to professionalize and commercialize the passion play, to which ends the Young Director, a draft-dodger with a fake English accent, is hired; he tangles with P who rejoins the production after his tour of duty. This section spans from 1969 until the present day and includes a number of appearances by Ronald Reagan.

Second Comings

In *Arguing the Apocalypse, A Theory of Millennial Rhetoric* (1994), Stephen D. O'Leary posits the "three essential topoi of apocalyptic argument" as authority, time, and evil (19). Through the apocalypse, the problem of the existence of evil, which would seem to be at odds with that of a beneficent God, is resolved once and for all at the end of time (51). In order to attract followers, any apocalyptic prophecy must be issued from a position of authority. A primary source of apocalyptic thinking in the Christian tradition is the New Testament Book of Revelation authored by John of Patmos, who envisions a final battle in which good triumphs over evil. In their introduction to *Millennium, Messiahs, and Mayhem: Contemporary Apocalyptic Movements* (1997), Thomas Robbins and Susan J. Palmer observe that the apocalyptic model is one of crisis-judgment-reward, in which divine forces destroy the oppressive antichrist, followed by divine judgment with punishment for the wicked and reward for the virtuous (5). They distinguish between apocalyptics, "who focus mainly on the catastrophic apocalypse," and millenarians, "who are more concerned with a utopian postapocalyptic order" (9). They further differentiate between postmillennialism and premillennialism; in the former, Christ returns after the millennial kingdom has been brought about by human agency, and in the latter, Christ must vanquish the Antichrist at Armageddon before the millennium may commence. The millennium itself is a 1000-year period of peace on earth presided over by Christ (9). In "Millennialism with and without the Mayhem" (1997), Catherine Wessinger suggests replacing the terms premillennialism and postmillennialism with the more descriptive phrases "catastrophic millennialism" and "progressive millennialism," respectively (48–52); her recommendation will be followed here.

Some versions of catastrophic millennialism incorporate the rapture, in which the saints, or faithful Christians, will be lifted into the clouds to be united with Jesus and thereby escape the tribulation (Robbins and Palmer, 11). The scriptural source for the rapture may be found in 1 Thessalonians 4: 16–17:

> For the Lord Himself will descend from heaven with a shout, with the voice of the archangel and with the trumpet of God, and the dead in Christ will rise first.
> Then we who are alive and remain will be caught up together with them in the clouds to meet the Lord in the air, and so we shall always be with the Lord.[1]

In "Constructing Apocalypticism: Social and Cultural Elements of Radical Organization" (1997), David G. Bromley delineates two methods for building religious authority—the priestly and the prophetic. The former builds continuity, and the latter emphasizes discontinuity, between the transcendent and phenomenal realms. The priestly mode upholds the existing social order whilst the prophetic challenges it (33–4). Stagings of the passion play operate in the priestly mode in the sense that they manifest the connection between the earthly and spiritual realms by reiterating the act that made possible the Christian salvation of all humankind.

Drawing upon theories of drama, O'Leary differentiates between tragic and comic versions of apocalypse. He notes that many scholars before him have analyzed Revelation in dramatic terms (66) and draws especially on the critical theories of Kenneth Burke and Susanne K. Langer. In the tragic, destiny is portrayed as fate; in the comic, as fortune. Whereas fate is predetermined and unalterable, fortune is open-ended and variable. In the tragic, evil is expressed "in terms of guilt," its "mechanism of redemption is victimage," and its plot advances toward sacrifice. In the comic, evil is expressed as error, resolution comes about through recognition, and the plot advances towards "the exposure of fallibility." In tragedy the moral order is restored through suffering; in comedy, "by exposing the foolishness of pretension and vanity." Comedy is episodic, tragedy progressive (68–9). It follows that a literal interpretation of Revelation will produce a tragic vision of the apocalypse as an event that will invariably include the sacrifice of the Lamb, which leads to the final restoration of the moral order through the banishment of evil. An allegorical reading of Revelation will tend toward a comic interpretation in that the struggle against evil is envisioned as a day-to-day battle in which the individual must strive to overcome his or her foolishness and resist temptation.

The passion and resurrection of Christ as enacted in the passion play would seem to fall, under O'Leary's definition, in the category of the tragic. Christ is the victim in a pre-ordained sacrifice that resolves sin in his followers. Ruhl disrupts the tragic depiction of the passion with versions of the second coming. In the first part, Mary 1 attempts to pass off the impending birth of her child as the second coming in order to legitimize her pregnancy. In the second, the Third Reich, which Hitler characterized as a 1000-year empire (Shirer, 5), functions as a secularized millennium. President Reagan manipulates fear of a nuclear holocaust as Armageddon in the third part. Ruhl presents various other counter-narratives to the passion itself in all three parts, as shall be seen.

Frye's Apocalyptic Imagery

In *Anatomy of Criticism* (1957), Northrop Frye diagrams the archetypical symbols of the Biblical apocalypse:

divine world	= society of gods	= One God
human world	= society of men	= One Man
animal world	= sheepfold	= One Lamb
vegetable world	= garden or park	= One Tree (of Life)
mineral world	= city	= One Building, Temple, Stone [141].

He positions Christ as the unifying meta-symbol:

> The conception "Christ" unites all these categories in identity: Christ *is* both the one God and the one Man, the Lamb of God, the tree of life, or vine of which we are the branches, the stone which the builders rejected, and the rebuilt temple which is identical with his risen body [141–2].

Frye associates the world of the apocalyptic with "the heaven of religion" rather than imagery of the demonic. The apocalyptic images represent "human desire, as indicated by the forms they assume under the work of human civilization," as opposed to the demonic, which portrays "the world as it is before the human imagination begins to work on it; ... the world also of perverted or wasted works, ruins and catacombs, instruments of torture and monuments of folly" (147).

Frye further notes that in apocalyptic symbolism, man cannot be confined to "his two natural elements of earth and air," but must pass through trials of fire and water when traveling to other realms. Poetic symbolism positions fire above life in this world, and water below. The passage to heaven necessitates traversing a region of fire that, like the heat of alchemy, serves a purifying and transmutational function. On the other hand, as the realm below human life, water represents a state of "chaos or dissolution which follows ordinary death, or the reduction to the inorganic. Hence the soul frequently crosses water or sinks into it at death" (145–6).

Ruhl introduces imagery of fish and birds that challenges the sovereignty of the Lamb and the unifying power of the Christ. The deaths of Mary 1 and Pontius in the first part are met not with images associated with heaven or hell, but with the appearance of large fish puppets that carry off the body of Pontius. The sacrifice is not of the Lamb, but symbolically of Pilate, the one who ordered the sacrifice of the Lamb. Whereas Christ calms the storm and is associated with the anchor in early Christian art, P incites the wind rather than attempting to overcome it, and hoists his anchor in order to sail across the sky. He thereby rejects the stabilizing, unifying symbol of Christ.

Undermining the Passion

Ruhl's inclusion of a wise fool character in the person of the Village Idiot/Violet provides a comic foil to the tragic passion. In *Satire: Spirit and Art* (1991), George A. Test tracks the wise fool as a type that reached its height during the late Middle Ages (210). The Christian humanist Erasmus provides a rich exploration of the wise fool in his "Praise of Folly" (1511), asserting that all men are fools; even the Savior "was made something of a fool himself," since he took the form of man, albeit in order to save mankind (148). Along similar lines, in "Sileni Alcibiadis" Erasmus discusses the Sileni, which he describes as small statues made out of wood, which, when opened, reveal inside the image of a deity. Erasmus reports that Alcibiades, in Plato's *Symposium*, compares Socrates to this type of statue, as his unattractive exterior conceals his great wisdom. Erasmus extends the metaphor to Christ, a divinity disguised in poor and humble trappings (Erasmus, "Sileni," 264). Shakespeare would almost certainly have been familiar with these works; regardless, his plays provide numerous examples of the wise fool. The fool in Shakespeare and elsewhere is granted "the freedom to speak forbidden, unwanted, or unrecognized truths" (Test, 210).

The positioning of even Christ as a wise fool counters a tragic vision of the apocalypse. A fool, even a wise one, is by definition prone to error, and so restoration of the moral order through the revelation of error takes precedence over suffering and sacrifice. Additionally, Ruhl's wise fool offers images and narratives that run counter to those of the passion play. In the first part, the Village Idiot disrupts the rehearsal by playing with a Jack-in-the-box. The image of Jack the puppet corresponds to Pilate as mere pawn, playing an essential, if unsavory, role in the crucifixion. This correspondence is mapped through the actor playing the part, named also Pontius. The script indicates a deformed physicality: he complains that the doctor did not sew up his umbilicus correctly at his birth (29) and that he can cry out of only one eye (33). In the 2007 Goodman Theatre production, actor Brian Sgambati accentuated this deformation by turning one foot in, walking with a limp, and hunching and twisting his spine. Pontius experiences himself as a puppet as he imagines a string pulling up and down on his head (16). His evokes the Village Idiot when he compares the moon to a dunce's face (29).

The Village Idiot speaks to her Jack-in-the-box as if he is Pontius, "bent and twisted" and with his "heart in a box" (22). Pontius keeps his heart in a box hidden from Mary 1, who is infatuated with John, fearful that he cannot compete with his more attractive rival. He consummates his desire for Mary 1 only after the virtuous John, oblivious to her advances, has rejected her. Pontius promises to keep their tryst secret, swearing that he will be as "silent as a closed box underwater" (40). If the biblical Pilate is a puppet, then his puppet master must be God. In this respect, the Village Idiot plays God to Pontius in Ruhl's play. Furthermore, the insertion of the Village Idiot into the play as Eve reinforces the concept that all people are fools as descendents of a foolish Eve.

In the second part of the play, Ruhl utilizes Violet to introduce narratives that counter that of the Oberammergau passion. Two of these narratives are in the form of fairy tales, and the third is a rewriting of Jesus's words during the Last Supper. When the Visiting Englishman encounters Violet in the street, she asks him to tell her the story of Little Red Riding Hood. He tells a version symbolic of the future Allies' complacency towards Hitler's rise to power, in which the little girl and the wolf become good friends and live happily ever after (85). At the conclusion of this part, Eric, who plays Jesus and is now a soldier, captures Violet in the forest, fating her to a concentration camp. He sets the record straight in regards to Little Red Riding Hood, noting that the wolf eats the little girl in the end (145). Violet disrupts a rehearsal of this virulently anti–Semitic version of the passion by reciting the story of Hansel and Gretel, dwelling on the part in which the witch threatens to push Hansel into her oven in reference to the gas chambers and crematoria of the concentration camps (102–5). Ruhl again draws on the fairy tale at the conclusion of part 2 when Violet, lost in the forest, feeds bread crumbs to a hungry bird rather than even attempt to use them to mark her way back out. This act of kindness and the resulting disorientation underscores her hopeless situation as a Jew in Nazi Germany, and implies a rewritten ending of Hansel and Gretel consistent with that of Little Red Riding Hood, one in which the children succumb to an overpowering force.

Violet (Polly Noonan, under table) feeds lines to Eric (Joaquín Torres) as Jesus during the Last Supper scene from Part 2. *Passion Play.* **Goodman Theatre, 2007 (courtesy Liz Lauren).**

During a rehearsal of the Last Supper scene, Violet feeds lines to the forgetful Eric, altering them to counter the anti–Semitic intent of the production. As Jesus, she promises to forgive sinners, but advises them that it would be better not to sin "in the first place." Her speech includes an admonition to beware the false prophet, Hitler, and a reminder of Jesus's Semitic origins, but her warning goes unheeded (120). For this transgression, the Director orders that she be locked in a basket without food for a week—a rather extreme punishment given the crime, but one that foreshadows an even bleaker destiny for the girl. Although the Visiting Englishman snaps photographs to document her internment, he again fails to intervene (121).

In the final part, Violet is the daughter of Mary 1 and ranges in age from three to 12 years. Her paternity is uncertain; her father is either Mary 1's husband, P, or his brother, J. She seems to retain some memory related to the Violet of the second part; she is obsessed with drawing birds and remembers dying in a war. When P returns from the Vietnam War, she is initially frightened by his strange behavior but overcomes this fear to bond with him. She shares in his visions of the tall ships flying in the wind and tries to "pluck the wars out of his head with her fingers" (193). Her role is reduced from that in the first two parts. Here she serves, not as a wise fool, but rather as an innocent with a metaphysical link to the past.

Violet (Polly Noonan) in cage in Part 2. *Passion Play*. Goodman Theatre, 2007 (courtesy Liz Lauren).

Foundational Imagery

Ruhl establishes a rich set of images in the first part upon which she draws in the second and third; much of this imagery is derived from biblical and Christian symbology, some of it associated with Revelation and apocalypse. These images include fish, water, the moon, the red sky, birds and air. The fish is an important Christian symbol. In the early church, the Greek word for fish (*ichthus*) was taken to be an acrostic for "Jesus Christ, Son of God, Savior" (*Iesous Christos Theou Huios Soter*) (Speake, 54), and early Christians secretly identified themselves to one another by drawing the symbol of a fish (55).[2] A number of Jesus's followers were fishermen, including the apostle John (Matthew 4: 21), as is the character of the same name in the first part of *Passion Play*. Jesus urges Peter and Andrew to become "fishers of men" (Matthew 4: 19), meaning that they should become savers of souls, and Matthew uses an analogy of the sorting of fish for judgment day, upon which the unworthy will be cast into a furnace as into hell (Matthew 13: 47– 50). Jesus performs a number of piscine miracles. On one occasion he feeds 5,000 people with two fish and five loaves of bread (Mark 6: 38–44; Matthew

15: 17–21; Luke 9: 12–17; John 6: 5–13), and on another he feeds 4,000 with a few fish and seven loaves (Matthew 15: 34–39). After the disciples have had an unsuccessful night of fishing, the resurrected, disguised Jesus instructs them to cast the net on the right side of the boat, upon which they draw in 153 fish (John 21: 1–14). Matthew compares the internment and resurrection of Jesus to Jonah's confinement to, and release from, the belly of the whale (Matthew 12: 40), with "whale" appearing as "fish" in early versions of the Bible (Roop, 124).

Lois Drewer analyzes the occurrences of what she terms "fish ponds" in early Christian art in "Fisherman and Fish Pond: From the Sea of Sin to the Living Waters" (1981). She notes, "The fish are usually recognized as symbols of Christian souls, while the fisherman is an image of Christ or the apostles who bring them into a state of salvation" (533). The current alternates, as water conveys contradictory meanings in these images as derived from early Christian writings, both as "the 'living water' in which Christian souls flourish" and as " the sea of this world, or as the bitter sea of sin" (534). The Christian soul is rescued from the sea of sin by the fisherman, but also enjoys eternal life in the living water of baptism. The fish-soul experiences a death to the world, that is the sea of sin, and then a resurrection through the effect of the living waters. Birds sometimes appear in early Christian art alongside fish and other sea creatures (540–2). Both fish and birds came into being on the fifth day of creation (Genesis 1: 20–21), and Tertullian associates birds with "the martyrs which essay to mount up to heaven" (qtd. in Drewer, 545). In *The Dent Dictionary of Symbols in Christian Art* (1994), Jennifer Speake notes that "birds may sometimes be symbolic of souls, which inhabit both the physical and the spiritual world as birds inhabit the earth and air" (19). Thus both fish and birds may represent the soul. The dove specifically symbolizes the descending Holy Spirit (45).

Another biblical image employed by Ruhl is that of the red sky. When asked by the Pharisees and Sadducees for a sign from heaven, Jesus replies:

> When it is evening, you say, "It will be fair weather, for the sky is red."
> And in the morning, "There will be a storm today, for the sky is red and threatening." Do you know how to discern the appearance of the sky, but cannot discern the signs of the times [Matthew 16: 2–3]?

Whereas in Matthew a red sky serves as a metaphor for changing times, in Acts and Revelation it foretells the apocalypse. In Acts 2: 20, it is prophesized that a sign of the second coming will be the sun going dark and the moon "turning into blood." In Revelation also, the moon becomes "like blood" (6: 12) and is associated with a pregnant figure:

> A great sign appeared in heaven: A woman clothed with the sun, and the

moon under her feet, and on her head a crown of twelve stars; and she was with child; and she cried out, being in labor and in pain to give birth [Revelation 12: 1–2].

Deriving from this vision, the crescent moon is associated with Mary in early Christian art according to F. R. Webber in *Church Symbolism* (180–1), published in 1938. Webber indicates that the rose also is associated with Mary (179). Although the moon is not mentioned, the Gospels note that the sky turned dark during three hours of Jesus's crucifixion, from the sixth to the ninth hour (Matthew 27: 45; Mark 15: 33; Luke 23: 44), which is equivalent to the span from 12:00 noon until 3:00 P.M. (Dake, 54).

Fish of the Sea

Ruhl associates the Pontius of the first part with fish, those that swim in the sea of the world rather than the living water of grace. He reeks of the fish that he guts for a living. His attractive cousin, John, who plays the Christ, spends his days upon the clean, living waters. Pontius equates the stench of fish with his own unworthiness, particularly in regards to Mary 1, whom he imagines will be repelled by the odor. She offers rose water as an antidote. Through association with the Virgin Mary, the rose connotes purity, and therefore rose water would have a cleansing effect. In the New Testament, Pilate washes his hands of Jesus's blood before releasing him to be crucified (Matthew 27: 24). Ruhl's Pontius is so immersed in the waters of sin that he lacks any means of washing the smell off of him. He begs of Mary 1 that she run off with him to bear her child, couching his plea in terms of the passion with himself in the role of the Christ, promising that she can scourge and crucify him every night. He flounders in a state of generalized primal sin. He expresses joy rather than remorse over Mary 1's out-of-wedlock pregnancy (51). Like the biblical Pilate, he is unable to wash away his sin.

An incident that Pontius relates from his workday is rife with symbolism:

> I gutted a fish today—I thought it was dead—I slit open its belly—and five live fishes squirmed out. They stunk of death. They wriggled and wraggled in the guts of their mother and they died one by one. The last one to go was a real wriggler. He watched everyone go before him—he swam around in their fishy guts—and then I slammed the knife down on his back. I couldn't stand to see one so alone and so alive, so I killed the poor devil to put it out of its misery [37].

The image of the lone survivor swimming around in "fishy guts" symbolizes, in a general sense, the lost soul floundering in the waters of sin. It may also be read in turn, specifically, as Mary 1, her unborn child, Pontius himself, the historical/biblical Pilate, Christ, and Pontius's cousin John. Pontius may be seen to have killed Mary 1 by impregnating her, causing her to be trapped in a set of circumstances from which she imagines suicide her only escape. The fish also represents Pontius killing himself with a knife over Mary 1's body. His suicide is foreshadowed at rehearsal, during which he stabs himself with a stage knife, miming puncturing his eyes and slitting open his belly as one might a fish (58). Although the New Testament does not narrate Pilate's death, speculations may be found in various sources. In *Pontius Pilate* (1999), Anne Wroe chronicles some of these, including a version related in the medieval *Golden Legend* in which Pontius preempts a death sentence with suicide (Wroe, 364). Wroe states that in the Rome of his time, suicide was often "performed for the sake of others," as the wishes of the deceased would be honored and the family's reputation salvaged (365). Also according to the *Golden Legend*, the emperor ordered Pilate's body thrown into the Tiber, but the river rejected it through the agency of devils that "made the air and water seethe" and attacked the city with storm and flood. Next the body was thrown into Vesuvius, which erupted, and thence into the Rhone, which also became troubled by devils. According to local legend, he was finally thrown into "a flaming pit somewhere in the Alps" where the demons were happy to claim their own (Wroe, 368–9). The "wriggling and wraggling" of the fish in their mother's guts evokes the seething waters that expelled Pilate's body.

 The fish stabbed by Pontius also represents the Christ. In this symbolic murder Pontius comes as close as he ever does to fulfilling his wish to kill his cousin, as expressed in his opening monologue. It is not his wish merely to kill him, he wants to take his place on the cross, to play the role of Christ (16). He imagines that crucifixion would straighten his twisted spine and sanctify him. It would function as a baptism, a dip in the living waters. His way to the cross would be through his cousin's crucifixion, his own holiness bestowed through punishment for the crime of murder. His yearning finds precedence in the Coptic account of Pilate, who is scourged and crucified as punishment for ordering the Savior's death. However, he is perceived as unworthy to follow in the Savior's path and his blood as defiling the Savior's crucifix, upon which he is hung (Wroe, 355–6). Since, according to Christian theology, Christ died on the cross to bear the burden of all men's sin, Pontius's following him to atone for his own sin is redundant and even heretical.

 Ruhl provides a counter-narrative to the Christian doctrine of salvation. Huge fish puppets appear to Pontius twice like pagan gods. They hint at fulfilling his wish for crucifixion by stripping him as Jesus was stripped before scourging. The fish are his allies and he belongs to them, as they provide his

VI. Apocalypse Deferred

Brian Sgambati as Pontius, with fish puppets in Part 1. *Passion Play*. Goodman Theatre, 2007 (courtesy Liz Lauren).

livelihood and he reeks of them. They reappear to carry him off after his suicide. These beautiful fish represent neither lost souls swimming in the sinful waters of the world, nor saved souls swimming in the living water of salvation. As an unrepentant suicide, Pontius's soul leaves the earth in an unclean state, undeserving of Christian grace. The grace that the fish bestow upon Pontius emanates from some other source. Their presence cleanses as signified by the sky turning from red to blue while they carry him off like a king. The fish challenge the primacy of Christ as the unifying symbol. They inhabit Frye's disintegrating element, water, associated as it is with death and the passage to the underworld. Yet they are native to this element, and for them it represents life, not the passage into death. They bear Pontius away as if to ready him for the next act and foreshadow, through association, his ability, as P in part three, to navigate currents, albeit those of the air.

Prior to his death, Pontius reports to Mary 1's corpse that the fish drink his cousin's tears. The author of Psalm 80 refers to the drinking of tears while pleading with God to answer the prayers of the Israelites to restore their good fortune (Psalm 80: 5–6). Drinkers of tears are, in this biblical sense, unfortunates whose prayers go unanswered. Earlier in the play, when John encounters Mary 1 alone at night, he wishes to drink her sorrow (33).

Brian Sgambati as Pontius and Kristen Bush as Mary 1, playing snake and Eve in Part 1. *Passion Play.* **Goodman Theatre, 2007 (courtesy Liz Lauren).**

This desire to shoulder Mary 1's troubles aligns him with the Christ. The trope is reversed, however, at the conclusion of the first part, as the fish drink John's tears, absorbing his sorrow.[3] John fishes across from Pontius and Mary 1's body "as if in a dream" (77), silhouetted against the lit backdrop and casting a net, as staged in the Goodman Theater production. The waterlogged corpse of Mary 1 represents one fish that he was unable to catch; Pontius's self-immolated body, another. It is left to the fish to absorb the Christ-figure's sorrow and to honor the sacrifice of Pontius. Rather than emblems of Christianity, they emerge as if from a Jungian collective unconscious. They remove Pontius's body to the beating of drums, as if honoring him in an ancient ceremony, granting him the respect he desired to earn on the cross. The central symbol of the One Man is thus displaced by a school of fish.

"The Smell of the Moon"

As noted above, the moon symbolized the Virgin Mary in early Christian art. Pontius notes that Mary 1 smells like the moon (37), and John poetically associates her with it as he treads a nighttime landscape, which he imagines is covered in "moonskin" (32). He expresses a readiness to die coupled with an aversion to breaking the skin, and this evokes Jesus on the night before his crucifixion, anticipating scourging and nails. The moonskin, however, is also associated with Mary 1, whose assumed virginity John cautions himself against breaching. Pontius expresses a complex relationship to the moon. He imagines it sequentially as "a laughing pitchfork" and a bewildered dunce, as a "white wedge" one evening and a full moon the next (29). The "white wedge" suggests a crescent, as associated with the Virgin Mary and by extension Mary 1. Pontius's perception of a laughing moon projects his fear of rejection by Mary 1. The sudden transformation into full phase foreshadows Mary 1's pregnancy, as the moon becomes as round and full as an expectant mother's belly. Suddenly the moon is no longer laughing; he looks "bewildered and afraid" as will the pregnant Mary 1. Only Mary 1 will witness Pontius's grief as she refuses to flee with him and publicly disavows earthly paternity.

Pontius makes one last reference to the moon before he commits suicide. It is once again in virginal crescent form, and is "cradled by the night" as Mary 1 is cradled in death. The rocking cradle evokes the unborn child, and Pontius assumes the role of child as well, with the prospect of death softened by thoughts of his lover/mother.[4] He vows to swim after her into the beyond (77). Within the narrative of Ruhl's cycle, he finds her once more in the third part, thereby resisting the disintegrative tendencies of water.

Red Sky

As noted above, in both Revelation and Acts the moon appears as though drenched in blood as a harbinger of the second coming. The sky ominously reddens in the first part of *Passion Play* on several occasions. Pontius notices it first, in the second scene, and complains that everyone is too busy to notice. The Visiting Friar next bears witness to the transformation at two o'clock in the afternoon (17), which hour falls within the time span of the darkened sky during Jesus's crucifixion. The Village Idiot next wills the sky red when the director ties her to a stump to prevent her from disrupting the rehearsal. She relates to her Jack-in-the-Box as confined in the dark while she does so (22). She turns the sky red with the power of God the Father and suffers as God the Son trapped in a box, symbolic of Christ in his moment of despair on the cross. The positioning of God the Father as wise fool transgresses Erasmus's formulation, reducing the eternal divine to mere humanity.

When Mary 2 asks the Visiting Friar why her dreams of embracing women are wrong, he defers her question to God the Father (28). The sky turns red

Nicole Wiesner (left) as Mary 2 and Kristen Bush as Mary 1, watching rehearsal in Part 1. *Passion Play.* **Goodman Theatre, 2007 (courtesy Liz Lauren).**

once again, as if in protest of a homophobic, patriarchal god. While rehearsing the annunciation scene, The Village Idiot blasphemously inserts the name Jack into the lines as she mimics Carpenter 1 as the Angel Gabriel (48). At this juncture, the sky turns red and the harnessed Carpenter 1 crashes to the ground. The fact of Mary 1's terrestrial pregnancy appears to impinge upon the enactment of immaculate conception. The Village Idiot's blasphemous substitution of the name Jack for Biblical names, including Jesus, provokes, if not the wrath, then perhaps at least the ire of a vengeful God. The Village Idiot disrupts Frye's archetype of Christ as the unifying One Man. "Jack" references the Jack-in-the-box, but is also a nickname for John, which designates both the character playing Christ and one of Christ's apostles. It refers to Pontius as well through his association with the Jack-in-the-box. The name Jack, through its many associations, signifies an everyman as opposed to the One Man and thus secularizes the Biblical story.

  The sky and moon portend a second coming, one that is aborted. The sky turns blue again when the fish gods carry Pontius away, but Mary 1 fails to give birth to the new fish messiah. Pontius's fish salvation fails to transcend earthly life, as he must return in the following two parts of the cycle in order to reenact the passion play. In both of those parts, he longs for release. As he escapes in a flying ship he transmutes from a fish immersed in the waters of sin to a bird-like Tertullian martyr ascending to heaven. The medieval passion was staged as representative of all time and meant to remind its audience of the impending endpoint, doomsday, and of the redemptive power of the crucifixion and resurrection (Kolve, 101–2). The repetitive nature of Ruhl's passion cycle however, with actors playing the same parts in successive sections, suggests reincarnation rather than redemption, which is philosophically consistent with Hinduism or Buddhism rather than Christianity. P's plea to be excused from the play brings to mind the cry of the weary soul, in Eastern philosophy, for release from the cycle of death and rebirth with its inevitable, and endlessly repeated, suffering. His escape in a ship, staged as a vertical ascent in the Goodman Theatre production, suggests enlightenment as defined as a release from the earthly, karmic cycle although, as will be explored below, his flight from the earth is not as completely liberating as it may seem.

Earthbound Birds

Ruhl sparingly redeploys images from the first part in the second, and delays the reincorporation of fish and air imagery until the third. Characters mention the moon twice in the second part, in the first instance as discussed by Eric and the Footsoldier as they surreptitiously flirt. Stage directions call for an orange moon, described by Eric as a judge, that mirrors the German officer who is observing, and disapproving of, their homosexual flirtatiousness; however, the moon also projects, as judge, the eventual indictment of the Nazi regime at the Nuremberg trials. When the Footsoldier removes his hands from Eric's eyes, the moon appears in gold, conveying a German optimism under Hitler's leadership (129). The moon is mentioned one more time as Eric rehearses, in a warning about the darkening of the sky that will occur with the emergence of false Christs and prophets (135). The passage refers to Hitler in the context of Matthew 24. Revelation also refers to a false prophet who is in league with the devil in three separate verses (16:13, 19:20, 20:10). Hitler referred to the Third Reich as a 1,000-year reign in a secularized millennium, one in which he implicitly assumed the role of messiah. When he is cast as a false prophet, his projected reign is inverted as a millennium celebrating the triumph of sin.

Images of birds and the red sky figure prominently in the second part, the former associated specifically with Violet. The director imprisons her in the basket that houses the doves released during the temple scene (121). The dove is generally recognized as a symbol of peace and in Christian symbology, particularly when descending, represents the Holy Spirit. The peaceable Violet replaces the doves in the basket in a foreshadowing of her eventual internment in a concentration camp. When Eric expresses a desire to join the army, his sister, Mary 2, relates an incident from their childhood in which he accidentally kills her pet bird. Afterwards, filled with shame, he despairs of anyone ever loving him again (114). This memory foreshadows the final scene of part two in which Eric, now a soldier, captures Violet. They play a word game in which they challenge each other with horrible dilemmas. The first poses the choice between cruelty to two innocents, the second between self-interest and self-sacrifice. Eric chooses to kill a dog rather than kick a baby, and to poke someone in the eardrum rather than become deaf since, as he explains, "It would be terrible to be deaf. I love music" (145). His decisions fail to correspond to what Jesus would do, in spite of his playing that role in the passion.

Violet disrupts a rehearsal as she tells the story of "Hansel and Gretel," a fairy tale in which hungry birds strand children in the forest. Even though Violet disavows breadcrumbs as trail markers to the Visiting Englishman (85), she finds herself in the position, later on, of using them for that purpose. When a giant bird appears in the forest, she kindly feeds him all of her stock, confident in her sense of direction. The unreliable bird immediately abandons her when she closes her eyes to sleep. In any case, it is too large to fly and therefore unable to provide rapturous transport away from the tribulation, and thus abandons Violet to her fate.

The red sky, which portends the death of Mary 1 and an aborted second coming in the first part, reappears here within a context that suggests a sky reddened by war or the glow from concentration camp crematoria. Violet claims to be turning the sky this color, as does her counterpart in the first part. Violet tells the Visiting Englishman that no one notices when she reddens the sky, and when the Director locks her in the birdcage, she unsuccessfully attempts to do so, which failure demonstrates her impotence within the context of the second part. A red sky overhangs Eric's capture of Violet in the forest. Violet carries with her a white ribbon that, as she has explained to the Visiting Englishman, represents "the white drool of a snake" (58). Through its association with the serpent in the garden of Eden, the ribbon would seem to represent evil or sin. In Nazi Germany, Jews were forced to wear the star of David and homosexuals a pink triangle as means of identification; like these markers, Violet's ribbon flags the immorality of the society that surrounds her. Whereas in the first part the sky turns from red to blue when the giant fish remove Pontius, in the second part it shifts from red to gray as the cast members look out to the audience to the sound of a train "speeding across tracks" (147), suggestive of Violet's journey to Dachau.

The sky color reinforces the bleak conclusion, evoking as it does the smoke from concentration camp crematoria.

Rapture Deferred

Ruhl carries into the third part imagery of fish, water, birds, the red sky, and especially the wind. Violet in this part is the daughter of Mary 1. She retains some memory of being involved in a war and is obsessed with drawing birds. Her dramatic lineage represents a fixation on the failed rapture of the second part and an anxiety over the possibility of an impending apocalypse. Early in part three, upon P's return from Vietnam, the three-year-old presents him with a picture of a bird; he frightens her with the compliment that it is lifelike enough to fly. His behavior scares her further when he insists on sleeping outdoors in order to keep watch, and then bids her "sleep with the angels," a goodnight wish that connotes death (191). Later, when she is in the sixth grade, she conveys her fascination with the "architecture of feathers" (222). Eventually she studies painting in college and, as P reports, her pictures become increasingly abstract (235). The Violet of the third part retains some of the fear associated with birds from that of the second, eventually transcending that fear and sublimating the traumatic into art.

P longs to absolve himself of guilt incurred in Vietnam, especially over the death of a girl Violet's age. He holds the girl's head as she is dying and her blood stains his hands; due to the conditions of war, he is unable to wash them over a period of several months and likens himself to Pontius Pilate without water (207). During a rehearsal, he hallucinates that the stage water is blood (198). Although he is unable to cleanse himself with water, the fish puppets nevertheless come to his assistance. In a battle scene set in Vietnam, he drags a bloodied fish across the stage as he holds a smoking gun. He announces that he has killed a fish and then exclaims, "My head" (174)! Like Pontius from the first part, he experiences himself as a puppet, in this case manipulated by the state. Queen Elizabeth asynchronously intervenes and orders him carried off the battlefield, a command that the big fish obey, reprising the conclusion of the first part.

Jesus performed a miracle in which he tamed both sea and air as described in Matthew 9: 23–27, Mark 4: 35–41 and Luke 8: 22–25. The disciples and Jesus were crossing the water in a ship when a storm struck. The frightened disciples woke up the sleeping Jesus, who "arose, and rebuked the wind, and said unto the sea, Peace, be still. And the wind ceased, and there was a great calm" (Mark 4: 39). In early Christian art, Christ is conceptualized as the "anchor of the soul" in reference to Hebrews 6: 19 (Webber, 81). P rejects the anchoring power of Jesus and learns to control rather than abate the wind. Even before his tour in Vietnam, he is obsessed with the wind and provides soothing audiotapes of it to his brother and wife as parting gifts. As he explains to Violet, he was the pilot of a ship in Vietnam, one that he imagines to have been wind-powered. Ruhl stages his vision of Elizabethan ships with the aid of a chorus. In the Goodman Theatre and Epic Theatre productions, the boats were manipulated on poles to striking effect. He also collects the wind in jars to give to his wife, as John and Pontius in the first part collect the night air for Mary 1. As Mary 1 fears the wind, however, this proves an unwelcome gift. When P's brother J seduces his wife, he does so under the guise of stopping the wind. J stops the wind as does Jesus, the character he plays; P stirs it up. P envisions a giant wind machine to expel bad air in the case of a nuclear holocaust. Human agency averts catastrophe in this comic representation of apocalypse. His mastery of the wind coincides with Violet's obsession with birds. Both of them have learned, over the course of the cycle, to negotiate the flow of life. The navigation of unpredictable winds requires improvisational flexibility, and this lies at the heart of P's transformation as he rejects the scripted passion.

 The red sky reappears in the third part as P drags the giant fish in Vietnam. President Reagan reinforces its association with war and promises to stop Armageddon, according to God's plan for him. Finally, though, the red sky is stripped of political and religious significance, and merely indicates the weather as Pontius imagines manipulating the wind to bring the ships home safely. At the conclusion of each part of the cycle, the sky turns a different color: blue in the first, gray in the second, and white in the third. These colors may be associated with three of the Greek elements, with the red sky symbolic of the fourth. Blue is associated with water and the fish that carry Pontius away. Gray represents the earth of ashen, burnt bodies. The color of clouds and sails, white is associated with the sky into which P flies. Red represents fire and its destructive properties. The Greeks held that the elements were transmutable. In the first part the giant fish transform the fire of destruction, which has burned away the lives of Pontius and Mary 1, into soothing blue waters. Red represents the fires of war and trauma that, in the second part, deposit a residue of human ash and from which, in the third, P escapes into the element of air. In Frye's analysis, man must pass through trials of fire and water when journeying to other realms. Pontius/P, however, rather than passing through these elements, learns to navigate their currents, not quite ascending in a rapture, which would entail passing through fire, nor sinking below the water in death.[5] The cosmology of the play resists not only a universal eschatology, but the demise of the individual as well. Pontius/P learns to inhabit what should be transitory states, the passages through water unto death and through air and thence fire unto the heavens. In this way Ruhl once again undermines the passion, which provides both individual and cosmos with a definitive endpoint. Pontius/P's navigational abilities indefinitely defer the second coming and judgment day.

"Queen, Fuehrer, President"

Ruhl presents historical leaders as characters in each of the three parts of her play. Queen Elizabeth forbids the enactment of the passion in the first, Hitler praises the anti–Semitic bent of the Oberammergau production in the second, and Reagan in the third campaigns for a second term at Spearfish. Elizabeth and Hitler asynchronously appear in the third part as well. Through these figures, Ruhl explores political responsibility and the nexus of performance, politics, and religion.

Queen Elizabeth's appearance in the Village Idiot's dream conflates her with the Virgin Mary. In *Elizabeth I* (1988), Christopher Haigh reports that Elizabeth cultivated a virginal self-image and was accordingly represented in poetry and portraiture as "the moon-goddess" (19). She was considered a special virgin, approaching the status of the Virgin Mary, and was presented as married to her subjects as a whole or to the kingdom itself (20). Elizabeth never bore an heir and resisted naming one for the sake of her own security, fearful that followers of whomever she might designate would attempt to depose her (19). In the dream, she appears in the sky naked and pregnant. The Village Idiot's description of Elizabeth's "privates" as a stage always covered with curtains emphasizes the theatrical nature of her leadership and the political use to which she put her image as the Virgin Queen (29). As Ruhl observes in the "Playwright's Note," Elizabeth ordered the cessation of passion plays in 1575 to reduce the influence of Catholicism (2). When the fictionalized Queen halts the passion, she emphasizes that she wears layers of white paint in order not to appear "old or ugly," but demands that her subjects not impersonate Christ (50). She reserves for herself the right of performance.

In the second part, Ruhl includes an historical speech of Hitler's that praises the Oberammergau passion play for its anti–Semitism (Ruhl, "Playwright's Note," x). Before delivering the speech, Ruhl's character claims that the people loved his voice, observes his own love of public speaking, and expresses pleasure at the cheers that always greet him. He quickly establishes himself as a character obsessed with, and proud of, his ability to manipulate

T. Ryder Smith as Queen Elizabeth. *Passion Play*. Goodman Theatre, 2007 (courtesy Liz Lauren).

his audience. He then demonstrates his highly theatrical rhetorical style by working up "a public rage" as he delivers the historical speech (103).

Ronald Reagan opens part three with a phrase from his television advertising campaign for reelection in 1984, "It's morning in America" (Raine). He then spews a disjointed series of slogans and anecdotes and links his replacing of Gorbachev's son's dead goldfish to the fall of the Soviet Union. Highly aware of his delivery, he expresses himself in newsworthy sound bites. He brags that his first job was announcing baseball games *in absentia*. His task was to make the game sound so exciting that listeners felt as if they were there, even though he himself was not, defining his ability to do so as a quality of leadership (228–9).

In *Ronald Reagan: The Great Communicator* (1992), Kurt Ritter and David Henry identify three stages to Reagan's secular, apocalyptic rhetoric, as employed primarily in the 1950s and 1960s while representing General Electric. He would begin with a lament of America's difficulties and warn of an even worse future, portray "a cosmic struggle between good and evil," and finally warn of an impending Armageddon and possible "dark millennium" to follow (15). The forces of evil included the communist threat both at home and abroad and big government at home. The Soviet Union threatened

T. Ryder Smith as Ronald Reagan. *Passion Play*. Goodman Theatre, 2007 (courtesy Liz Lauren).

America with Armageddon, and Reagan identified Karl Marx as the Antichrist, the messiah of "a Godless religion" (qtd. in Ritter and Henry, 18). He supplanted the utopian vision of an earthly millennium of peace with one of tribulation (19). He maintained, however, that the apocalypse could be averted by voting Republican (26–7). His vision of the apocalypse is thus a comic one in that it may be forestalled by human action. Reagan functioned in prophetic mode at this stage of his career, positioning himself in opposition to the political status quo. Later, particularly in the role of president, he would function as priest-in-chief in order to solidify the status quo. Ritter and Henry characterize President Reagan "as a sort of secular pastor to the nation" who delivered "emotionally appealing messages" that promulgated "value-laden themes" (61).

In *Passion Play*, Ruhl depicts a Reagan who is somewhat absent both mentally and physically. She contrasts Elizabeth, who addressed her soldiers on the battlefield (Hammer, 4), with Reagan, who never served in the military (Ruhl, *Passion Play*, 232). Elizabeth appears in Spearfish to bless P the day before he enters military service (158–9). Later, when she visits P in Vietnam, she expresses bewilderment over his willingness to engage in battle without the corporeal presence of his leader (174). As Reagan was not actually president during the Vietnam War, her indictment may be directed at modern leaders in general. As Reagan dedicates the Vietnam War Memorial and says a few words over the tomb of the Unknown Soldier, he appears to be more concerned with the effectiveness of his speech than the import of the occasion. He states that although he never served in the military, he made training films for soldiers during the war and learned how to salute at that time. Insensitive to the pain and suffering of veterans such as P, he remembers it as "one of the happiest times" in his life (232). Considering Ruhl's disparaging comments aimed at President George W. Bush in the "Playwright's Notes," and her assertion that she wrote part three with urgency before Bush's second presidential election (xii), it is quite clear that she had him in mind, and the military intervention in Iraq, while writing Reagan into the work. The leader's absence from the battlefield may more widely be interpreted as a lack of concern for the welfare of the soldiers, and an eagerness to engage in war without adequately weighing the human toll.

A Canadian Passion

Denys Arcand's French Canadian film *Jesus of Montreal* (1989) explores the same thematic territory as Ruhl's cycle, examining the effect that staging the passion play has on the actors so engaged, particularly on the one playing Jesus. The events in the film mirror those of the New Testament. Daniel, who plays Jesus, gathers actors around him as if disciples; he destroys camera equipment at an audition for a beer commercial in a scene that mimics the destruction of the moneylenders at the temple, and he dies of a concussion suffered when the cross upon which he is playing the crucifixion accidentally falls on top of him. His resurrection occurs through the donation of his organs: his heart revitalizes a dying man and his eyes bestow sight upon a blind woman. Hired by a Roman Catholic priest to update the passion as staged at his church for 35 years, Daniel's revision invites charges of heresy. He challenges the divine paternity of Jesus by suggesting that a Roman soldier fathered him and suggests that the Savior's miracles may have simply been cheap magic tricks. The outraged Father Leclerc insists on shutting down the production. The actors defiantly mount a final performance, during which the fatal accident occurs.

The film tracks Daniel's transformation as he becomes increasingly Christlike. He watches over Mireille, the Mary Magdalene figure, destroying the equipment at her beer commercial audition. He clashes with the priest, who functions as the bastion of religious tradition, paralleling the Pharisees and

Sadducees of the New Testament. After Daniel's accident, paramedics rush him to an overcrowded public hospital. He regains consciousness in the waiting room and the actresses playing both Marys escort him away from the chaotic emergency room. He sorrowfully imparts wisdom to his companions as they descend onto the subway platform where he moves from passenger to passenger, gently touching them and warning them of the coming judgment. He tells them to beware of false prophets and his final line is "You know not when ... the Judgment ... watch!" He then collapses and dies shortly thereafter. The film contrasts this saintly figure with those who would take advantage of him: talk show hosts, agents, and a devilish lawyer who offers wealth and stardom. He forms a tight community with the actors in his company but they remained besieged, as it were, by the outside world. The film portrays the plight of the artist as the actors support their fondness for alternative theater with commercial acting work, modeling, and voiceovers for pornographic films and planetarium shows.

Whereas Arcand has undertaken a modern retelling of the Passion, Ruhl uses it as a lens through which to examine issues of community, leadership, and religion. In her work, the mounting of the play operates in priestly mode, reinforcing the religious status quo; threats of apocalypse come from outside of the staging. In the film, the play challenges the status quo without actually venturing into prophetic territory. Only at the end, immediately before his death, does Daniel prophecy a second coming, but his message falls on deaf ears as the waiting passengers board the next train. By implication the false prophet triumphs, as in the final scene the satanic figure of the lawyer discusses with the remaining actors establishing a theater in Daniel's name, one that will remain true to his principles while at the same time, he promises, turning a profit. It seems that the whore of Babylon from Revelation has triumphed at least temporarily, and a second coming will be required to vanquish her. The narrative of the film thus mimics the passion and the prophecy of apocalypse, in contrast to that of Ruhl's play, which offers an alternative, non-biblical conclusion.

Millennium Deferred

Ruhl began work on the third part of *Passion Play* in response to Arena Stage's request for a play about America. She figured that "there's nothing more American than the nexus of religious rhetoric, politics, and the theater" (Ruhl, "Playwright's Note," xi). Tony Kushner's *Angels in America* deals with these issues as well. In comparing these epic works of Ruhl and Kushner, it would be wise, first of all, to delineate the ways in which they are profoundly different. Kushner is centrally concerned with the AIDS epidemic and gay identity in the 1980s, and his cast of characters encompasses a range of racial, ethnic, and religious backgrounds as well as political beliefs: Jewish, Mormon, WASP, black, as well as liberal and conservative, in various configurations. Most of his characters articulate their strong political beliefs. Exclusive of the second part, which presents a Nazi/Jewish binary, Ruhl does not specify the racial and ethnic makeup of her characters, although the historical setting of the first part suggests homogeneity. The social and political oppression of homosexuality is depicted, but the exploration of gay identity is not a concern. Outside of the historical figures, Ruhl's characters do not articulate strong political beliefs.

The playwrights take differing approaches to history, as well. David Savran, among others, has noted the influence that Walter Benjamin's explication of Paul Klee's painting, "Angelus Novus," had on the formulation of *Angels in America* (Savran, "Ambivalence," 16–7). According to Benjamin, Klee's angel, driven relentlessly forward by a storm from Paradise, looks back helplessly upon the rubble of history (Benjamin, 257–8). Kushner establishes this history in various ways: Rabbi Isadore Chemelwitz speaks of the hard life that Louis's grandmother fled in Eastern Europe (1: 9–11), Aleksii Antedilluvianovich Prelapsarianov laments the failure of Soviet communism (2: 13–5), Prior's ancestors refer to earlier plagues (1: 85–9), and Ethel Rosenberg returns to haunt her nemesis, Roy Cohn. The purpose of this background is to pinpoint the present moment, the approaching millennium heralded by angelic visitation, questioning whether or not the millennium will redeem the catastrophic course of history. In contrast, Ruhl's work is a triptych bound together by the presentation of the passion play. She takes snapshots of these various time periods without building historical momentum towards millennium. She approaches the very concept of millennium with more subtlety than Kushner, suggesting a second coming through biblical imagery rather than plunging an angel spectacularly through a bedroom ceiling. Another significant difference between the two works is that Ruhl's is essentially a backstage drama that counterpoints the passion; although Kushner incorporates two former drag queens, his play does not focus upon a shared theatrical endeavor.

The two works ultimately converge in their conceptualization of a deferred millennium. Prior resists the Angel's call for stasis, which would put an end to history, and makes a demand for "more life," which, once met, postpones the end of time indefinitely. This deferral switches the apocalypse from tragic into comic mode. As discussed by Stanton B. Garner, Jr., in "*Angels in America*: The Millennium and Postmodern Memory" (1997), this deferred millennium is a postmodern one. Garner contends that "postmodernism is deeply informed by the rhetoric and psychosocial preoccupations of Cold War millenarianism, with its utopian imaginings and its even stronger apprehension of catastrophe" (175).[6] Nevertheless, postmodern theorists exhibit an uneasiness with millennialism, practicing "what Jameson calls an 'inverted millenarianism,' problematizing the ideas of finitude and conclusion even as they advance them" (Garner, 175). Even as Kushner establishes the "urgency of apocalypse" he continually undermines it with "currents of indeterminacy and persistence" (178). The epilogue of the play, set in 1990, four years after the previous scene, provides ample evidence of this as four friends, including AIDS survivor Prior, gather before the Bethesda Fountain in Central Park. Prior has, so far, escaped death and his visions of Angel and apocalypse have apparently been relegated to the past.

The threat of the millennium has torn apart some relationships, and sutured others together. Nevertheless, as Savran observes in "Ambivalence, Utopia, and a Queer Sort of Materialism" (1997), in the dialectic of communitarianism/individualism, the former is "read as being preferable" (22). Prior confronts the Angel terrified and alone in his apartment, abandoned by his lover; one reward for undergoing this trial is reunion with some sort of community. In Ruhl, inversely, individualism is valued over communitarianism. In the first part, Pontius and Mary 1 die because they are unable to conform. In the second segment, conformity with the Third Reich is portrayed as sinful. In the third, P comes to question his blind obedience to state and religious performance. His mental illness isolates him, and eventually he learns to survive on his own. As he strives for self-definition, P rejects the leadership of Ronald Reagan and the notion of one nation under God. Ironically, Reagan projected himself as the rugged individual, the cowboy riding horses and chopping wood on his ranch, and the lone sentry warning of the coming apocalypse. Ultimately however, as president, he becomes a figurehead for his own particular brand of conservatism and the unifying symbol of a political community.

In the last part, professionalism dissolves the amateur community gathered around mounting the passion. Here again, the individualism of P is offered in place of religious community and representation. Rejecting her mother's biblical role, Violet turns to the visual arts and ever more abstract depictions of birds, aligning herself with her presumed father's fantasies of flight. This, however, is a freewheeling aerial dance, not a rapturous ascension at the end of time through the realm of fire to meet the maker. Navigation replaces transfiguration. In both Kushner and Ruhl, the millennium is deferred indefinitely: in the former, a communal future is envisioned; in the latter, the individual learns to make his or her own way.

In *In the Next Room or the vibrator play*, Ruhl restricts her focus to just two rooms in a house with potent results. The alternating currents of desire are most pronounced in this work, as they course through the characters and wreak havoc with their lives. The implement of the subtitle initiates waves of pleasure that expand outward with far-reaching consequences, threatening a doctor and his wife's marriage and home. Although none of the characters flies off into the sky, the liberating conclusion is just as fantastical as that of *Passion Play*.

VII

Alternating Currents of Desire: *In the Next Room or the vibrator play*

Bringing Down the House

In *In the Next Room or the vibrator play*, Ruhl stages a house divided. Two rooms are visible, a so-called operating theater, or doctor's treatment room, and a living room. In one room the husband, Dr. Givings, cures patients of hysteria through the application of vibrator therapy; in the other, the wife, Catherine Givings, frets and fusses like a caged bird, or even an undiagnosed hysteric. She chafes against her restricting role as Victorian housewife and, unable to produce sufficient milk, grieves her insufficiency as a mother. The house's structure isolates her. The central wall separates along gender lines and situates the power object, the vibrator, in the male domain. Catherine breaches the wall to experiment with the device and uncovers that to which her husband, and indeed the 1880s medical establishment, is blind: the paroxysms that the instrument induces are sexual in nature. In the process, she discovers her own sexuality. The released flow of energy ultimately blows away the walls of her home and deposits husband and wife together in the garden. The patriarchal structure of house and home dissolves, replaced by a blissful winter scene that stages a return to the garden by way of sexual intimacy. In a reversal of the biblical expulsion propelled by a female hunger for knowledge, Catherine's newfound sexual intelligence reopens the gates of heaven.

A primary thematic of flow and blockage plays out across various domains. Female hysteria is conceived as congestion in the womb, from which pent-up fluid is released by the application of vibrator therapy. The therapy also unleashes the male hysteric's arrested creativity. Catherine's unhappiness as a mother is due, in part, to an insufficient flow of breast milk. Electricity flows into the house to power miracles of modern technology, inclusive of the vibrator and the incandescent light bulb. Flow is associated with vitality and health, and blockages must be removed, with or without the aid of technology, in order to release or increase that flow. Flow need not be unidirectional, as expressed by the thematic of alternating current. Borrowed from electricity, the term refers to a flow that switches direction and is deployed by Ruhl in two senses, as ambivalence and reciprocity. The former surfaces in complicated relationships, for example those between Catherine and her baby, and the wet nurse Elizabeth and the baby, marked not only by love but also guilt, grief, inadequacy, and even hatred. In the sense of reciprocity, an alternating flow of information and sexual energy ultimately erodes hierarchical power structures to take down the house.

Flow itself is associated not only with life but, alternately, with the marking of death. The linking of fluidity with bereavement harks back to *Eurydice*, in which water is associated with tears and grief. Indeed, Elizabeth cries on two occasions as she grieves her infant: first, when she nurses Letitia for the first time (26), and again as Mrs. Daldry plays a sad tune on the piano (31). In *In the Next Room*, grief is also associated with the flow of milk. Elizabeth expresses a desire for the flow to stop so that she may forget her buried child; the increasing health

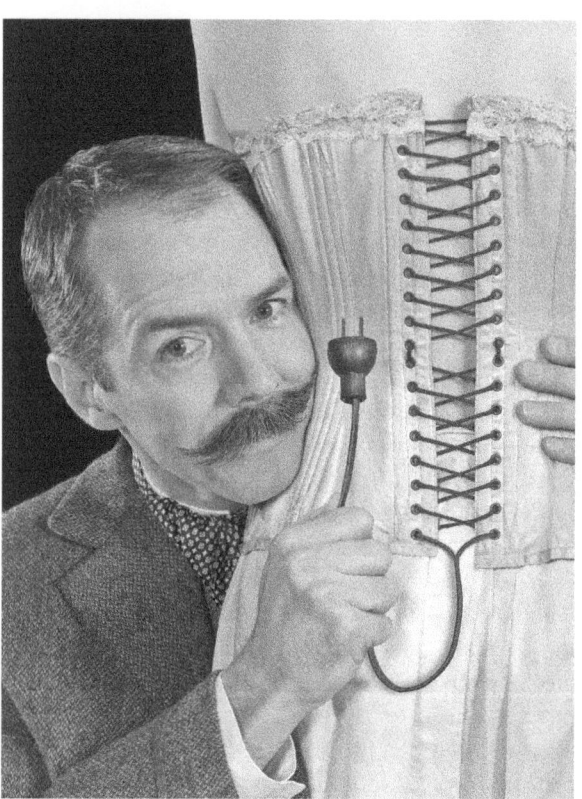

Paul Niebanck as Dr. Givings and Maria Dizzia as Sabrina. Promotional photograph: corset with power plug. World premiere of *In the Next Room (or the vibrator play)* at Berkeley Repertory Theatre, 2009 (courtesy Berkeley Repertory Theatre).

of Letitia, nourished by the flow, keeps her grief alive. Breast milk both grants life and reminds of death. Catherine perceives her own insufficient flow as a failing, and conflates tears and milk when she laments that her body is weeping gray milk (54). This buildup of a complex of emotions around flow is characteristic of Ruhl's thematic attention to ambivalence throughout.

The Givingses' house occupies a lot in the long row of domiciles that stretches back through the history of modern theater. In *Staging Place: The Geography of Modern Drama* (1995), Una Chaudhuri identifies the home as a space of personal experimentation, a place in which to approach a definition of self. Ruhl's characters certainly engage in this struggle; what is unusual is not that certain of them must flee the constraints of the Givings' home, but that the structure itself is unable to contain, and is transformed by, the experiments with identity. Chaudhuri has coined the term *geopathology* to designate "the characterization of place as problem" (xii). Certainly the architecture of the home, and the social structures that it represents, is implicit in the problems faced by the characters. However, as the doctor and Catherine redefine themselves, they also reconfigure the seemingly stable structure of their home. Not only do they act *within*, they act *on* their environment. Catherine's experiments in selfhood release the flow of her sexuality and activate the alternating current of reciprocity in her marriage; this in turn reconfigures her home so that flight, the primary option of many of her dramatic predecessors, becomes, for her if not for other of the characters, unnecessary.

Ruhl's thematic structure corresponds to the architecture of the Givings's home; that is, themes are structured as dualities that, in quite a few cases, align with the split setting. These include work space/domestic space, male/female, science/art, science/religion, visible/invisible, and intellect/body. Another spatial division is significant as well, that of indoor/outdoor. Other pairings are less clearly tied to the setting, and these include public/private, animal/angel, and sexual/spiritual. The binaries collapse, in a sense, along with the house at the conclusion. Only in *Eurydice* has Ruhl employed such a markedly dualistic thematic structure. In both plays, she brings about a massive synthesis at the conclusion, favoring death in *Eurydice*, and life in *In the Next Room*.

In the Next Room or the vibrator play was a 2010 Pulitzer Prize finalist and Tony Award nominee. It premiered at Berkeley Repertory Theatre in February 2009 and introduced Ruhl to Broadway in November of the same year in a production at the Lyceum Theatre under the auspices of the Lincoln Center Theater. The Berkeley Repertory Theatre presented the play with the subtitle in parentheses: *In the Next Room (or the vibrator play)*. Les Waters directed both productions with the same design team, including sets by Annie

Smart, costumes by David Zinn, and lighting by Russell H. Champa. Action takes place simultaneously in both rooms throughout. The plot concerns the comings and goings of patients around the doctor's troubled marriage, although it is up to his wife, Catherine, to determine what the marital issues are, or even their existence. It is the 1880s, and Dr. Givings is a gynecologist who incites "paroxysms" in his patients through the application of vibrator therapy as a cure for hysteria. Catherine becomes curious when she overhears him treating a patient, Mrs. Sabrina Daldry, and demands her own session. He refuses, and while he is out she and Sabrina break into his operating theater and experiment with the vibrator on one another. When the doctor finally gives in to his wife's demands and administers the treatment, he is appalled when she tries to kiss him, as he considers the procedure a strictly medical one and is oblivious to its sexual aspect. As tensions rise between doctor and wife, he diagnoses a new patient, an artist named Leo Irving, as suffering from male hysteria, a rare condition addressed by anal vibrator treatments.

Catherine suffocates in the role of Victorian woman, and is unable to even participate fully in child-rearing duties, as her flow of breast milk is inadequate. Her husband hires the Daldry's African-American housekeeper, Elizabeth, as a wet nurse. She has recently lost her baby to cholera. Catherine falls in love with the dashing and flamboyant Leo, and is caught by her husband with her hand upon Leo's cheek, a flagrant indiscretion given the Victorian setting. Invigorated by his treatment, Leo begins to paint again and insists on composing a portrait of Elizabeth nursing Catherine's baby as Madonna and Child. The doctor is further scandalized when he stumbles upon the portrait session in his living room. Leo falls in love with Elizabeth, but she scorns his advances and he flees to Paris. Sabrina and the doctor's assistant, Annie, surrender to their mutual attraction and share a kiss on the piano bench, but then vow never to see one another again. Dr. and Mrs. Givings resolve their disagreement in a spectacular finale. They reassert their love for one another, and she undresses him as snow begins to fall and the winter garden replaces their house, the walls of which fly away. With him now naked, they together make an angel in the snow as Catherine calls out for God.

"Impossibly Strange": The Vibrator, Electricity, and Wet Nursing

In the "Playwright's Notes," Ruhl asserts that which seems "impossibly strange" in her play is true and has been drawn from three nonfiction sources:

The Technology of Orgasm: "Hysteria," the Vibrator, and Women's Sexual Satisfaction (1999) by Rachel P. Maines, *AC/DC: The Savage Tale of the First Standards War* (2006) by Tom McNichol, and *A Social History of Wet Nursing in America: From Breast to Bottle* (1996) by Janet Golden. Ruhl skillfully weaves the material from these sources through the fabric of her play.

Maines chronicles the history of hysteria and the electrical vibrator. The Greek root for "hysteria" means "that which proceeds from the uterus," and the term "hysterical" connotes negative aspects of femininity, and the irrational (21). The disease paradigm persisted from as early as the fifth century B.C. until removed from the books by the American Psychiatric Association in 1952; during that span, it was "one of the most frequently diagnosed diseases in history" (11). Maines's sources reveal a great deal of confusion over exactly what hysteria was (22). Commonly listed symptoms included "fainting ... congestion caused by fluid retention ... nervousness, insomnia, sensations of heaviness in the abdomen, muscle spasms, shortness of breath, loss of appetite for food or sex with the approved male partner, and sometimes a tendency to cause trouble for others" (23). Maines notes that many of the symptoms of hysteria are those of chronic sexual arousal (8).

According to Maines, the biological function of female orgasm is still not clearly understood. The common assumption has been that penetration to male orgasm, which fulfills the biological need for procreation, should satisfy both men and women. As reported by sex researchers including Alfred Kinsey and Shere Hite, as many as 70 percent of women fail to consistently achieve orgasm through penetration alone (Maines, 5). It remains a mystery as to why, biologically speaking, more than half of women require stimulation of the external genitalia (6). The androcentric model of sexuality helped cloak the sexual nature of paroxysm as it advanced the belief that female gratification could be induced only by vaginal penetration. By definition this model focuses on the male and consists of three stages: foreplay, penetration, and male orgasm.

Specific details from Maines include the large Chattanooga vibrator, designed specifically for men; the hydraulic vibrator that Dr. Givings envisions; and the classical diagnosis of hysteria as caused by congestion in the womb, treatable by inducing "paroxysm" in the female patient. Dr. Givings's analogy that inducing paroxysms manually was like the child's game of patting the head and rubbing the stomach simultaneously refers directly to a complaint made by physician Nathaniel Highmore in 1660 (Maines, 4). Annie's observation that many patients desire to sleep after treatment echoes a statement published by American gynecologist William Goodell in 1890 (Maines, 40). The phrasing of Dr. Givings's promise, as he treats Mrs. Daldry, to "invite the juices downward" (14) comes from an essay on the water cure, as applied to female dysfunction, from 1752 (Maines, 73).

From McNichol come references to electrocuting animals that demonstrate both enthusiasm for and anxiety over technology. As his title indicates, a standards war raged in the late 19th century over the adoption of alternating over direct current in the United States. The chief proponent of direct current was none other than Thomas Alva Edison, who envisioned an electrical delivery system to power to his improved, long-burning incandescent light bulb. His chief opponent, on the side of alternating current, was George Westinghouse. Edison lent material support, including the use of his laboratory, to an enterprising salesman named Harold P. Brown. As he had built his career on promoting direct current systems, it was in Brown's interest to side with Edison (McNichol, 89). In an attempt to prove alternating current the more dangerous, Brown electrocuted a series of animals, including dogs, calves, a horse, and ultimately an elephant, under decidedly unscientific conditions to skew the results in his favor. Most of the experiments occurred in 1888.

Brown escalated his campaign against alternating current by convincing New York's Medico-Legal Society to recommend it for the execution of criminals. Death by hanging, the standard procedure at the time, was deemed cruel and unusual punishment, as slow strangulation and decapitation occurred regularly (96). In part due to Brown's experiments and testimony, the state of New York pioneered execution by an electric chair using alternating current on August 5, 1890 (124–5). Despite Brown's best efforts, alternating current was winning out over direct current, primarily because it could be transmitted through electrical wires over much longer distances. The execution by alternating current of the troublesome elephant Topsy, who had killed a number of its handlers, on January 4, 1903, at Coney Island, was a last-ditch effort to discredit alternating current. The event is recorded in the Edison film *Electrocuting an Elephant* (see McNichol, Chapter 10).

Ruhl references the electrocution of animals, and particularly Brown's experiments, a number of times. Dr. Givings rushes off to his club, and away from an argument with his wife, to witness the electrocution of dogs by "Mr. Edison's man," who will attempt to demonstrate the danger of alternating current. Sabrina mentions the Coney Island elephant as she and Catherine fantasize about the electrified future. In the second act, Catherine touches on both the danger and promise of electricity when she asks Leo what can "put a man to death and also bring him back to life again" (51). The story of Benjamin Franklin electrocuting a turkey for Christmas Eve, as related by Dr. Givings, also comes from McNichol (16). He intends to calm his patient's fear of electrocution from the vibrator, although in his enthusiasm for the new technology he perhaps overlooks that the image of Dr. Franklin in convulsions, before breaking free of the electrical circuit, and the fate of the bird itself, may fail to have the desired effect.

McNichol supplies other electrical miscellanea as well. Dr. Givings expresses support for Edison in his effort to win the standards war (32), even though elsewhere he scoffs at the claim that alternating current is more dangerous than direct current (35). Sabrina marvels over Edison's recording device, capable of preserving the "last wishes of the dying" (37), which was indeed one of the inventor's stated applications of the phonograph (McNichol, 38). When Leo relates the praise accorded the glow of Edison's electrical light, comparing it to "the sunset of an Italian autumn" (46), he is quoting from an editorial in the *New York Herald* published on December 21, 1879 (McNichol, 52). Dr. Givings's anecdote about releasing sparks by stroking a cat, and wondering if God stroked nature's back in order to generate electricity (56), is a story from the childhood of Nikola Tesla (McNichol, 71–2). Tesla was an inventor whose perhaps greatest contribution (among many) was to design an efficient induction motor for generating alternating current (74–5).

Ruhl draws upon her third source for the particulars of wet nursing. Golden thoroughly documents the fear of contamination, both morally and physically, that the upper and middle classes expressed towards their lower class wet nurses. The spread of disease through nursing, including tuberculosis and syphilis, was not uncommon (J. Golden, 143)—hence Dr. Givings's examination of Elizabeth. Furthermore, the belief that the moral character of the wet nurse could be transmitted through her milk was commonplace among physicians and families alike (151–3). Wet nurses were generally regarded as a necessary evil, essential in some cases for the survival of an infant, but nevertheless potentially disruptive. Since reliable wet nurses could be difficult to procure, a woman in this position generally yielded more clout than other servants in the household and could therefore place additional demands upon the employer (62). Ruhl's characters express these anxieties. Mr. Daldry's assertion that most wet nurses are "nine parts devil, one part cow" (19) paraphrases a statement that John Lovett Morse, a professor of pediatrics at Harvard Medical School, recalls a colleague making (J. Golden, 155). Mr. Daldry soothes the Givings' fears with his recommendation of his housekeeper Elizabeth as a religious, church-going, married woman. At least one woman reported jealousy over the bond between wet nurse and infant (175), an unsurprising response shared by Catherine.

Golden indicates that a black wet nurse, such as Elizabeth, would have been somewhat unusual in New England. In the North, white servants greatly outnumbered African-American ones, and this proportion would have most likely held within the wet nursing occupation (72). The employment of black nurses to suckle white babies was no doubt much more common in the South, simply due to the makeup of the labor force. Indeed, during the antebellum period, plantation mistresses were known to nurse the children of slaves in order to preserve the wealth, in manpower, of the plantation. Given the greater prevalence of cross-racial nursing, Southerners were much less likely to believe that the character of the wet nurse would be transmitted to the infant (73–4). In the North, Irish women dominated the wet nursing marketplace; the anti–Irish prejudice expressed by Dr. Givings would have been commonplace at the time (J. Golden, 72).

Catherine wrestles with guilt and anxiety over her desire to employ a wet nurse whose baby has died. To contemporaneous thinking, there were advantages and disadvantages associated with the death or survival of the wet nurse's own child. If the child were alive, it could be examined to determine if the mother was producing wholesome milk. An examination of the mother provided by a doctor, such as that administered by Dr. Givings, would obviate this advantage. Were the child alive, however, the nurse might favor it over that of her employer (J. Golden, 57). Tragically, as physicians acknowledged, "wet nursing often involved trading the life of a poor baby for that of a rich one" (97). The wet nurse often could not afford to provide sufficient care for her own child, who would suffer from the lack of mother's milk. Another class factor that may have increased the popularity of wet nursing was the perception, present in both popular and professional medical literature, that middle- and upper-class women were too weak and too "sensitive and excitable" to nurse their own children (53). The sturdy lower classes were considered much more suitable to the task.

Home and Garden: Home

Although Catherine's insufficient milk flow, and the need to hire a wet nurse, troubles the Givings home and family, their problems run much deeper. They suffer from a geopathology rooted in their home's bifurcated structure. The architecture expresses a hierarchical relationship of binary pairs, favoring the first term, corresponding to the operating theater and living room as has been noted: work space/domestic space, male/female, science/art, science/religion, visible/invisible, and intellect/body. The operating theater is clearly the work space of the male, medical scientist, and the living room the domestic arena of female-gendered activities such as breast-feeding and child rearing, as well as entertaining. The painting session of Madonna and Child introduces art and religion into the living room as well. Although the doctor treats bodies in the operating theater, his is a disembodied knowledge, based on a theoretical understanding rather than embodied experience, as evident in the misunderstanding of paroxysm. The breast-feeding that occurs in the other side of the house as a necessary component of child rearing qualifies as embodied, and even sexual, experience. The setting itself foils Dr. Givings's attempts to keep work and home separate, as patients must pass through the living room to reach the operating theater. The doctor's wife and baby are expected to not only not be seen but also not heard. Catherine is forced to hide behind the piano at Sabrina's first entrance while Dr. Givings hides the baby in the nursery; the patient's encounter with the baby impinges, from the doctor's perspective, on the therapeutic process. Indeed, during the first session the women of the household, including even the doctor's assistant, are clearly expected to disappear, as stage directions indicate that Annie sits "invisibly in the corner" during the consultation (9).

Ruhl demonstrates that each sphere contains elements of the other. Commerce, for example, occurs in both to mark the buying and selling of labor and services: Mr. Daldry speaks to the doctor about paying for his wife's treatments; Elizabeth asks Catherine about payments for breast-feeding; Dr. Givings promises to pay Elizabeth handsomely, but not so much so that she will leave the Daldrys' service; and Leo offers Elizabeth an exorbitant fee to sit for the portrait of Madonna and Child. Dr. Givings's medical expertise is for sale, as are Elizabeth's services on a sliding scale, with domestic work at the bottom, next up breast-feeding, and modeling at the top. All of these services address or employ the female body and, apart from Elizabeth's employment at the Daldrys', induce or exploit the flow of bodily fluids. Through the specific of breast-feeding, domestic tasks are positioned as labor and the worth of a woman's efforts within the home elevated. Technology in the form of electricity flows into both spaces, notably to the vibrator on the one side, and the lamp on the other. Through experimentation in the operating theater and conversation in the living room, Catherine acquires bodily knowledge of the vibrator therapy. Ultimately, however, the house must be dissolved in order to completely break down the architectural division and hierarchy that it represents.

Domestic Hazards

Ruhl defines home around the concept of family. Domestic activity, to a great extent, revolves around the bearing and raising of children, which is presented as the right and proper purpose of the Victorian family. The play catalogs the hazards of this vocation and demonstrates alternating currents of ambivalence in the feelings of characters towards it. Catherine and Elizabeth's love for their children is evident, as is Sabrina's desire to start a family and the feelings of tenderness elicited by Catherine's baby. Nevertheless, both Sabrina and Catherine express anxiety about childbirth: Sabrina imagines it as "torture" (18), and Catherine describes the intense pain and terror wrapped up in the bloody spectacle of birthing Letitia (30). Catherine is unable to provide sufficient milk and Sabrina has been unable to conceive, and Elizabeth has lost her youngest to cholera. An awareness of the high infant mortality rate slips out with Catherine's comment that she and her husband plan to have "extra children, just in case" (25). Of the three marriages, Elizabeth's appears the most solid despite her loss, as two boys survive and she and her husband would seem to share mutual respect for one another. The enervated Sabrina and frustrated Mr. Daldry hardly seem compatible, and the Givings' crisis provides much of the dramatic action. Leo's fiancée has fled him, and his love for the married Elizabeth, across lines of race and propriety, cannot be requited. The same-sex attraction between Sabrina and Annie, likewise, fails to fulfill any mainstream Victorian model for partnership.

Mrs. Givings (Laura Benanti) with her baby. *In the Next Room or the vibrator play.* Lyceum Theatre. Produced by Lincoln Center Theater, 2009 (courtesy Joan Marcus).

The primary function of marriage as a social arrangement that facilitates procreation is complicit with the androcentric model of sexuality. The pain that Sabrina suffers in the dark at the hands of her husband is acceptable under this model, as long as semen is delivered, with pleasure a secondary consideration. The pleasure that might be experienced between partners of the same sex falls outside of the model as nonproductive. The use of the vibrator as therapy is legitimized, but its potential to deliver pleasure is rendered irrelevant. Ruhl implicitly critiques this model and celebrates the combined pleasures of sexuality and intimacy apart from, or in addition to, the goal of procreation.

Sabrina offers an anecdote during medical consultation that illustrates the restrictions faced by Victorian women and suggests that hysteria might be the result of social rather than psychological factors. Sabrina identifies a cause of her illness as dirty, green, haunted curtains, which she relates to her childhood home. The curtains appear to have been inspired by the short story "The Yellow Wallpaper" (1892) by early feminist Charlotte Perkins Gilman. In "Hysteria, Mysteria" (2009), an article included in the *Lincoln Center Theater Review*, which was on sale in the lobby when the play appeared on Broadway (and which is also available online at www.lct.org), Helen Horowitz notes the similarity between Sabrina and the protagonist of the short story. The connection between play and story is indeed significant. The story is derived from Gilman's own experience of a resting treatment, prescribed by a prominent nerve specialist, that almost drove her insane. The protagonist's husband, a doctor, diagnoses her as suffering from mild hysteria and forbids her from working. She spends most of her time in an upstairs bedroom and gradually comes to perceive a woman trapped in the wallpaper. As the figure becomes more real to her, eventually she identifies with it completely.

Gilman's autobiography strikingly illustrates the problems faced by an independently spirited woman during the late 19th and early 20th centuries, on whom the effects of social repression were apt to be diagnosed as illness. Gilman's first marriage demonstrates Chaudhuri's trope of the home as shelter and prison, with the emphasis on the second term, just as effectively as her short story does. From a young age, Gilman voiced a strong sense of purpose, accompanied by a powerful work ethic, in her desire to help humanity. She entered into marriage reluctantly, fearful that it would impinge on her aspirations. It turned out that her fears were well founded, as she plunged into depression whenever she stayed at home with her husband, Charles Walter Stetson (Knight, 13–15). Motherhood only compounded her agony: she wept painful tears even as she nursed her "lovely child" (Gilman, "Breakdown," 59). It was during her marriage that she underwent the calamitous resting treatment fictionalized in "The Yellow Wallpaper." Eventually the marriage ended in divorce; unfortunately, Gilman never completely recovered from her breakdown. Prior to her marriage, she was involved for four years in a loving relationship with her long-time friend, Martha Luther, which ended painfully for Gilman when Luther married and moved away (Knight, 12). Societal pressures foiled her happiness, as mirrored in the play in the truncated romance between Sabrina and Annie.

Sabrina paints an idealized vision of the past, inclusive of a strong, healthy mother who fulfilled her household duties by cleaning the drapes on a weekly basis, and by processing grapes from the family arbor into jam. (The "grape-covered arbors" are probably derived from a brief mention in Gilman's story [Gilman, "Yellow," 25].) The mother's attention kept the drapes clean and transparent, through which Sabrina could view the grapes and celebrate their ripening in the autumn. The memory is one of fertility, abundance, and nurturance anchored in the figure of the calm and productive mother, in sharp contrast to Sabrina's current condition of weakness, which may at least be partially attributed to the middle-class, late 19th-century expectation that she not work. Like Gilman's protagonist, Sabrina complains that all she does is rest, and Mr. Daldry reports wooing her with a promise to take care of and protect her. He assumes that women are the weaker sex, requiring the protection of a husband. The dynamic of this power differential positions husband as father and forecloses the possibility of an equal partnership. The significant age difference between husband and wife in the marriages of the Givings and the Daldrys reinforces the impression of a father/daughter relationship, with the father figure in control.

The grape arbor assumes Edenic significance, as does the other garden in the play, that planted by Catherine. The arbor represents the domestic paradise lost. Significantly, Sabrina's father is absent, and all the goodness in this landscape emanates from the mother. This vision conforms to the woman-centered religion with which other characters flirt: Elizabeth imagines a male God unable to comfort infants in heaven, and Catherine wonders if a woman might not better fulfill the function of sustainer than Jesus does. Sabrina's nostalgic world includes "long walks out of doors" (10), an activity that links it with Catherine's winter garden, which frequently accommodates walks. In the case of Catherine's garden, walks are associated with eroticism; the vigorous fecundity of the grape arbor suggests a parallel function.

Sabrina's fall from the Eden of the past is presented as a problem of impaired vision and absence. The dusty curtains block the view to a grape arbor that no longer exists, and would seem to require an exorcism rather than a good beating. Although Ruhl frequently catapults her characters into the afterlife, an actual haunting is unusual but may be found in the example of Matilde's parents in *The Clean House*. There, the parental ghosts operate in a magic realist sense as reminders of the past, and as a lineage of succession to which Matilde aspires, and they manifest Matilde's process of bereavement. Conversely, the ghosts in the curtains of *In the Next Room* are the shadow or negative image of Sabrina's mother as the ideal, traditional woman; they represent failed marriage and motherhood. Further, the obfuscation caused by the dirty curtains represents an obstruction of sorts, and as such fits into the thematic binary of flow/blockage. They symbolize Sabrina's decreased vitality, and impaired vision was regarded as a common symptom of hysteria. The absence of a grape arbor in Sabrina's yard demonstrates the divorce between her and her idyllic past. It also represents infertility, which surfaces in Sabrina's frustration at her inability to conceive. The grape arbor of her past links happiness and fecundity, and sexual pleasure is missing from her current life. Ultimately in this play, the garden represents happiness, knowledge, and sexual fulfillment. A home without a garden, such as the Daldrys', is an unhappy one indeed.

The Buried Child

The lack of a child distresses Sabrina; the loss of one grieves Elizabeth. The devastating impact of the death of a child on a family has been well documented in the American play. Chaudhuri identifies the buried child as a common trope in American drama, appearing in O'Neill's *Long Day's Journey into Night*, Albee's *Who's Afraid of Virginia Woolf?*, and Shepard's *Buried Child*, to name a few examples. The buried child (an imaginary one, in Albee's case) represents the "hidden secret" of realist drama—the skeleton in the ground rather than the closet—which, unearthed, brings to light the source of the family's problems. Those problems have to do with "the animosity between the generations, powerlessness as impotence, family as pathology" (110). In Chaudhuri's reading, Shepard's work comments on the trope itself, as the small bundle of bones brought onstage at the conclusion fails to clarify anything. His move is an intertextual one, referencing external dramatic texts rather than revealing deep structural meaning.

The buried child of *In the Next Room* belongs to the black wet nurse, Elizabeth. It was not uncommon for the infant of a wet nurse to die from lack of attention and sustenance from its mother, although, in Elizabeth's case, her baby's death from cholera predates her employment in this capacity. The trope assumes a racial dimension as Elizabeth is charged with nursing her white employer's baby, and the familial problems customarily addressed widen in scope to assume nationalist, racial dimensions. The play is set in the 1880s, merely two decades after the Civil War. The sustenance of the white body by the black one represented by Elizabeth's nursing of Catherine's infant symbolizes the legacy of slavery and continued exploitation of black labor. The familial issues typically wrapped up in the trope of the buried child may be rewritten as the animosity between the races rather than the generations, and racial policies and practices, rather than family, as pathology. The conceptualization of powerlessness as impotence, usually laid upon the patriarch, assumes racial and class dimensions as well.

Elizabeth (Quincy Tyler Bernstine, left) and Mrs. Givings (Laura Benanti) with baby. *In the Next Room or the vibrator play.* **Lyceum Theatre. Produced by Lincoln Center Theater, 2009 (courtesy Joan Marcus).**

Chaudhuri has identified the figure of America as another frequent presence in modern drama, and although it may not be Ruhl's primary concern here, it is implied in the play's setting and its racial politics. Indeed, the figure of America replaces that of the family in these reconfigurations of the significance of the buried child. Elizabeth takes to wet nursing reluctantly, driven by financial necessity. Her feelings towards her ward are anything but simple, as revealed in her explosive farewell speech in which she likens Catherine's baby to a tick filled with the blood of her own child, one that she would like to burst; nevertheless, she displays, also, a tenderness towards the baby. The depiction of a lone minority character is a hazardous one for a playwright, since critics will be alert to stereotypical renderings. Ruhl opens herself to attack in this regard in her positioning of Elizabeth as the one female who is cognizant of sexual pleasure, in contrast to her clueless white counterparts. Her complex characterization, however, counteracts the simplifying force of stereotype. Elizabeth is the most proper of the women, and the most conscientious of her marriage. Her feelings towards Catherine's child, as noted above, are depicted as intricate and deeply human. She treads carefully in the home of her white employer, selects her words with care, and only reveals her feelings when pushed to the point of exasperation, and when it is safe to do so. She is a black woman negotiating a white man's world, and the sexual knowledge that she shares with Catherine and Sabrina allies her, at least briefly, with the other women in the play. The recasting of paternal impotence in racial terms as brought forth by the trope of the buried child, as suggested above, is not entirely correct. Although a second- or third-class citizen, as defined by race and gender, Elizabeth demonstrates potency in her impact on Catherine and in a presence strong enough to attract Leo's ardor. Although disadvantaged, she is not without agency.

This is not the first time that Ruhl has buried a child. She dispatches Eurydice to the underworld not to unearth family secrets, but rather to reestablish a father-daughter relationship and place it at odds to that between husband and wife. She entombs Jean of *Dead Man's Cell Phone* with Gordon just long enough for her to discover the open secret that her fantasy lover is not a nice person. Although not buried, Blue of *Late: a cowboy song* is staged as invisible and thus conceals the family secret, that of her intersexuality. As they attempt to name her, her parents tussle over her gender and identity; the reconfiguration of family at the conclusion, expanding beyond the heteronormal model, would seem to allow for visibility. Again, however, Ruhl's usage of the trope does not conform in a strict sense to the pattern identified by Chaudhuri, as the invisible child is, so to speak, in plain sight throughout and represents possibility rather than pathology.

Likewise, the unearthing of Elizabeth's baby, Henry Douglas, in her farewell speech, reveals an open secret about race relations. The plot has not been structured around this disinterment; rather, it is an event in a series that leads to the disintegration of the doctor's home. The trope of the buried child crosses not only race and class lines here, but intersects with issues of religion when the English artist Leo insists upon painting Elizabeth with Catherine's baby as a Madonna and Child "for our times ... after the Civil War" (51). Ruhl stages the sitting in the Givings' living room, providing the visual of a black Madonna nursing a white baby Jesus. On the surface, this portrays an idealistic vision of America, depicting as it does harmony between the races within a religious setting; one may extrapolate from this the American ideal of equality. Nevertheless, the legacy of slavery cannot be erased from the image, in the nurturance of a white body by a black one, and in the ghost of Elizabeth's child hovering in the background. A white child has been substituted for a black one as the Christ figure; this loving vision is predicated upon the sacrifice of the black infant. A gap opens between the real and the ideal in the figure of America presented here.

Left to right: Melle Powers as Elizabeth, Hannah Cabell as Mrs. Givings, and Joaquín Torres as Leo. Leo paints Elizabeth and Mrs. Givings's baby as Madonna and Child. World premiere of *In the Next Room or the vibrator play* at Berkeley Repertory Theatre, 2009 (courtesy Berkeley Repertory Theatre).

An Alternative to Departure

Although robust and seemingly healthy, with her child above ground, Catherine is nevertheless trapped within her domicile and the social strictures it represents. Her escape route follows a path of self-discovery. When Catherine urges her husband to experiment on her with the vibrator, she invokes the tradition of home as a place of experimentation with definitions of selfhood, a feature of modern drama as demonstrated by Chaudhuri (8). Chaudhuri analyzes Ibsen's *A Doll's House* at some length as she develops her definition of geopathology. *In the Next Room* parallels Ibsen's play in significant ways. *A Doll's House* premiered in 1879, which is approximately the time at which Ruhl's work is set. Both works trap their female protagonists within Victorian gender roles and, by extension, the family home. Ibsen's drama is an early example of realism; Ruhl adheres to many of the conventions of the genre. Chaudhuri credits Ibsen, in *A Doll's House*, with discovering the true subject of modern drama as "the problematic of home." She positions Nora as a descendant of the fallen woman of bourgeois drama and melodrama; one of the new drama's revolutionary breaks from the past is that it will stage the fall rather than present its aftermath (61). Nora's shocking solution is a heroic departure that entails leaving husband and children; she must abandon home and family in order to pursue her experiment in selfhood. In dramas that would follow, the dilemma of leaving or staying would become a central moral issue, with the inverse of a heroism of departure expressed as a victimage of location (63). Chaudhuri notes that Nora's actual escape would endure as the exception rather than the rule; later "falling" characters would be more likely to resort to suicide as a solution to the problematic of place. Examples include Strindberg's Miss Julie, and Ibsen's Hedda Gabler, Rosmer and Rebecca, and Master Builder Solness (62).

Ruhl finds an alternate solution to Catherine's geopathology that departs from realist conventions: she makes the house, rather than the protagonist, go away. A precedent may be found in *The Ghost Sonata* (1907), at the conclusion of which Strindberg wished to dissolve the haunted house into white light. However, that work is an expressionistic rather than realistic one. What is unusual in Ruhl is that the appearance and conventions of realism are maintained up until the final scene, inclusive of Catherine's attempt to escape with Leo to France, which would involve abandonment of husband and baby. This differs from Nora's solution in that it entails leaving one man for another. True, it represents the choice of artist over scientist, and the promise of completion; Catherine confesses to Leo that she imagined herself the half-finished woman on the threshold of self-discovery of which he spoke. However, even as she is drawn toward fulfillment, she is willing to compromise by vowing to be silent so as not to interfere with Leo's work. She begs him to draw her soul out from her body, from where he says it is locked, to hover two inches before her eyes, which is where he located his fiancée's soul. Although she yearns for completion, she is all too willing to place the brush in Leo's hands.

Catherine's threatened escape would leave her dependent upon a man. Nora's entails emancipation from a man, but also the great risk of self-sufficiency for a woman in 1879. Home functions for Nora, as it will in many dramas to follow including *In the Next Room*, as both shelter and prison (Chaudhuri, 8). Carl H. Klaus, Miriam Gilbert, and Bradford S. Field, Jr., identify the central issues of *A Doll's House* as those of misunderstanding and lack of communication rather than the suppression of woman, as both husband and wife are denied their human rights in this situation (548). The same might be said of *In the Next Room*, as both Dr. and Mrs. Givings suffer due to their inability to discuss the latter's dissatisfaction and the effect of the vibrator. The doctor is a caring husband who wants to make his wife happy; as he himself admits, he has not known how. He is willing, finally, to be taught, and his wife is still around to teach him, in contrast to Nora who rejects her husband's final pleas for reconciliation. The solution, or failure to arrive at

Dr. Givings (Michael Cerveris) and Mrs. Givings (Laura Benanti) share a serious moment. *In the Next Room or the vibrator play.* **Lyceum Theatre. Produced by Lincoln Center Theater, 2009 (courtesy Joan Marcus).**

one, lies within the relationship of the couple; the suppression of woman restricts the man as well.

Ultimately, Catherine escapes only as far as the garden, although with far-reaching consequences. The garden has been associated with eroticism through the act of walking as an expression of Catherine's vibrant, unfulfilled sexuality. As early as the first scene, her references to being wet and dry, ostensibly referring to the rain, excite Mr. Daldry, who later attempts to kiss her. After walking with Annie, Sabrina returns for her hat in a flustered state as if sexually aroused, "over-excited" and "faint" to the point of requiring additional treatment (32). Finally, at his insistence, Leo walks Elizabeth home and earns a slap when he confesses his "affections" for her. Elizabeth's husband sees him walk her to their house, and insists she discontinue her employment with the Givings. The threatened interracial affair is thereby cut short by Elizabeth and her husband. The walks, and transgressions that they suggest, represent an escape from the bourgeois, and stifling, domesticity of the Givings' home.

Characters frequently refer to precipitation, which clearly has to do with more than the weather, as they consider venturing outside. In *The Birth of*

Pleasure (2002), developmental psychologist Carol Gilligan speculates, "Maybe love is like rain," as both bring life (3; 235). In reference to *In the Next Room*, one may ponder, less poetically, if perhaps "love is like precipitation," inclusive of both rain and snow. In this vein, Catherine employs the umbrella as a barometer of personality. She finds a person who dares the elements without one, who risks a drenching, to be a romantic. She claims to not know what type of person she is, as her husband has always been in charge of the umbrella; this statement helps to establish the need for her experiments in selfhood. If love is like rain, then a romantic is likely to expose him or herself to it, and Dr. Givings's constant employment of an umbrella protects him against experiencing the fullness of his wife's love. Love is like snow as well, as Catherine writes her name in it for her future husband, and makes angels in it, and it blesses the final scene in the winter garden. Her inattentive husband fails to notice, first, her name in the snow, and subsequently the first snow. He urges her to wear her wrap when she rushes outside, not comprehending that she does not require insulation against love. When the winter garden replaces the house, and precipitation cannot be denied, he fully sees her. The coldness of snow invigorates Catherine when she makes a snow angel by herself, and enlivens both her and her husband when they come together at the conclusion. Leo's characterization of snow as kind, as it falls and meets the ground or an eyelash slowly, links it to tenderness, a quality which is in ample evidence in the final scene. In the Lincoln Center Theater production, Michael Cerveris as Dr. Givings played against the line to strong effect, shivering violently as he denied that he was cold. This choice only enhanced the tenderness as an act of self-sacrifice to his wife's desires and to the fullness of their marriage.

Resting on Air

Ruhl does not so much undermine the foundations of home as represent it as something that must be weighed down to keep it from flying away. To do so, she deploys oppositions between heaviness and lightness, and permanence and impermanence. After Leo returns to retrieve his scarf, he and Catherine sip tea in the living room while they wait for Sabrina's treatment to finish. They overhear her moans from the next room as Catherine primes Leo to ask him about the use of the vibrator on a man. She describes the home as anchored and held together by objects such as plants, teapots, and statuettes, and refers to her experience with the vibrator, as assisted by Sabrina, as capable of shattering the house, or making it fly away. She links the experience to electricity. This conversation occurs before her husband experiments on her, and before she has compared notes with the other women, and thus before she has linked the vibrator to sexuality. From her perspective at this point, paroxysm is a technologically-induced, and novel, sensation. Her house is being loosed from its moorings in other ways, as she begins to fall in love with Leo and by implication doubt the solidity of her marriage. She is already alienated from her child through her inability to breast-feed, so the increasing strain on her marriage further divorces her from family.

It appears that Catherine took the lead in courtship when she wrote her name in the snow while still a girl, for her future husband. He failed to notice this act of devotion; Catherine claims that he was always one step behind her and married her in order to be able to see her face. Ruhl plays here with the binary of permanence and impermanence. A house, the site of a home, would ideally be solid and permanent. Yet ultimately, what is written in snow is ascribed with greater staying power. Catherine insists that "a gift must be unnecessary—for it to be good," and that her name in the snow, written for her husband alone, would "exist for all time" (58). She doubts her scientist husband's ability to have even appreciated the gift. A tension between science and aesthetics, between the useful and beautiful, undergirds Catherine's criticism of her husband and counterpoints the binary of permanence and impermanence. As a scientist, he puts his faith in cause and effect, in the necessary conditions for a given outcome. Catherine places her gift outside of causality and within a timeless realm of aesthetics. Her name in the snow endures because the visible signifies the invisible; with the act of writing, she signs herself over to him. The promise outlasts the act of promising. Yet the melting of the snow signifies the impermanence of the seemingly permanent, of marriage and the home as unstable containers under siege by any passing artist.

The images of love and marriage are lightened further by the teachings of the Greek philosopher Thales, transmitted from Annie to Sabrina. Like Thales, the doctor's assistant has never married, presumably due to sexual orientation. According to her, Thales envisioned the world as suspended on water, to which Sabrina compares her ideal image of love as a girl, to be "surrounded and lifted up ... for eternity" (75). She has found that marriage rests instead on air, a less substantial, and invisible, element. Ruhl's handling of the house demonstrates her philosophy of lightness. She systematically subtracts weight as Catherine's vibrator experiments threaten the solidity of the house, and as she ascribes permanence to her name in the snow, and as Sabrina discovers that the world rests on air, not water. The playwright ultimately dissolves the seemingly solid patriarchal structure of the Givings home to demonstrate that that which appears heavy may actually be light.

Experiments in Selfhood: Electric Sex and Flames of Desire

As the play begins, Catherine flicks on and off an electrical lamp to entertain her baby. This action introduces several themes, including those of electricity and technology, the stopping and starting of flow, and the binary of light and dark. Catherine acquires knowledge through her experiments in selfhood, which help her see possibilities beyond the walls of her home. Technology facilitates vision, both in the physical and metaphorical sense, and may be divided into a binary of new and old: the new forms harness electricity, and include the vibrator and electric lamp, and older forms involve flame, and include candles and gaslight. New technology elicits both wonder and anxiety. As a stalwart man of science, Dr. Givings is enthusiastic about the potential of electricity, and he utilizes it in his office to power the vibrator and in his home to light the lights. Both Sabrina and Leo are cured of their symptoms through treatment with the electric vibrator: they become converts to the new technology. Sabrina and Catherine envision a brave new world with electrified cooking, poultry farming, prosthetics, and fireflies, and recordings of the last wishes of the dying.

But they register loss as well. Sabrina recoils at the thought of an electric piano. Catherine laments the passing of the candle, of the solemnity needed to carefully walk a dark hallway heedful of starting a fire, and of the beauty of blowing out a candle "with one's own breath" (37). The older technology is trusted and familiar, albeit not without danger; the newer technology excites but also raises anxiety, as the hazards of electrical current are feared. In a reference to alternating current, Catherine speaks of changing one's mind many times in a second as easily as flipping a switch and thereby becoming empowered as gods, an outcome that neither she nor Sabrina seems to relish. And yet, within a few lines Catherine demonstrates her ambivalence as she discovers how to turn on and eagerly commandeers the vibrator, formerly solely the province of her husband.

As channeled through the vibrator, electricity is linked with sexuality as revitalizing. Paroxysm/orgasm releases the flow of fluid and life energy. Vibrator therapy revivifies Sabrina and Leo, and jumpstarts the Givingses' marriage. Sabrina directly conflates electricity and sexuality when she describes her experience of paroxysm as electrocution as though "struck by a terrible lightning" (36). Leo articulates a theme when he associates fire with love and desire, and light without flame to the mechanical act of sex, in his example with a prostitute. The failure of Sabrina's second vibrator treatment reinforces this theme, as the doctor repeatedly ramps up the instrument in a futile attempt to induce paroxysm and accordingly blows a fuse.

Leo (Chandler Williams) makes an impression on Mrs. Givings (Laura Benanti). *In the Next Room or the vibrator play.* Lyceum Theatre. Produced by Lincoln Center Theater, 2009 (courtesy Joan Marcus).

As Catherine lights candles in the living room, Annie enters and the flow of desire between her and Sabrina achieves what, in this instance, the flow of electricity could not. Catherine's experiments with electricity ignite her sexuality; however, the last scene, in which currents of love and desire freely course between her and her husband, is lit by gaslight. Moments of intimacy are unplugged. The current of life flows not just from an object, the vibrator, to humans, but in the opposite direction as well. According to Catherine, a piano deprived of touch is a languishing "piece of dead wood" (24), and furniture is "dead" and "sad" without children climbing all over it (25). People animate the objects that anchor a house and hold it together; family and friends bring a habitation to life, make a house a home.

Light, and lightness, may be interpreted in a number of ways. Lightness figures predominately in Ruhl's work, as has been discussed, as a strategy for subtracting weight from heavy topics, as is evidenced in the humor and whimsy in this and her other plays. As the addition of light, illumination enables eyesight on the physical plane, and the acquisition of knowledge on the conceptual. Illumination figures in both the scientific and artistic realms. As a man of science, Dr. Givings attempts to shed light, through experimentation, on the mysteries of the universe. Both his patients complain of maladies of vision: Sabrina is sensitive to light, and Leo's vision is impaired. The doctor's cure has ramifications that extend beyond the physical realm. After his first treatment, not only does Leo see better, he is better able to perceive beauty; the stage directions indicate that "he would fall in love with whatever creature crossed his path," and accordingly he is dazzled at Sabrina's entrance (48). This sudden receptiveness to beauty sparks his creative urge and he rushes off to create "a thousand paintings" (49). The electrical treatment not only cures his eyesight but also restores his aesthetic sensibility as a function of perception.

Science and love intersect elsewhere as well. Sabrina expresses love in scientific terms as she compares Annie's dark eyes to magnets to which she is irresistibly drawn. After Dr. Givings admits that he missed his future wife's name in the snow, he attempts to redeem himself as a caring and attentive husband in the best way he knows how, through science. On his wife's departure after the disastrous treatment, another invention occurs to him: that of a hydraulic vibrator intended for excitable patients like Catherine. A doctor moved to the "point of invention" for the benefit of his wife or lover occurs in *The Clean House* as well, as Charles emulates the example of the surgeon Halsted who invented rubber gloves to protect the chapped hands of his nurse wife, as he pursues a natural cure for Ana's cancer.[1] This is a scientist's attempt to express what poets do with verbal elegance; as Dr. Givings later tells his wife, he has tried to love her, but has not known how.

Sight and blindness parallels the binary of light and darkness. In commenting on the pain induced by the electrical light, Sabrina links religious ecstasy to blindness, conjuring Tiresias and other blind seers. An intuitive, embodied knowledge does not require external light; indeed, religious mystery is best conceptualized as shrouded in darkness, and is thus opposed to knowledge acquired by empirical means. Scientific enlightenment also has its blind spots. After Leo relates the story of the friend who was shocked by his bride's pubic hair, having only seen the female form represented in marble, Dr. Givings notes that what men's intellect prevents them from seeing would fill volumes. His comment resonates with irony, as he himself is blind to the sexual aspect of the treatments he administers.

The scientific project attempts to shine light into the dark corners of the universe. In order to calm his wife's fears about electricity, Dr. Givings links it to nature in the story about exciting sparks by stroking a cat, taken from Tesla. He reasons that electricity is safe because it comes from nature. This strategy is similar to that taken by Edison's supporters who promoted electric light by comparing it to an Italian sunset. This vision of a benign nature erases its shadows and the world's mystery. As a child, Dr. Givings wondered if God stroked nature's back in order to produce lightning; as an adult, his explanation replaces God with natural law. Although his patients cry out for God at the therapeutic climax, the doctor regards his treatments from a scientific vantage point, free of religious overtones. He decouples vibrator therapy from sexuality, and sexuality from religion. Leo assumes a more romantic stance towards lightness and darkness. He equates light with hope as he shows Catherine the lights coming on in the neighborhood as darkness falls. In a brief but profound speech, each lit window represents others' lives—apart, hopeful, and unknowable, not unlike Dickens's separate carriages as cited in *Dead Man's Cell Phone*. Leo's comparison of partially lit houses to incomplete paintings illustrates the limits of illumination, in both a physical and conceptual sense. He insists that an unfinished painting captures life more accurately than a finished one. He cites Michelangelo's *Virgin and Child with the Angels* as an example of a work of art that, had it been finished, would have proved unbearably beautiful: as is, it intimates "the incomplete lines of God" (48). The artist values the mystery that science would eradicate.

Above, Ruhl's play has been situated in relation to the theatrical genre of realism. Its close relative, naturalism, promised a "contract of total visibility" and knowledge (Chaudhuri, 29). Émile Zola, a founding theorist of the genre, envisioned it as a scientific form that demonstrated the influence of environment on identity. According to Chaudhuri, the naturalist approaches the unknown with a scientific curiosity, regarding it as an "enigma, conundrum, and puzzle" to be solved, rather than as a mystery in the religious sense. She examines Strindberg's *Miss Julie* as an, or even the, exemplary work in this genre, and states that in it the playwright attempts to shed light on the unknown through the "powerful explanatory systems" of sex and class (31).

As a 21st-century playwright, Ruhl charts the complexities of these systems rather than attempt to map the unknown with them. The naturalist environment functions as a petri dish of sorts that contains experiments worked out on characters as subjects, and every attempt is made to create a setting as true-to-life as possible. That environment is inviolable; to destroy the illusion is to ruin the experiment. Exclusive of the final scene, Ruhl's unit setting would be appropriate to naturalism and realism. Ruhl's staging of even gynecological treatments would seem to adhere to the naturalist promise of total visibility. However, the replacement of the house with the winter garden shatters the stage illusion, showing it to be just that, and thereby reneges on the contract. The naturalistic and realistic appearance of the set establishes an expectation that Ruhl vigorously foils. Ruhl reinjects mystery and wonder, in a religious and mystical sense, when she dissolves the house.

Maria Dizzia (left) as Mrs. Daldry and Hannah Cabell as Mrs. Givings. World premiere of *In the Next Room or the vibrator play* at Berkeley Repertory Theatre, 2009 (courtesy Berkeley Repertory Theatre).

Recovering the Sexual Voice

Catherine's research into her sexual identity passes through a number of stages. She first discovers the vibrator with Sabrina, then undergoes the treatment from her husband, compares data with Sabrina and Elizabeth, and finally meets her husband in the winter garden. The doctor resists his wife's initial inquiries into the nature of his therapeutic sessions. Her curiosity is piqued when she overhears one of Sabrina's treatments. Her husband asserts that she would not understand and would be bored by the science. As in *A Doll's House*, a lack of communication, or rather the male partner's inability or unwillingness to engage in it, lies at the heart of marital discord. The doctor locks the door of his treatment room to assert his control over the flow of information.

After Dr. Givings flees to his club, a male bastion, Sabrina returns for her gloves and provides Catherine with the opportunity to pursue her research. Catherine interrogates Sabrina, who whets her appetite by describing her experience of the therapy in binary terms as combining pleasure and pain, sensations of electricity and heat, and impressions of lightness and darkness. Ever more intrigued, Catherine engages Sabrina and her hat pin as allies in her quest to uncover what lies behind the locked door. The excursion proves empowering, as Catherine discovers that the vibrator treatment, cloaked in the mystery of medical science by her husband, is available at the flip of a switch. Ironically, he has employed science, a discipline intent on discovery, to conceal. Under Sabrina's guidance, Catherine experiences the treatment as both "awful" and irresistible as it moves her to tears (38). In this first stage of experimentation, the two women have combined forces in order to uncover knowledge suppressed by the male figure. Sabrina has already experienced the vibrator, but only in the role of female patient subjected to the authority of the male doctor. Catherine is impudent enough to toy with the master's machine. The vibrator is a blatant phallic symbol, and as Catherine appropriates it, she poses a serious threat to patriarchal structures of knowledge and power. The sharing of knowledge continues the next time they meet. Catherine expresses a desire to find out why the therapy has an opposite effect on each of them, in another example of the thematic of alternating current: it energizes Catherine, and puts Sabrina to sleep.

Maria Dizzia (left) as Mrs. Daldry and Hannah Cabell as Mrs. Givings. World premiere of *In the Next Room or the vibrator play* at Berkeley Repertory Theatre, 2009 (courtesy Berkeley Repertory Theatre).

The Givingses' marriage arrives at a crisis point when the doctor finally yields to Catherine's call to experiment on her. He regards the treatment as an experiment because he considers her to be healthy and free from the symptoms of hysteria. He finally consents on the grounds that perhaps her body has retained an excess of the fluid of milk. He expresses unease, however, since the procedure brings the realms of work and home much too close together for his comfort. He demands her silence to protect his reputation. The experiment runs amok when Catherine insists that he kiss her during the procedure; her husband regards this desire as a perversion. Besides conflating work and home, the incident demonstrates the sexual nature of vibrator therapy, which the doctor would prefer to continue to overlook. Catherine realizes the sexual potential of the vibrator without being able to articulate it as such.

Catherine's experimentation reconnects her with embodied knowledge. In "When the Mind Leaves the Body ... and Returns" (2006), Gilligan charts the course of dissociation that occurs in both boys and girls. At a certain age, in early childhood for boys, and in adolescence for girls, mind dissociates from body in an adaptive move to align with social expectations. The individual denies what he or she knows in his or her body in order to conform, and much of this adjustment occurs along gender lines. Qualities associated with masculinity are favored over those gendered as feminine, so that mind is privileged over body, thought over emotion, and self over relationships (60). Male and female are opposed as hierarchical, binary opposites, with manhood defined as "not being a woman and also being on top" (61). Gilligan cites Freud's "Civilized Sexual Morality and Modern Nervous Illness" (1908), in which the founder of psychoanalysis traces "the so-called intellectual inferiority of women to their sexual suppression." Divorced from their sexuality, women limit their intelligence in the sense that they must "keep their minds out of their bodies" (Gilligan, "When the Mind," 65).

Gilligan identifies the recuperation of the sexual voice as the point at which dissociation is undone. Bolstering her argument with an example from literature, as Freud himself was wont to do, Gilligan calls on the bearer of Nathaniel Hawthorne's scarlet letter, Hester Prynne. What releases Hester from the psychic prison implied in the term "goodwife" is not so much the act of sexual transgression, but the "freeing of a sexual voice, the joining of mind and body" (64). The suppression of the sexual voice occurs within the structure of patriarchy, often generically understood as the suppression of women by men. In *The Deepening Darkness* (2009), Gilligan and philosopher and constitutional law scholar David A. J. Richards offer a more precise, anthropological definition as "a rule of priests ... in which the priest ... is a father." Patriarchy sets up a hierarchy that "elevates some men over other men and all men over women," and within the home places the father in the position of authority over women and children (22).

A significant step in Catherine's freeing her sexual voice is the sharing of knowledge with other women. Notably, Leo resists her questioning about the treatment, allying himself with Dr. Givings as he blocks the flow of information. Sabrina and Elizabeth are more cooperative as the women puzzle out the sensations of paroxysm, which the latter identifies as sexual in nature. The women tread on dangerous ground as they situate themselves somewhere between Madonna and whore. As noted by Gilligan and Richards, this age-old division "justifies male dominance in the name of protecting women's purity and also alienates women from one another and from vital parts of themselves." Love is divorced from sexuality and virtue from pleasure (238). This reinforces the dissociation of mind from body and mutes the sexual voice. Ruhl provides examples of both archetypes, in Elizabeth posing as the Madonna, and in Leo's description of sex with a prostitute. In reference to the former, Leo wonders why it is so rare to see the baby Jesus actually "[give] suck" (62). The answer may be found in the anxiety experienced by Catherine and Elizabeth over the return of the doctor, who is shocked to find an exposed breast in his living room.

The setting of the exposure, rather than the act itself, is what unsettles Dr. Givings who, only a few scenes previously, conducted a gynecological examination on the wet nurse. What is appropriate in one room is not in the next, because a bared breast in the parlor takes on sexual significance further complicated by the act of nursing. The reason the baby Jesus is so rarely depicted at the teat may be attributed to anxiety over the relation between breast-feeding and sexuality. The status of the Virgin Mary as pure and chaste might be sullied by the implied flow of bodily fluid. In "Maternal Experience and the Boundaries of Christian Sexual Ethics" (2000), theologian Cristina L. H. Traina interrogates the ethics of maternal sexuality. The experience of motherhood as "sensuous, erotic, or sexual" is a common one (370). The author begins with an anecdote of her own experience of orgasm while nursing, an unexpected and uninvited occurrence, but nonetheless a startling demonstration of the erotic potential of the mother-child relationship. The phenomenon has been relatively unexplored until fairly recently because it brushes up against fears of incest and sexual abuse. Traina maintains that the loving touch between mother and child may contain an erotic pleasure that is beneficial for both. She positions eroticism or sensuality as a superset of experience that contains that of sexuality focused on "genital relations," and thus allows for an erotic, non-genital, non-orgasmic, and nonabusive intimacy between mother and child (383).

Traina summarizes research to support the contention that not only breast-feeding, but childbirth as well may be regarded as a sexual event. She parallels the sequence of childbirth to that of orgasm and relates that for some women, "birth is an orgasmic event." Both suckling and sexual stimulation may provoke "nipple erection and milk ejection," and "coital sexual pleasure" and "successful labor and milk ejection" are inhibited by the same stimuli. The hormone oxytocin is implicit in all three processes, which are also typically "followed by caretaking behavior" (373). Moreover, she argues against linking sexuality solely with pleasure, noting that pain is a factor not only in childbirth, but also at times in association with coitus and breast-feeding. This complex of events associated with procreation and child-rearing, that is coitus, childbirth, and breast-feeding, may thus be regarded as sexual ones, inclusive of sensations of both pleasure and pain. Traina notes that in many non–Western cultures maternal sexuality is the accepted norm, incorporating even direct sexual stimulation of infants. This perspective is at odds with the model of asexual motherhood that persists to this day in Western cultures and that was certainly the predominant one during the Victorian era. The Virgin Mary is the paragon of this model, as she has bypassed coitus. However, if childbirth and breast-feeding are defined as sexualized activities, the depiction of a nursing Madonna and Child threatens the image of the supreme asexual mother.

As Catherine, Sabrina, and Elizabeth redefine, in so many words, paroxysm as orgasm, they explore the boundary between asexuality and hypersexuality as delineated in moral terms. The split between Madonna and whore reinforces that between mind and body and the women must venture into the middle ground in order to rediscover their sexual voices. Leo represents a male gaze that atypically fixes on this median, where he situates his Italian fiancée. He implies a sexual relationship with her, as he explains that she kissed with her whole body and states his own intention to explore the naked female form so as to avoid the fate of his friend, who was repulsed by his wife's pubic hair on his wedding night.[2] As an artist, Leo is unfettered by convention and does not demand a chaste bride. He himself is feminized as suffering from hysteria, and further by Dr. Givings for being an artist (45). As the figure of the artist and foreigner, albeit an English one, he escapes rigid gender identification and exemplifies a more fluid model of masculinity, and is himself more comfortable with female sexuality than the other male figures in the play: Mr. Daldry is only able to communicate about sex in winks and nudges, and the doctor has carefully divorced his love life from what happens in the next room. Like their women, the husbands are dissociated from their sexual voice. The final phase of Catherine's experimentation, in which she meets her husband in the winter garden, stages a rediscovery of embodied knowledge for both of them that replaces the polarizing images of virgin and whore with a fuller and freer conception of womanhood.

The Female Jesus

This concept of womanhood challenges even the suitability of a male God as sustainer of life. Elizabeth loses faith in God when He reclaims her infant son. She balks at her mother's advice that all loved ones are borrowed from God, and must be returned to Him sooner or later. She offers two visions of heaven, one maternal and the other paternal. In the former, the child flies back willingly, like an angel, to the "milk in the clouds" (43). In the latter, the infant is imprisoned in a "horrible cabinet" by a male God who is unable to offer comfort and sustenance (78). In the first, the relationship between child and God is reciprocal and voluntary; in the second, the soul is stored as a possession and against its will. The second vision references the patriarchal structures of slavery and racism as well, evident in Elizabeth's subservient position as determined by skin color and gender. Traina, after Rita Nakashima Brock, asserts that Jesus Christ as the son of God must have been nurtured in a "maternal" sense towards "autonomous mutuality," rather than in a patriarchal one, as "property to be disposed of according to a father's wishes" (Traina, 397). Elizabeth intuits that to position God as a sort of omniscient pawnbroker is to grant him power in the non-reciprocal, patriarchal sense; or rather, is to restrict the flow of power to a direct, unidirectional current from God to believer rather than allowing an alternating current between the two.

Catherine's account of childbirth also questions the adequacy of a male God. She wonders if the first emotion is a hunger to eat—not food, but one's own mother. Catherine casts hunger, surprisingly, as an emotion rather than an urge; she elevates a lower brain function into the upper part of the brain. Within the same speech, she characterizes herself with the oxymoron "rational creature," foolish to contemplate undergoing the agonizing process of childbirth a second time. The effect is to position humans as both animal and rational, and then spiritual as she draws Jesus into her speculation. Ruhl seems to suggest that the hunger for another person, in the sense of the Eucharist, is a multivalent impulse, emanating from animal, human, and spiritual urges. The male mammal lacks the gland for which his class within the animal kingdom is named and is thus unable to turn his body into food. The spiritual sustenance offered by Jesus lacks a basis in biology and therefore fails to unify the three strata. The portrait of Mary nursing the baby Jesus is rare because it brings the both of them down to earth inclusive of their animal natures, and thereby opposes the patriarchal vision of the pure, celestial virgin.

Catherine reasons that because the mother gives up blood during childbirth, and manufactures milk from her body, she better fulfills the role of sustainer than a father figure possibly could. The bloody terror of her description suggests childbirth as a female passion. Along these lines, theologian Bonnie Miller-McLemore addresses the giving of body and blood during childbirth as "wrongly appropriated" by the male church in rituals of communion and baptism in *Also a Mother: Work and Family as Theological Dilemma* (1994). The rituals fail to reflect the embodied, female experience (129). The killing of animals by electricity mentioned at various points in the play represents the repression of the animal nature in humans necessary to desexualize the Virgin Mary and reassign the role of sustainer to a male Jesus. The repression of the body is also the defining act of dissociation.

In reference to the unfinished paintings of Michelangelo, Leo has asserted that a partially completed woman is the most appealing to a man. Angels receive mention several times in the script, and a dichotomy between angels and humans is hinted at; or rather, to be an angel is to approach humanhood. Most directly, Elizabeth claims that babies are still angels while nursing and become animals when they start to eat, after which there is no returning to heaven. Leo identifies the unfinished figures in Michelangelo's *Virgin and Child with the Angels* as "women or angels ... coming into being," and states that a young woman who is just about to know herself is most attractive to a man (48). A woman with body hair may also be regarded as a beast, as in the case of Leo's friend who is repulsed by his bride. Angels are disembodied beings, and so for a woman to become whole she must come into her animal, or bodily, aspect. Leo describes Catherine as "a fallen angel" when he retrieves her from making an angel in the snow (59). She earlier claims to not know who she is, which positions her alongside the unfinished women in the painting but, like the baby who starts to eat, as she falls to earth she approaches her full humanity.

FINGERPRINTS

To reclaim one's sexual voice is to more fully embrace one's individuality as one is freed from proscriptive gender norms. Ruhl artfully advances the themes of individual identity and sexual tolerance through her depiction of hands. She employs the hand synecdochically to represent the entire body and, by extension, personality. Leo confides that the primary goal in his paintings is to express the memory of a person's hands, especially the hands of someone he has loved. He claims that hands "have personalities as intimate as faces" (63). Even though he disguises Elizabeth's face in the painting, her husband identifies her by her hands, proving both that Leo has done his job well as an artist and also intimating his love for Elizabeth. Within this context, Dr. Givings's discovery of his wife with her hand upon the artist's face is especially damning. It provides the doctor an opportunity to specify that there are "many shades and degrees of love" (61) in his attempt to minimize the impact of the encounter. This apparent lack of concern may be countered effectively by subtext, as played by Cerveris; his doctor was practically doubled over in physical pain as he professed indifference, in a powerful demonstration of dissociation of mind from body.

When the doctor later recalls his wife's hand on Leo's face and asks if she loves the artist, she responds in the affirmative, but reminds him of his claim that there are many different types of love. The involvement of the hand, and Leo's suggestion that hands are as intimately individual as faces, suggests as many types of love as there are individuals. This perspective validates the same-sex attraction between Sabrina and Annie, and opens up the possibility of numerous other configurations as well. It prepares for the disintegration of the Givings' bourgeois and heteronormal household. In another example of alternating current, science and love converge when Catherine urges her husband to express his own specific love for her. The doctor has downplayed the significance of a hand on the cheek as merely "muscles, skin, facts" (61), and Catherine's disinterest in science is well established. This time lips, rather than hands, do the touching as he tenderly kisses and labels the parts of her face in medical Latin, an act so intimate that it causes her to weep. The language of science comes to the service of love.

Home and Garden: Garden

Ruhl achieves miracles in the final scene between Dr. and Mrs. Givings, especially given that it occupies only seven pages in the script, with ample white space. Most spectacularly, she addresses the victimage of location by transforming the environment, thus providing an alternative to flight. Ruhl takes an activist stance that suggests that familial and societal change is possible; the organisms in Zola's petri dish stage a revolution. Catherine's reaching out to her husband in an intimate, vulnerable, and sexual way, and his response in kind, shatters their bifurcated home and dissolves the patriarchal structure that has held them apart. The walls are swept away before powerful currents of desire. Ruhl collapses as well the binaries associated with the dual structure of the house and stages a return to the garden with Eve in the lead.

The flow of the scene effects change across a number of registers, not the least significant of which involves the stripping away of clothing to reveal a naked individuality. Communication opens between the couple with increased vulnerability as they undress. Considerable stage time has been devoted to the undressing and dressing of the doctor's patients, which functions dramaturgically by allowing for scenes in the living room to play out. Apart from this, clothing serves, obviously enough, as protection. The Victorian woman covers

VII. Alternating Currents of Desire

her modesty thoroughly, and part of Annie's job is to assist with unpeeling and reapplying layers of clothing. After the doctor cuts his wife's session short, her exit is delayed by the necessity of fastening her many buttons, with which she requires his assistance. Performed badly and with much fumbling, the act of buttoning relays the state of their marriage, within which she is restricted, as if in a corset, along gender lines. Furthermore, the doctor is dressing her when her desires demand he do the opposite. He remains, of course, fully clothed and in control in his roles of doctor and husband. The final scene reverses the hierarchy as the male strips entirely naked while the female remains covered in her Victorian undergarments. He drops his authoritative persona with his trousers, and stands exposed before her. The relative infrequency of full male nudity on the stage, compared to that of women,

Hannah Cabell as Mrs. Givings and Paul Niebanck as Dr. Givings as they undress in the winter garden. World premiere of *In the Next Room or the vibrator play* at Berkeley Repertory Theatre, 2009 (courtesy Berkeley Repertory Theatre).

only heightens the impact. Ruhl reverses gender to present the doctor as partially drawn, as opposed to the incomplete female figures described by Leo; Catherine admires her husband's body, which she has never seen before, etched in moonlight. She comments on the lines but also the shadows; he emerges in chiaroscuro, bathed in darkness never completely to appear. For male and female alike, identity is a state of becoming more than one of being. In a delicate stage direction, Ruhl reinforces this theme: underneath the snow rest trees that "in the spring flower with pink flowers" (83). The winter garden itself represents potentiality; from its dormancy will burst new life.

Sharing of knowledge has occurred in the separate spheres, as represented by the doctor's involvement in the scientific community, and in Catherine's discussions with the other women about the vibrator therapy. As the doctor and Catherine reconcile, they finally openly share information about their wants and needs with one another, and this draws them together physically. Catherine's experiments in selfhood continue, now with husband as collaborator. They escape home not only as a prison, but also as a shelter, as they undress in the snow. Comfort and complacency are implicated in the figuration of home as restrictive, and risk and discomfort as necessary in the search for identity and freedom. Coldness invigorates. To the extent that comfort inhibits becoming, home is a prison *because* it is a shelter.

The scene flows away from technology. It begins with Catherine unsuccessfully attempting to stimulate herself with the vibrator; she is too sad and lonely for the device to work. Electricity, and the vibrator, have been associated with sexuality; gas and candlelight with love and intimacy. The scene begins with electricity and ends with gaslight and finally darkness, as Catherine moves from attempting to stimulate herself technologically to her experiment with her husband of combining sexuality with love and intimacy. Embodied knowledge supersedes empirical knowledge as the light dims. An earlier scene in which the doctor and his wife are interrupted as they prepare to make love in the living room would indicate that their sex life is more cordial than that of the Daldrys. Nevertheless, Catherine's experiments clearly indicate that female orgasm lies outside of her marital experience. With her investigation in the garden, she intends to integrate it. Technology has provided invaluable data but is left behind at the point of human intimacy, as in Annie's digital (phalangeal, not electronic) stimulation of Sabrina. Similarly, in *Dead Man's Cell Phone*, Ruhl's other "technology" play, the titular device leads Jean to her idealized lover, Gordon. Her picaresque journey to the afterlife convinces her that the man she left at home, Dwight, is the one for her after all; on her return they are free to hang up their cell phones and retreat to their stationery store sanctuary. At the conclusion of the first act, the store bears some resemblance to Catherine's garden, lit as it is by the glow of paper lanterns in place of gaslight, and with stationery falling through the air like "a snow parade" (Ruhl, *Dead Man's Cell Phone*, 56). Precipitation shortcircuits technology in both plays, as lovers come together in a setting that, at the least, simulates nature.

The house disappears at Catherine's impractical request, followed by a kiss, that her husband undress her in the winter garden in December. She insists that their "whole future happiness" depends on it (82). Her wish blows away the house that her experiments have been loosening and lightening. That which seemed permanent is proved impermanent, and a love that seemed as insubstantial as a name written in the snow endures. The woman leads the way, and the commitment she demands from her husband is total, consisting of giving up his operating theater and loving her for his job "all day long" (81). In a politely subversive moment, the beautiful stage magic marks a paradigm shift, one that might well be lost on an enchanted audience. In the inaugural 2009 productions directed by Les Waters at Berkeley Repertory Theatre and the Lyceum Theatre on Broadway, with the same design team, the stage magic was spectacular. As the doctor finds his wife alone with the vibrator, isolated snowflakes flutter, increasing to a heavy downfall by the final blackout. The transition from house to garden is accomplished as the walls fly up and the garden rotates forward on two turntables, stage right and left, consisting of snow-blanketed trees and shrubs. Gaslights flicker in the background. The transition as staged frames a tender moment of reconciliation, while sweeping away power structures. Ruhl provides both magic and message, as husband and wife are released from the restrictive architecture of their home into the invigorating coldness of the garden.

In the final staged image, the celestial and earthly intermingle as husband and wife make the beast with two backs even as they trace an angel in the snow. Woman earns reentry into paradise as she integrates body and spirit to reclaim her sexual voice. Indeed, the related duality of sexuality and spirituality finds resolution in this image as well. Earlier, Sabrina calls out for God as she climaxes, as Annie reassures her that many patients do. In the stage directions, Ruhl slyly states that Dr. Givings gestures "heavenwards" with the vibrator as he thanks Benjamin Franklin for his electrical experiments (16), and that Catherine and Sabrina look in that direction as well, to transcendent music, while they experiment with the vibrator. She thereby reinforces the connection between sexuality and spirituality and religion. Indeed, the theme of woman-centered religion receives its final iteration in the last scene in a retelling of the story of Genesis. Gilligan identifies the biblical word *da-at* as "referring both to the tree of knowledge and to Adam's knowing of Eve" ("When the Mind," 65). It is an embodied knowledge arrived at through experience. Catherine has eaten of the tree of knowledge through her experiments in selfhood and in conference with her female companions, and this emboldens her to stage a return to the garden with Adam in tow. In this reversal, Eve's acquisition of knowledge reopens the gates to paradise rather than slamming them shut. She retrieves sexuality from sin and facilitates the reacquisition, for both herself and her husband, of the sexual voice. Animal, intellect, and spirit converge as the two couple while tracing an angel in the snow and Catherine cries out for God. Who exactly that God is, and His or Her gender, has been brought into question. Ruhl's dramaturgy challenges the structure of not only the Givingses', but God's house as well.

Depornification

With *In the Next Room*, Ruhl practices *historification*, a Brechtian term that means to stage the past in order to comment on the present. The issues of race, class, and gender that she addresses in the 1880s persist to this day, even though they differ somewhat in form and degree. Gilligan's recent work on dissociation, which has been applied to this play, addresses current gender politics. Although the contemporary Western woman faces far fewer restrictions than her Victorian counterpart, patriarchal structures still define, to a great extent, male-female relationships, and influence the formation of the individual psyche. These structures are implicated as well in race relations and attitudes towards homosexuality. Ruhl's interest in religion, so central to *Passion Play*, here raises concern about the dangers inherent in leaving the man on top.

Her handling of sexuality might be termed *depornification*. In her description of Sabrina's first paroxysm, she reminds the reader and actor that the occurrence predates digital pornography and warns against a clichéd vocalization of orgasm. This stage direction raises the issue of the impact that the media and technology have had on the modern conceptualization of sexuality. Sabrina and Catherine's play with the vibrator brings a level of innocence to the experience of paroxysm/orgasm, freed as it is from all the social taboos associated with sexuality. The suggestion of a maternal sexuality in this work further widens the scope of the term, and a woman-centered religion might function to loosen strictures around sexuality as it banishes the strict, disapproving paternal God, in favor of a nurturing, reciprocal maternal deity. Both male and female pleasure are framed positively and as mutually beneficial as Ruhl counters the androcentric model of sexuality with a gynocentric vision of religion.

The grief and whimsy so prominent in earlier Ruhl works, such as *Eurydice* and *The Clean House*, are here integrated as two elements amongst many. Certainly Elizabeth's grief over her buried child is a significant factor, but an overriding emphasis is placed upon unleashing the flow of life. Whimsy is confined mostly to Catherine's personality; she is prone to non-sequiturs and fanciful turns of phrase, which translated delightfully as charm in Laura Benanti's performance for the Lincoln Center Theater production. Ruhl's trademark magic is, without a doubt, powerfully demonstrated, although she withholds it until the final minutes. Structurally, the play is her most impressive to date. The themes interweave seamlessly and constantly and surprisingly demonstrate, over and over, an alternating current. The analysis offered here only cracks open the door to the wealth of riches contained within.

VIII

Other Works

Ruhl's works not discussed in the body of this study will be presented briefly below. These consist of the short *Dog Play*, a study in grief that predates *Eurydice*; a full-length adaptation of Virginia Woolf's novel *Orlando*; one-act adaptations of two of Anton Chekhov's short stories and the full-length play *The Three Sisters*; *Virtual Meditation #1*, a multimedia, interactive piece realized with the assistance of students from Carnegie Mellon University's Entertainment Technology Center; *Demeter in the City*, a Cornerstone Theater commission based on the lives of 20-year-olds living in Los Angeles, and structured around the Greek myth; and *Snowless*, a one-act that draws attention to global warming.

Dog Play

In 1998, Ruhl's *Dog Play* was given a reading at the Ten Minute Play Festival at Chicago Dramatists (Ruhl, *Dog Play*, 1). Clearly derived from the exercise written for Vogel in 1994, the play explores the death of a father from the perspective of the family dog and lays the foundation for the later *Eurydice*. The lights come up on "a huge glowing puppet of a moon" to the sound of "a dog baying as though his heart is breaking." The title character, played by a male or female actor in a mask, washes the dishes and remembers the paramedics recently taking the father away (2). It turns out that the deceased father has been staying mostly in the moon. He converses solely with the dog, as no one else is able to see him, including the daughter, who desperately wishes to do so. The mood is dreamlike and, at times, nightmarish. A doctor looks into the daughter's mouth while she tells a sad story to see if she is crying inside. As the family fishes together, they snag a large creature and scream and turn to the audience in slow motion; it turns out to be the family dog, hooked in the mouth (14–5). As a group of mourners follows the moon, baying at it, subtitles relate a mundane conversation about funeral arrangements.

The play is stark, conveying the shock and unreality of fresh grief. One scene demonstrates the inadequacy of ritual in the face of death, as the family stands over the grave discussing trivialities, concluding with a prayer that asserts the futility of prayers for the dead. The dog itself is growing old, and expresses dismay at both its declining physical condition and the foolishness of the young, particularly as demonstrated by the new puppy that the family has adopted. A dark sense of humor is in evidence. In one scene, a flashback, the grandfather and his new wife sit silently in a fishing boat while prerecorded voices express their thoughts. The grandfather revels in the silence while his wife vents her frustration at the lack of conversation, and her hatred of fishing. When the grandfather asks out loud if she is happy, she replies, reassuringly, "Oh, yes" (7–8).

The father of this play resembles that of *Eurydice*, based as they both are upon Ruhl's own. Stories told by the father in *Eurydice*, in all their detail, appear first in *Dog Story*: his own father loved duck hunting and fulfilled his wish to die in a duck pond, the guide Old Frank was skillful at calling the ducks, the take was limited to ten ducks, the hunters took measures to deceive the warden, and the normally taciturn grandfather waxed loquacious when it came to hunting. The dog commiserates, as it was itself a participant in the hunt. The element of water, so crucial to *Eurydice*, figures here as well, in the duck hunting stories, the grandparents' fishing honeymoon, and the fishing nightmare. The moon, however, is associated with the deceased father in *Dog Play*, rather than the living groom, as in *Eurydice*. Out-of-tune-singing, which functions as a bonding ritual between father and daughter in the latter as they attempt "I've Got Rhythm," indicates longing in the former as the daughter sings "Blue Moon" to an empty chair, seated in which she intuits the ghost of her father. Later, at the conclusion, she does at last sense his presence, at which point the lights go down and the moon is brought on one last time (21). Certain aspects of this play will reappear in *Passion Play* as well, including images of the moon and water. Additionally, in *Dog Play*, a renaissance queen takes tea with the father on the moon (18), foreshadowing Queen Elizabeth's presence in the trilogy.

Whereas in *Eurydice* Ruhl depicts various stages of the bereavement process, in *Dog Play* she focuses on the sense of shock and unreality that occurs immediately after the loss. The earlier play is rawer and more condensed. Ruhl demonstrates an early interest in theatricality and a disregard for realist convention. Dog and human ways of mourning are juxtaposed throughout, with the huge, puppet moon linking the two modes of perception. Dogs bay at the moon on which the deceased father is now residing to convey bereavement on the animal level. Yet the dog also engages in civilized conversation with the father as they listen together to a jazz recording, complaining about the rude manners of other dogs. The dog assumes a humanness in its possession of memory, and the theme of the centrality of memory to human life will be expanded upon in *Eurydice*. In *Dog Play*, Ruhl tries out themes that will be developed at length in *Eurydice*; nevertheless, it does not read as an immature, undeveloped work, but stands strongly on its own merits.

Orlando

Joyce Piven commissioned Ruhl's adaptation of the Virginia Woolf novel and directed it at the Piven Theater Workshop in 1998 and subsequently at the Actor's Gang in Los Angeles in 2003 (Ruhl, *Orlando* 1; Hitchcock; Shteir). The novel and play follow Orlando through three centuries, across his transformation from male to female. Ruhl includes the protagonist's major love relationships, his brief encounter with Shakespeare, and his/her musings on gender and his/her ongoing effort to write a poem about an oak tree. Orlando and Sasha are to be played by women, with a chorus assuming all other roles. The play is composed as a mixture of narrative and dialogue, with Orlando and the chorus sharing the role of narrator. Ruhl preserves the verbal playfulness of the novel as is consistent with her own style, one perhaps originally inspired, at least in part, by Woolf. In the play and in the novel, for example, when Orlando first sees and instantly falls in love with the Russian Princess Sasha, he calls out, in his astonishment, a seemingly unrelated list of objects: "melon, pineapple, olive tree, emerald, fox in the snow" (Ruhl, *Orlando*, 25; Woolf, 24). This playful whimsicality runs throughout both play and novel.

Elements present in this early adaptation will reappear in Ruhl's later plays. Whereas a generic Renaissance queen serves tea to the father in *Dog Play*, which had its first reading in the same year that *Orlando* premiered, in the latter, Queen Elizabeth adopts the young protagonist as her consort. The English queen will show up in *Passion Play* as well. The queen refuses to remain in her own time period, appearing at the end of *Orlando* to remind the protagonist of her past, in *Dog Play* to represent the long-dead, and in *Passion Play* to demonstrate that styles of leadership have changed over the centuries. The focus on gender in *Orlando* will reappear again in Ruhl's *Late: a cowboy song*, with its androgynous cowboy and intersexual baby. Another significant theme in *Orlando* is that of the loss of a loved one; the protagonist frequently longs for Sasha, the Russian princess who is her first true love and who abandons her to return to her native country. Needless to say, loss figures prominently in much of Ruhl's work. Although an adaptation, *Orlando* nevertheless sets the tone and introduces much of the thematic material that Ruhl would be working with for years to come.

Chekhov Adaptations: Short Stories and *The Three Sisters*

When pressed by interviewer Peter Gianopulos to sum up the thematic essence of her work, Ruhl responded with "love and death" (Gianopulos). In her two adaptations of Chekhov short stories, the focus is on love or the lack of it. Joyce Piven commissioned these adaptations as well and presented them as part of the program *Chekhov: The Stories* in March 2000 (Ruhl, "The Lady," 1). In these adaptations, as in *Orlando*, characters switch between representational and presentational modes, engaging in dialogue as well as narration. One of the adaptations includes a proper chorus, out of which various characters emerge, and the other contains two generic characters that fulfill a choric function.

"The Lady with the Lap Dog" chronicles an affair between Gurov, a middle-aged man, and Anna, a young woman, both of whom are married. In each other, they find an intimacy and excitement that is lacking in their otherwise unhappy and mundane lives. Ruhl faithfully reproduces the ambiguous conclusion, having her characters split the lines of Chekhov's narrator. The man expresses hope for the future; the woman, dismay over the difficulties that they are bound to face. The second adaptation, "Anna around the Neck," also features a spring-autumn relationship, an unhappy marriage between 18-year-old Anna and 52-year-old Modest Alexeich. Anna has married for money, her mother having passed away and her alcoholic father barely able to provide for Anna and her two brothers. She finds herself intimidated by her husband, a dull and unappealing but well-off government official who keeps her in a state of virtual poverty. She comes into her own, however, when she is introduced to high society, which she dazzles with her beauty and grace. After this coming-out, she is able to demand of her husband that all of her financial needs be met, as he recognizes both her newly found influence and power as well as the benefits of having such a charming and popular wife. Anna's transformation changes her relationship with her family as well. Although in the early stages of her marriage she dines with her father and brothers daily at their home, she later ceases to visit them. At the conclusion of both play and story, as she passes her father and brothers on the street in a carriage, the embarrassed sons prevent the father from calling out to her.

As with *Orlando*, these adaptations reflect Ruhl's ongoing concerns. In "The Lady with the Lap Dog," Chekhov imbues what would otherwise be a rather pedestrian love story with a sense of the mystery and beauty of life, particularly in one passage in which the lovers take a ride to the beach at Oreanda after their first tryst. The author conveys through his description of nature a contradictory sense of both the insignificance and consequence of human endeavor, as he describes the rumbling sea that promises both eternal sleep and never-ending progress towards perfection (419–20). This passage situates the developing relationship within a larger context and introduces an alternating current in the form of paradox. A similar affair set against a wider backdrop may be found in Ruhl's *The Clean House*; Charles and Ana claim that their liaison has been preordained, but their transgression is ultimately overcome by questions of life and death when Ana succumbs to cancer.

The theme of fathers and daughters occurs in "Anna around the Neck," as it will in many of Ruhl's plays. In this instance, the daughter has lost her father to alcoholism rather than a fatal illness. Once she assumes her place in high society, she essentially abandons him; as in *Dog Play*, the connection between father and daughter is severed. In the later *Eurydice* and *The Clean House*, daughters will reunite with their deceased fathers, if only temporarily. The arc of a disempowered woman freeing herself from the oppression of a male partner will be traced by Ruhl once more in *Dead Man's Cell Phone*, as Jean escapes from her isolated existence and fully enters society through her liaison with Dwight only after she has broken free from her fantasy of Gordon.

Ruhl's adaptation of *The Three Sisters* was commissioned by the Cincinnati Playhouse, and premiered there in October 2009 under the direction of John Doyle. Ruhl reveals her unique approach to the adaptation, which will be briefly summarized here, in her notes to the unpublished manuscript. As she does not speak Russian, she enlisted the aid of several collaborators and referenced other translations. Elise Thoron, a playwright, director, and Russian scholar, provided a literal translation and cued Ruhl to three qualities of Chekhov often lost in translation, namely "luminosity, transparency, and spareness" (2). Conversations with her native-Russian-speaking sister-in-law convinced Ruhl that her goal should be to get to the root of the original Russian, instead of bending the text to her style—although this choice in and of itself left Ruhl's stamp on the adaptation. For example, she decided to leave some idioms intact, even if it left them somewhat opaque to English-speaking audiences, such as Masha saying, "Life is a raspberry—one little bite and it's gone" (27)! The playful whimsicality of this line is, after all, consistent with Ruhl's style. In addition to working with Thoron's translation, she consulted those of Kristin Johnsen-Neshati and Stark Young, the former for its clarity and modernity, and the latter for its literal adherence to the content, rhythm, and punctuation of the Russian original.

She also consulted with her childhood teacher Joyce Piven, with whom she had collaborated on her adaptations of Chekhov short stories. In the 1960s, Piven studied in New York with the Russian acting teacher Mira Rostova, who counted Uta Hagen among her pupils. Rostova identified five melodies of speech, which she called "the doings." Ruhl pinpoints three as especially significant to her adaptation: the "lament with humor," the "defy," and the "discovery." The first is associated with the acceptance of unalterable circumstances, the shrug of the shoulders and laugh that indicate a surrender to fate. Ruhl differentiates this from the complaint, an expression to which Americans seem especially prone and which contains an element of self-pity. Ruhl avers that the complaint should be avoided at all costs, especially in Chekhov. Ruhl also prefers the "defy" to the complaint—she contends that the sisters frequently defy their fate with their dream of Moscow, rather than complain about it. As an example, the last line of the play is often translated as: "if only we knew, if only we knew." There is no pronoun in the literal Russian, as is often the case, and the line is not necessarily in the past tense. Thus Ruhl expresses the defy in her translation: "To know, to know!"

Ruhl approached the text as a student of Chekhov and attempted a faithful translation in terms of phrasing, rhythm, stage directions, and even punctuation. After Chekhov, she omitted pronouns in many cases. For example, a phrase from one of Irena's speeches often translated as, "I am crying," Ruhl renders literally as "tears are flowing." The syntax with pronoun "implies bodily agency, self-pity, and self-awareness," whereas Ruhl's phrasing indicates the "discovery" of a condition, which is the third of Rostova's melodies (3). Consistent with this, Ruhl respected the fragmentation in the language of the original as Chekhov's purposeful expression of character. The end product is an adaptation that is lyrical and poetic, and characterized by those often lost qualities of luminosity, transparency, and spareness; not coincidentally, those three terms describe Ruhl's original works as well.

Virtual Meditation #1

As with the adaptations of Chekhov's stories, love is the theme of *Virtual Meditation #1*. The Actors Theatre of Louisville commissioned and produced it as part of the Humana Festival of New American Plays in March 2002. Students at Carnegie Mellon University's Entertainment Technology Center programmed the technical elements (Ruhl, *Virtual*, 1). The play was remounted at Carnegie Mellon University in April and May of the same year ("Virtual Meditation #1"). The play consists of three scenes structured around two volunteers from the audience, called A and B. Throughout, digital images of the faces of the volunteers are projected on the faces of two mannequins. These facial images have been programmed to represent various emotions that change according to stage directions in the script. Actors have pre-recorded the dialogue between A and B. A screen behind the mannequins projects various images that are influenced by the volunteers' heartbeats and the pressure of their hand-holding. One of the mannequins holds a white helium balloon, the other a black umbrella.

The first scene is set in a park and rain is projected on the screen. The rate of rain varies depending upon the hand pressure of the volunteers, as does the color of the sky. Tulips appear on the screen in a quantity proportional to the volunteers' heart rates. The names of the volunteers, recorded earlier, are inserted into the dialogue as the characters introduce themselves to each other. The second scene takes place in a museum against the backdrop of a Rothko painting. The characters have now known each other for a long time. The saturation of the painting varies with the volunteers' combined heart rates, and the top and bottom of the painting move towards each other in response to the hand pressure. The last scene takes place by the sea, and the projection is the surface of a lake reflecting the full moon. The combined heart rates create slow ripples in the water, and the hand pressure alters the brightness of the moon. The characters argue about swimming and discuss marriage.

The dialogue is simple throughout and the piece relies upon sophisticated computer programming. The water and moon imagery hark back to *Dog Play*. Rothko will reappear in *Late: a cowboy song*. As of the date of this writing, a brief documentary about the performance is available at the Carnegie Mellon University site for the project ("Virtual Meditation #1"). It chronicles the arrival of the audience, the selecting of volunteers, the hooking up of the monitors, and shows clips from the performance. The last few minutes of the documentary focus on the interactions between various sets of volunteers (the performance was run numerous times), which appears to have constituted a significant facet of the play in performance as two people, possibly strangers, were brought into close proximity to one another and their reactions observed by the audience.

Demeter in the City

Cornerstone Theater commissioned Ruhl to write a play about 20-year-olds in Los Angeles; it was presented at REDCAT in June 2006 (W. Jones). Ruhl considers the script to still be a work in progress (Ruhl, "Re: Checking in"). The playwright interviewed young people across the city from a wide demographic. She found that many subjects were concerned about the separation between parents and children and the struggle to define oneself after leaving home. Ruhl found that the myth of Demeter and Persephone resonated with the young mothers at Shields Healthy Start, many of whom had lost their children to foster care due to drug addiction (Ruhl, "Program Notes," 4–5). In the Greek myth, mother and daughter are separated when Hades steals Persephone away to the underworld; in her despair, Demeter, the goddess of agriculture, neglects the Earth's crops. In order to avert famine, Zeus intervenes and a compromise is reached wherein Persephone spends half her time on earth and half in the underworld, with these times corresponding to summer and winter ("Demeter").

Ruhl structures her plot on this myth. Demeter is a young mother whose child is taken into foster care after a social worker finds used heroin needles in her apartment. The judge fulfills the role of Zeus, and a Young Republican that of Hades, who seduces a now 20-year-old Persephone at the beginning of the second act and whisks her away to the underworld. After 20 years, Demeter has recovered from her addiction and tracks down Zeus, now retired, in a gated community in Palm Springs. The central characters, including Hermes, who was the bailiff and is now Zeus's driver, come to realize that they are indeed Greek gods. Zeus works out the compromise and Persephone is reunited with her mother. The play draws attention to the plight of drug-addicted mothers who have lost their children, indicting the foster care system without exonerating the mothers. It focuses on the human toll caused by the separation of parent and child. The work is Brechtian in nature, highlighting political and social issues and commenting on the action through song. The use of a Greek chorus, consisting of "at least three mothers, all different ethnicities" (Ruhl, *Demeter*, 2), contributes to the alienation effect. Whereas Ruhl adapts Greek myth in *Eurydice* in order to stage personal grief, in *Demeter in the City*, myth is utilized for a more overtly political purpose.

Snowless

Snowless, a one-act play, first appeared at the Chicago Humanities Festival in November 2007 ("Chicago Humanities Festival"), then at the New York University Humanities Festival in April 2008, in both instances on bills of plays concerned with global warming (Robertson, "Nine Writers," 7). The first of two scenes, set at an indeterminate time in the future, consists of a conversation between two groups of three characters each; one group is composed of elders, the other of children. As the title suggests, snow no longer occurs. The older characters attempt to describe snow and its effects to the children. As the scene progresses, water rises from the characters' toes to their chins.

At the beginning of the second scene, an older couple sits over breakfast as the Woman reads aloud an article concerning climate change from the *New York Times*. The article includes the statistic that the honeybee population has declined by 70 percent. Absorbed in his own reading, the Man fails to respond to his wife's growing sense of alarm until a bee buzzes through the window and stings him on the arm. At this point the Woman calls on their Belgian, beekeeping neighbor, Maurice, for advice about bees. Maurice quotes at length from Maurice Maeterlinck's *The Life of the Bee*. In a sudden plot twist characteristic of Ruhl, Maurice and the Woman lie down together in the garden and, before long, start kissing. Snow begins to fall. Three grandchildren appear in the garden and the voices of the three ancients from the first scene once again relate memories of snow. In unison, and in what appears to be an homage to the children's book *Goodnight Moon*, a work that Ruhl reports having read to her daughter ("A Promising Playwright's Summer Reading"), all of the characters wish good-night to a long list of things, including snow, bees, elephants, and trees. The sound of the bees grows louder, then falls silent as a blackout ends the play.

The play is unusual for its inclusion of long passages from a work of nonfiction. These passages from Maeterlinck serve to educate the audience about bees and provide instructions on how to best address the threat of global warming through the manufacture of a "cerebral substance" created by humans as naturally as bees make honey (Ruhl, *Snowless*, 14). In a touch of magic realism, the kissing of the Woman and Maurice produces snow in May, in reference to which the woman claims that she is making honey for her grandchildren and their descendents. The play optimistically suggests that human ingenuity will solve the problems posed by global warming.

IX

Conclusion

Light Currents

In the preceding pages, Ruhl's light handling of alternating currents of desire across heavy themes has been examined. Like Perseus, the conqueror of Medusa, she walks on the wind and clouds as she approaches her horrible foe, who is often Death himself. She subtracts weight from her burdensome subjects through fantasy, magic realism, whimsy, and humor. She captures the complexities of love, loss, and longing. She selects every word with poetic precision as her keen intelligence shapes dramas rich in imagery. Although her dramatic structure is, to a great extent, traditional, her work exhibits a postmodern intertextuality and asyncronicity. The weight of her father's death is felt more keenly in her earlier work than in later efforts. This progression is clearly discernible in *Passion Play*, the first two parts of which were composed significantly before the third. The first two end in catastrophe: a drowning and suicide and imprisonment in a concentration camp. The third ends hopefully, with the Vietnam veteran P's secular ascension. This trend is readily apparent across separate works as well: for example, the sorrowful longing of *Eurydice* gives way to the manic gyrations of *Dead Man's Cell Phone* to the life-affirming flow of *In the Next Room*. Throughout, Ruhl's characters cling to and find meaning in human relationship in a universe that frequently spins out of control in unexpected ways. Ruhl often combines multiple genres within a single work. Generic transitions transport the spectator through a tonal wonderland of sorts and support the coexistence of lightness and heaviness. The fantastic is always close at hand, sometimes taking the form of magic realism. Ruhl stages the fantastic not as escapism, but rather to metaphorically reveal subjective experience.

Ruhl's Place in American Drama

It is no doubt too early to definitively position Ruhl within American drama. Nevertheless, it is possible to discern affinities with other American playwrights and further illuminate her *oeuvre* by comparison. Ruhl's lineage may be traced back through Tony Kushner to John Guare and Thornton Wilder. Each of these playwrights resists the tendency towards realism that has dominated the 20th, and, so far, 21st century. The theories of Bertolt Brecht serve as a useful touchstone when discussing these dramatists. Brecht espouses revealing the theatrical means of production in order to denaturalize events occurring on stage, in contrast to realists, who by definition strive to present the illusion of everyday life (Worthen, 725–6). Techniques used in the service of *Verfremdungseffekt,* or the alienation effect, include direct address, "songs, scenic titles, projected slides and an almost completely bare stage" (Helmetag, 66–7).

Wilder would almost certainly have been familiar with Brecht's practice and writings, and goes to great lengths in his own works to destroy theatrical illusion, as is discussed by Charles H. Helmetag in "Mother Courage and Her American Cousins in *The Skin of Our Teeth*" (1978). Lacking Brecht's political agenda, Wilder rather employs these techniques to illuminate archetype. Kushner, the most political of the American playwrights under discussion, acknowledges a great debt to Brecht, as the title of his interview with Carl Weber, "I Always Go Back to Brecht" (1994), indicates. He has called for an American form of Brechtianism (Weber, 113), and if anyone has achieved this, it has been Kushner in his *Angels in America*, with its focus on the AIDS crisis and the American religion of Mormonism. Characteristically, Kushner admits in his stage directions, "It's OK if the wires show" (Kushner, *Angels in America*, 1.5).

Guare's application of Brechtian techniques such as song and direct address shows more of an affinity with Wilder than with Kushner, as his concerns lie with the archetype of the little man pursuing the American dream rather than with any overtly political agenda. He paints on a smaller canvas than does Wilder, detailing the angst and neuroses of his characters rather than sketching the cosmos at large. Ruhl has utilized all of the Brechtian techniques listed above in various combinations. Like Wilder, she captures the big picture, often inclusive of an afterlife, while at the same time conveying an intimate sense of character, as does Guare. Even a Ruhl play that incorporates political figures, such as *Passion Play*, tends more towards the personal and metaphysical than political. Unfettered by the conventions of realism, these playwrights are free to venture into metaphysical geographies, something that Ruhl, Wilder, and Kushner do frequently and with enthusiasm. Ruhl, Wilder, and Guare craft poetic dialogue, wringing new connotations out of words and arranging them in startling juxtapositions. Although Kushner certainly writes commanding dialogue, it is typically in a conversational rather than poetic mode.

Wilder's Town

Fittingly, John Guare provides the introduction to *The Collected Short Plays of Thornton Wilder, Volume I* (1997). In it, Guare discusses Wilder's attempt to rebirth language, to rescue words from the weight of a literary tradition that burdens them with an accretion of meaning. Wilder drew inspiration in this endeavor from Gertrude Stein, whom he met when she lectured at the University of Chicago in 1935, at his invitation, and with whom he formed a close friendship (Burbank, 82). Stein exhorted the artist to re-instill the "excitingness of pure being" into what had become "stale literary words" (Stein qtd. in Guare, "Introduction," xxii), advice that Wilder took to heart. According to Guare, she "validated his gift of capturing the poetry of common speech," and Guare gives as an example this line from the Wilder short play *The Happy Journey to Trenton and Camden* (1931): "Goodness, smell that air, will you! It's got the whole ocean in it. —Elmer, drive careful over that bridge" (qtd. in Guare, "Introduction," xxii). Although Guare refrains from analyzing this line, it clearly operates as poetry in its employment of both image and juxtaposition: the air contains the "whole ocean" and the character abruptly switches from marveling at this to monitoring her husband's driving. This sudden zoom-in from the vast to the mundane demonstrates Wilder's overarching goal to situate the banalities of everyday American life within the greater patterns of the cosmos.

Further examples of Wilder's gift for the poetry of prosaic speech may be found in the dialogue of the Stage Manager in *Our Town* (1938). Early in the first act, as he is introducing the setting, he laconically states, "There's some scenery for those who think they have to have scenery" (6). The repetition of the word "scenery" both emphasizes that word and provides a rhythm to the line. He heralds the first intermission with another poetic repetition, this time of the word "smoke": "That's the end of the first act, friends. You can go and smoke now, those that smoke" (29). He delineates the acts in a folksy manner: "The First Act was called the Daily Life. This act is called Love and Marriage. There's another act coming after this: I reckon you can guess what that's about" (31). Wilder weaves a rhythmic poetry into the language of everyday speech.

Ruhl likewise juxtaposes words to keep them fresh, as when Matilde characterizes the perfect joke as existing "somewhere between an angel and a fart" (Ruhl, *Clean House*, 24). In another example, the Other Woman exhorts Jean to become comfortable with putting on makeup in public:

JEAN: I've always been embarrassed to put lipstick on in public.
OTHER WOMAN: That's crap. Here—You have beautiful lips
[Ruhl, *Dead Man's Cell*, 15].

The word "crap" humorously clashes with "beautiful lips." A more prevalent tendency in Ruhl's writing, which may even be characterized as a hallmark of her style, is the evocation of unusual, startling, and whimsical imagery. Instances abound in *Eurydice*: the Nasty Interesting Man scoffs at Orpheus's "long fingers that would tremble to pet a bull or pluck a bee from a hive," fingers that compare unfavorably to his own "big stupid hands like potatoes" (355); the Loud Stone conveys the hushed language of the dead: "Like if the pores in your face/ opened up and talked" (359); and Orpheus dreams Eurydice's hair as streaming faucets (371–2).

The characters in *Our Town* are archetypal American small-town residents. Wilder once again drew support from Gertrude Stein in his belief that America occupied a special place in history through an identification with world destiny (Burbank, 83). The American thus stands, in certain of Wilder's works such as *Our Town* and *The Skin of Our Teeth* (1942), for humanity as a (limited) whole. In these two works, he attempts to place the archetypal American in relation to the cosmos, albeit with a rueful sense of irony. In *Our Town*, he brings Emily back from the dead to appreciate the beauty contained in even the most banal moments, as the living seem unable to do. In *The Skin of Our Teeth*, Wilder paints on a broader canvas, positioning Antrobus as an everyman as he and his family face natural disaster and human destructiveness. He incorporates biblical mythology as well, modeling family dynamics on Adam, Eve, and Cain. By Wilder's own admission, the play was strongly influenced by James Joyce's *Finnegan's Wake*, a work itself greatly concerned with archetype (Castronovo, 106–7). A controversy erupted in 1942, a month after *The Skin of Our Teeth* opened on Broadway, when two Joyce scholars accused Wilder, in *The Saturday Review of Literature*, of plagiarizing *Finnegan's Wake*. Wilder's borrowings from Joyce, which in actuality fall far short of plagiarism, are outlined by David Castronova in *Thornton Wilder* (1986) as "conflation of time, mixing of images, cyclical patterning, and finding correspondences between the lives of ancient and modern man" (21).

Ruhl is also greatly concerned with archetype, although in a different way. Wilder can perhaps best be categorized as a Christian humanist, and accordingly situates his American characters in a biblical cosmos. Although raised Catholic, Ruhl does not claim any particular religious affinity, and the worlds of her plays do not reflect the philosophy of any specific faith or denomination. Whereas Wilder sets out to demonstrate a relationship between character/archetype and cosmos, Ruhl shapes the myth to suit her purpose. In *Eurydice*, she fashions a personalized portrait of bereavement. In *Demeter in the City*, she cobbles together stories of 20-year-old Los Angelenos, focusing on drug-addicted mothers who have had their children taken away from them. As she describes in the program notes, she brought the myth of Demeter to these women and they identified with "her anger, her sense of powerlessness before fate and before the judging eyes of Zeus" (Ruhl, *Demeter*, 4). The Greek archetype enabled them to express their particular frustration. With *Passion Play*, Ruhl draws on the story of Christ while producing a work that is neither pro- nor anti–Christian. Rather, the consequences of either emulating or resisting the archetype are examined. Whereas the Antrobuses match the pattern of the original biblical family, the "actors" in *Passion Play* respond to, rather than exemplify, the archetype.

For both Ruhl and Wilder, stage reality encompasses both the living and the dead. In *Our Town*, Wilder has borrowed his vision of the afterlife from Dante's *Purgatory* in order to "find a value above all price for the smallest events in our daily life" (Wilder, "Preface," xi). The cemetery, home to the dead and Emily's resting place, functions architecturally as part of the greater structure of town and cosmos. In Ruhl, the afterlife catalyzes personal transition. Like Emily, Eurydice comes to prefer the land of the dead to that of the living, however she does so because of the presence there of her father. In *The Clean House* and *Dead Man's Cell Phone*, the dead push the living back towards life. Matilde's parents cease to haunt her once she accepts their loss, and Jean's quick visit to hell convinces her that she is in love with the wrong man.

Degrees of Separation

Like Ruhl and Wilder, Jean Guare is a non-realist with a poetic style. Isolation is a frequent theme of his. Many of his characters pursue celebrity and/or the American dream, and in doing so are drawn away from living in the present moment; their obsessions prevent them from establishing meaningful relationships and thus result in alienation. Although it would be absurd to categorize Guare along with Wilder as a Christian humanist, a statement he made about plot in an interview with David Savran indicates some affinity to Christian values, or at least a particular interpretation of them. He stated that the "only two plots" are *Cinderella* and *Jack in the Beanstalk*, which both convey "the message of Christ, in the best sense": "the little man" has value, and power enough, even, to "topple the empire" (Savran, 98). Indeed, the Guare protagonist is generally the "little man" struggling to achieve his dreams. In his introduction to the above-cited interview published in *In Their Own Words: Contemporary American Playwrights* (1988), David Savran observes that, in Guare's plays, frustrated characters "almost inevitably ... turn their losses into unexpected gain" (85). The same may be said of Ruhl's works, which almost always end hopefully.

Savran singles out Guare's dramaturgy as most similar, among his contemporaries, to that of Chekhov, and describes it as "intricately plot-driven" with "major reversals and ... little ironic surprises ... that force characters incessantly to reevaluate their situations" (85).[1] Ruhl's works follow the same pattern; her protagonists constantly adapt to often ironic shifts in the environment. Like Wilder and Ruhl, Guare reinvigorates language through the employment of poetic dialogue and tends towards the quirky, whimsical, and frequently incongruous turn of phrase. In *The Loveliest Afternoon of the Year* (1966), a character named simply "He" warns of some dangerous pigeons: "All those pigeons had *foam*—... Were foaming at the mouths ... at the *beaks*? Pigeons were foaming at the beaks—all of them" (21). One of numerous vainglorious, overachieving characters in *Marco Polo Sings a Solo* (1977) builds a strange metaphor that equates a punctuation mark with weaponry: "Hear the exclamation points I'm talking in. My mind makes spears out of exclamation points and nails me right onto the world of Art" (45). Even in a work with a more serious tone, the dialogue typically has a rhythmic, poetic quality. In *Six Degrees of Separation* (1990), Paul fabricates stories about Flan, whom he claims to be his father, for the benefit of a young couple in Central Park. His words flow in a stream of consciousness:

> He went down South as a freedom marcher, to register black voters—his friends were killed. Met my mother. Registered her and married her in a fit of sentimental righteousness and knocked her up with me and came back here and abandoned her. Went to Harvard. He's now a fancy art dealer. Lives up there. Count six windows over. Won't see me [47].

Guare masterfully constructs quirky situations as well. The first act of *Bosoms and Neglect* (1979) consists of a conversation between the newly acquainted Deirdre and Scooper, who share a psychoanalyst. Deirdre, a book dealer, stores her inventory of first editions in the living room of her apartment. The act builds to a climax as Scooper, spurned by his lover over the phone, takes to destroying Deirdre's books. In retaliation, she stabs him repeatedly with a letter opener. They pause when they spot their therapist leaving his office across the street, lament his leaving on vacation, and express remorse for attacking each other. Nevertheless, in despair over their lack of psychoanalytic progress, they quickly resume their struggle: "They punch each other. They stab each other. They are weeping and hitting and attacking each other" (39). The curtain falls on this battle, which combines pathos and humor.

Ruhl also specializes in quirky scenarios: the chorus of stones in the underworld whose lord is a petulant child who grows to be ten feet tall, the housekeeper who hates to clean, the shy woman who commandeers a dead man's cell phone, and the spurned lover whom melancholy transforms into an almond, to name a few. And yet there is a qualitative difference between the quirkiness, and indeed the overall tone, of the two playwrights. In Guare, the characters tend to talk past each other, wrapped up as they are in their own fantasies. In Ruhl, the characters ultimately succeed in connecting with one another. Eurydice defies the Stones and reestablishes her relationship with her father, a community of women gathers to nurse Ana, Jean ultimately unites with the gentler brother, and the characters in *Melancholy Play* celebrate becoming almonds together. Guare's world is colder and has sharper edges. When, at the conclusion of *Landscape of the Body* (1977), Betty goes to the detective who has interrogated her over the death of her son, it is an act of desperation in a life that has been emptied of meaning. Her sister has died in an accident, her gentleman caller proven to be insane, and her son murdered and decapitated by his best friend who has evaded all suspicion. In contrast, when Eurydice joins her father, they reestablish a warm and meaningful relationship even as they approach, finally, oblivion and forgetfulness. Whereas Ruhl's characters love and sometimes lose, Guare's oftentimes never truly love.

Guare frequently employs techniques that break the theatrical illusion. In an interview with Steven Drukman, he remembers the revelation of seeing Wilder's *Our Town* as a boy and realizing that the fourth wall could be broken and the rules of naturalism violated (Drukman). In this vein, his characters often break into song and, at times, speak directly to the audience, as Flan and Ouisa do in *Six Degrees of Separation*. His perhaps most non-naturalistic work is *Four Baboons Adoring the Sun* (1992), in which two archaeologists, Philip and Penny, have left their spouses for one another. Their children come to join them in Italy for the summer, a vacation that the Greek god Eros fashions into a tragedy. Singing all of his lines directly to the audience, Eros lures the couple's two oldest children into an ultimately fatal sexual liaison, and in the process makes a mockery of Philip and Penny's vows of love. Guare's use of the god as directing but outside of the action differs markedly from Ruhl's deployment of Greek myth in *Eurydice* and *Demeter in the City*.

In Ruhl, myth serves as a template to be inhabited by mortals lacking the powers of the gods. Guare, in contrast, manifests the god Eros as an embodiment of the sex drive.

Ruhl claims to be more of a Jungian than a Freudian in her interest in universality over individual neurosis, and in seeking connection rather than probing for secret wounds (Royce). The analysis of joke as incantation in the chapter on *The Clean House*, with its invocation of shamanism, demonstrates this Jungian bias. In *Dead Man's Cell Phone*, Jean's voyage to the underworld to encounter Gordon may be read as the kind protagonist's encounter with her own animus or male aspect, or dark side, from which she emerges whole and free to couple with Dwight. The reliance on archetype, so common in Ruhl's plays, is another indication of a Jungian disposition.

Even when incorporating myth, Guare's work discloses a Freudian influence. In *Four Baboons*, figures from Greek myth represent the sex and death drives, Eros obviously the former and Icarus the latter. A male adolescent jumps off of a cliff believing, as Icarus did, that he can fly and predictably plummets to his death. In *Bosoms and Neglect*, Guare features the Freudian, wounded individual that Ruhl finds unappealing, stating that he hopes that his play provokes the audience to ask themselves, "What secrets are there lurking in our lives that we're not noticing" (Guare qtd. in Plunka, "Freud," 93)? Gene A. Plunka pursues a psychoanalytic approach in "Freud and the Psychology of Neurosis: John Guare's *Bosoms and Neglect*" (2000). He makes the case that the characters in this play are unable to connect to one another because they, themselves, have been wounded. Scooper's mother's breast is rotten with cancer, symbolic of the failed bond between mother and son (97). His poor relationship with his mother taints those with women in general, and the characters neglect one another because they are self-absorbed and riddled with neuroses. *Six Degrees of Separation* lends itself to an Oedipal interpretation, as Paul insinuates himself with mother figure Ouisa while enraging the father figure Flan. Although Guare and Ruhl's styles are similar in a number of ways, the difference in underlying psychological model is a significant distinguishing factor.

Guare depicts the supernatural with much less frequency than either Ruhl or Wilder. One play in which he does so is *Landscape of the Body* in the person of Betty's deceased sister Rosalie, who performs thematic songs and comments on the action, functioning not unlike a Greek chorus in this regard. In stark contrast to Wilder's Emily, who witnesses the beauty of life from beyond the grave, Rosalie expresses relief over her state: "The earth is small. We're gone. We're dead. We're safe" (57). Her relief highlights the difficulties Betty has faced and continues to face among the living. As

discussed above, Ruhl summons the afterlife for quite a different purpose—
that of achieving completion and closure.

Uneasy Angel

As do Guare, Ruhl, and Wilder, Kushner creates non-realistic theater and incorporates realms beyond the ordinary. His work is the most overtly political of the four playwrights under discussion. He employs various Brechtian techniques, such as song in *Hydriotaphia* (1997) and projected images in *A Bright Room Called Day* (1987). His notes to *Angels in America* (1993) reveal his preference for exposing the theatrical means of production, as he calls for "minimal scenery" and swift scene changes, and astonishing stage magic behind which, nevertheless, "it's OK if the wires show" (Kushner, *Angels in America*, 1.5). This theatricalism serves the biblical and mythical elements in his work. Like Wilder, he situates the everyday in relation to a greater cosmos. A ravenous Death hovers around Browne's bed throughout the course of *Hydriotaphia* as the ill man's personified soul cringes behind the headboard, begging for release. The Devil makes an appearance in *A Bright Room Called Day*, chronicling how his job has changed over the years. Priscilla seeks out the grave of Cain as she searches for clues to her mother's disappearance in *Homebody/Kabul* (2001). However, in Kushner, in contrast to Wilder, the character as often as not is fighting against the supernatural, rather than harmonizing with it. In *Angels in America*, Prior resists the Angel's command to "stop moving," ascending even to heaven to return the book of prophecy, a heaven that is in shambles because God has deserted it. The intrusion of, or references to, the biblical and supernatural rarely comforts or reassures, but rather threatens and unsettles. Kushner's employment of the celestial realm serves as a reminder of the overriding importance of human agency, functioning in a Brechtian sense as a prod for audience action in the political realm.

In contrast, Wilder paints an especially clear picture of an orderly universe and humankind's place in it in *Pullman Car Hiawatha* (1931). The Stage Manager orchestrates a parade of beautiful girls representing the hours, who quote from famous philosophers, followed by the planets, who whistle and hum the music of the spheres. Then the archangel Gabriel appears with his cohort to claim a soul. Although mortal characters suffer in this scenario, they inhabit a world of purpose and harmony. Ruhl's deployment of the supernatural differs from both of these models. In her works, the afterworld is a place of reconnection and mourning as in *Eurydice* or *The Clean House*, or a place in which illusions are set aside, as in *Dead Man's Cell Phone*. It functions predominantly on a personal level, rather than an overarching theological one as in Wilder, or in a political capacity as with Kushner.

American Dreams

It remains to discuss what marks each of these playwrights as distinctly American, and the similarities and differences between them in this regard. Wilder grants the American a privileged position in the course of history and situates him in the cosmos as a representative of the human race, although he does so with a sense of irony. Guare locates his characters in a celebrity-obsessed culture and chronicles their disappointment and tenacity as they struggle to achieve the American dream. Kushner protests American politics, finding the Reagan administration particularly abhorrent, as a reading of *Angels in America* confirms. Even *A Bright Room Called Day*, set in Nazi-era Berlin, may be read as a metaphor for the costs of political complacency in the United States during the 1980s. He addresses the 1960s civil rights movement in *Caroline, or Change*. He ventures overseas with work such as *Homebody/Kabul*, *Hydriotaphia*, *Slavs!*, and his adaptation of *Brundibar*, yet even in these cases his eye is always on the American political system to a greater or lesser degree.

Ruhl usually sets her plays in America and deals with American concerns. Even in *Eurydice*, the father is a Midwesterner who equates the Mississippi with the River Lethe. Yet she does not grant Americans a privileged position in the cosmos as Wilder does. She contrasts American culture with that of Europe in *Melancholy Play*, and although Lorenzo, the European psychologist, is a rather ludicrous character, Ruhl also indicates that the cellist who underscores the action with haunting melodies should be from outside the United States. She counterpoints the vapid absurdity of one non–American with the poignant musicality of another. The work valorizes European melancholy over American depression as a mood to be savored rather than medicated away. Overall, she contrasts cultures in order to gently point out the virtues and foibles of each. Her work is less politicized than Kushner's. This may be demonstrated by comparing the play by each that focuses on domestic servitude, Kushner's musical *Caroline, or Change* against Ruhl's *The Clean House*. In Kushner, Caroline is a victim of a racist system; however, she herself lacks the will to fight. It is up to the next generation in the person of her daughter to engage in the civil rights movement. In Ruhl, the immigrant housekeeper integrates into a community of women across nationalistic and cultural boundaries. The characters change, but political change is not on the agenda.

Although Ruhl's characters do not pursue the American dream with the same ferocity as Guare's, nevertheless some do aspire to it and find it lacking. The seemingly perfect marriage of two successful doctors residing in a "metaphysical Connecticut" falls apart in *The Clean House*, a veteran returns home a broken man after serving his country in Vietnam in *Passion Play*, and in *Demeter in the City* some of the less fortunate inhabitants of Los Angeles struggle to improve their lives. The American dream is not alive and well in these works and the characters do not pursue that broken dream with the maniacal obsessiveness found in Guare. In *Bosoms and Neglect*, Deirdre quotes E. M. Forster's directive to "Connect. Only connect" (Guare, *Bosoms*, 33). In this regard, Guare's characters usually fail; Ruhl's, on the other hand, typically succeed.

Waves of the Future

Ruhl is only in her mid–30s at the time of this writing, and perhaps her best work still lies ahead. *Eurydice*, *The Clean House*, and *In the Next Room* stand out as her strongest works to date for the way in which they combine her signature lightness and whimsy with a powerful emotional impact. The early, unpublished, short *Dog Play* impresses with its raw, emotional power, although it lacks the alternating flow between lightness and darkness that characterizes the longer works. Although still considered by its author to be a work in progress, *Demeter in the City* is also a powerful piece, calling as it does on Greek myth to bring attention to current political and social issues. The highly ambitious *Passion Play* contains moments of stunning theatricality, particularly at the appearances of the giant puppet fish and sailing ships. *Dead Man's Cell Phone* is an accomplished farce.

Ruhl has apparently moved beyond writing plays of mourning, although one expects that the themes of love and death will continue to dominate her work. Her current works contain a larger measure of lightness than darkness. In his profile of Ruhl in *The New Yorker*, John Lahr reports on commenting on the "oddness" of the "ironic detachment" and "unabashed optimism" of *Dead Man's Cell Phone* to Mark Wing-Davey. The director replied, "Why shouldn't it be? [sic].... Right now Sarah's life is great—a young child, newly married, the darling of the American theatre scene, her plays are done" (Lahr, "Surreal Life"). No matter what the tone, it may be expected that Ruhl will continue to draw on a wide range of subject matter and to create complex, flowing, and intriguing works in her own unique voice.

Appendix: Chronology of Play Premieres

Passion Play (first part). Directed by Peter Dubois. Trinity Repertory Company, Providence, Rhode Island. 1997.
Dog Play. Reading. Ten Minute Play Festival, Chicago Dramatists. 1998.
Orlando. Directed by Joyce Piven. Piven Theater Workshop, Evanston, Illinois. 1998.
The Lady with the Lapdog and *Anna around the Neck*. Chekhov: The Stories. Directed by Joyce Piven. Piven Theater Workshop, Evanston, Illinois. 2000.
Virtual Meditation #1. Directed by Brenda Harger. Humana Festival of New American Plays, Actors Theatre of Louisville. March 2002.
Melancholy Play. Directed by Jessica Thebus. Piven Theater Workshop, Evanston, Illinois. June 2002.
Passion Play (workshop of first two parts). Directed by Mark Wing-Davey. Tristan Bates Theatre, London. July 2002.
Late: a cowboy song. Directed by Debbie Saivetz. Clubbed Thumb, Ohio Theatre, New York City. April 2003.
Eurydice. Directed by Richard Corley. Madison Repertory Theatre. September 2003.
The Clean House. Directed by Bill Rauch. Yale Repertory Theatre. September 2004.
Passion Play (as trilogy). Directed by Molly Smith. Arena Stage, Washington, D.C. September 2005.
Demeter in the City. Directed by Shishir Kurup. Cornerstone Theater, REDCAT, Los Angeles. June 2006.
Dead Man's Cell Phone. Directed by Rebecca Bayla Taichman. Woolly Mammoth Theatre Company, Washington, D.C. June 2007.
Snowless. Chicago Humanities Festival. November 2007.
In the Next Room or the vibrator play. Directed by Les Waters. Berkeley Repertory Theatre. February 2009.
The Three Sisters (adapted from Chekhov). Directed by John Doyle. Cincinnati Playhouse. October 2009.
Stage Kiss. Directed by Jessica Thebus. Goodman Theatre. April 2011.

Chapter Notes

Introduction

1. Vogel has since left Brown University for a five-year appointment as chair of the playwriting department at Yale School of Drama beginning July 1, 2008 (Robertson, "Paula Vogel").

2. A 2009 study by Emily Glassberg Sands investigates the underrepresentation of women playwrights in production with startling results; most surprisingly, she uncovers an apparent bias against women playwrights on the part of female artistic directors and literary managers. For a summary of the study, see Cohen.

Chapter I

1. Ruhl utilizes string as one indicator of the shift in Eurydice's allegiance from husband to father. In the overworld, Orpheus proposes by tying a string around her finger; in the underworld, the father builds her a room out of string.

2. In one of the most fascinating moments of the play, the Father recounts how he remembered Eurydice's name by seeing it inside the rain. Through its association with the River Lethe, water erases memory. Paradoxically, in this instance it restores memory. According to Freud, melancholy differs from mourning in that that the lost object remains hidden in the unconscious. Through discovering Eurydice's name in the rain, the Father's lost love object passes from the unconscious to the conscious mind, and the Father, from a state of melancholy to one of mourning.

3. Ruhl reports that not every production has presented the Stones as ghouls. They have been depicted variously as lifeguards, bratty English school children, and teenage slackers, and have been played by children ("Turning the World," 3). In a workshop production, they functioned as a kabuki-style chorus that made things happen in the underworld, such as pouring water to provide the rain in the elevator (Weckwerth, 29).

4. In a radio interview, Paula Vogel states that the father is indeed returning to his childhood home, noting that this scene typically initiates weeping in the audience ("Paula Vogel").

5. In *Metamorphoses*, Zimmerman physicalizes this action in her staging of Ovid. As Orpheus turns, Hermes pulls Eurydice away from him while the lovers reach for one another. They repeat this action five times as the narrator attempts exegesis (43–4).

Chapter II

1. Ruhl also has a daughter named Anna.

2. The essay I am citing initially served as the preface to Carpentier's novel *El reino de este mundo* (*The Kingdom of This World*, 1949), and was later published in expanded form in 1967. I reference the later version as translated by Zamora and Faris.

3. The terms "magic realism" and "magical realism" may be used interchangeably. I prefer the former, after Hegerfeldt, "as it can be read as a double noun phrase and thus better reflects the relationship of equality between magic and realism that is a fundamental aspect of the mode" (Hegerfeldt, 1).

4. Why Charles bears a pickax rather than an axe for chopping down the tree, is not explained in the script.

5. Ruhl allows for the substitution of dif-

ferent jokes in various productions, should "more perfect Brazilian jokes" be found (112). Nevertheless, it must be assumed that the ones published with the text achieve the desired tone.

6. The source italicizes quotations. The italics have been removed for readability.

Chapter III

1. This imaginary, cinematic Europe is akin to the one in Vogel's *The Baltimore Waltz*, as discussed in the chapter on *The Clean House*.

2. This notion that an individual must have a history built on memory in order to merit bereavement is consistent with the thematic content of *Eurydice*.

3. The playwright confirms that the word in "a dead language" that means "to be so melancholy that you turn into an inanimate object" (316) does not, to her knowledge, actually exist (Ruhl, "Re: Melancholy question").

4. Vogel spoofs *The Third Man* in *The Baltimore Waltz*, as discussed in the chapter on *The Clean House*.

Chapter IV

1. All citations refer to, and all quotations are taken from, Theatre Communications Group's 2008 edition of *Dead Man's Cell Phone* rather than the 2007 First Look edition.

2. The lost innocent appears frequently in Ruhl's plays: Eurydice journeys to an underworld that is likened to Alice's Wonderland; Matilde struggles to survive as a housekeeper in a foreign country; Tilly navigates the currents of her mood swings and the entanglements of her relationships; Mary frees herself from her abusive spouse; and Violet, from the third part of *Passion Play*, struggles to come to terms with war. In each case, except for that of Eurydice, the innocent succeeds in emerging from the rabbit hole perhaps because of her naïveté. A hidden hand guides these characters, who are essentially good at heart, imparting the moral that perhaps, after all, goodness is its own reward.

Jean's assumption that humans are basically good enables her to fall in love with the deceased Gordon. After his funeral she is immediately thrown into the hell of dinner with his family, one that begins about as badly for her as it could: she is a vegetarian seated at a meal consisting entirely of meat, Gordon's mother berates and belittles her, she suffers an attack of the hiccups, and her inappropriate gift to Mrs. Gottlieb sends the matron upstairs in tears. Nevertheless, the evening turns out well for Jean as Dwight, whom she will come to love the most, takes her shopping for broccoli and zucchini.

Chapter V

1. Ruhl has obtained permission to use excerpts from the *All New Joy of Cooking*, with copyright dates ranging from 1931 through 1997, for this passage, as is noted on the copyright page of *The Clean House and Other Plays*. She has, however, rearranged the material and quotes, and draws them from an edition other than the most recent. She draws from pages 146, 488, and 489 as found for example in the 1973 edition, which is titled *Joy of Cooking* (Rombauer and Becker).

2. As the word "crick" is cowboy slang for creek, the name of Ruhl's character may be linked to George's suicide attempt. George is reborn after symbolic baptism in the river, which marks his initial encounter with his guardian angel. As Red teaches Mary to ride a horse, Mary musters courage to cross a river (172), just as she must overcome her fear of Crick in order to escape the boundaries of her marriage.

Chapter VI

1. This and other passages are taken from the New American Standard Bible.

2. The intersection of the circles of the *mandorla*, as discussed in conjunction with *Melancholy Play*, was known as the *vesica piscis*, or "fish bladder," and "was an early symbol of Christ in glory" ("Mandorla").

3. The drinking of tears occurs also in *Melancholy Play*, where it is associated with death and the transmission of melancholy, resulting in the almond state.

4. This image brings to mind a lullaby from *Late: a cowboy song*, in which are iteratively cradled a mouse by a cat by the sun by the moon by the sky. Ultimately, the cowboys "cradle the sky to sleep" (164). As a symbol of the Virgin Mother, the crescent moon reflects the light of the "Sun of Righteousness, Jesus Christ" (Webber, 181). The lullaby takes on a quirky theological meaning when read in this respect. The lying of cat with mouse substitutes for that of lion with lamb in Edenic tranquility. The Virgin Mother cradles her son to sleep; she herself rests in the infinity of the open sky, suggestive of God the Father. The cowboy is absurdly apotheosized as Father-of-the-Father.

5. See the chapter on *Eurydice* for a discussion of the four elements in that work.

6. Garner's usage of the term "millenarianism" diverges from the definition presented earlier in this chapter, which refers specifically to a utopian outcome. His usage may be equated with millennialism in both its positive and negative sense.

Chapter VII

1. The use of a directed water current in the treatment of hysteria actually predates the electric vibrator by more than a century (Maines, 73).

2. In "The Source of Happiness" (2009), Phyllis Rose identifies the likely source of Leo's friend as the English art critic John Ruskin, who testified to his lawyer that he was horrified at his wife's pubic hair on their wedding night in 1849 because he had seen none in classical sculpture. He considered his wife deformed and her body disgusted him. Their unconsummated marriage was annulled six years later (4).

Chapter IX

1. That Guare's plays share some characteristics with Chekhov's is not surprising, considering that Chekhov was Guare's favorite playwright when he was younger (Plunka, *Black Comedy*, 14).

Bibliography

Anouilh, Jean. "Eurydice (Legend of Lovers)." In *Five Plays*, translated by Kitty Black, 55–120. New York: Hill and Wang, 1958.
Archer, John. *The Nature of Grief: The Evolution and Psychology of Reactions to Loss*. London: Routledge, 1999.
Ashok, and Peter Skafte. "Interview with a Killing Shaman." In Narby and Huxley, 234–7.
Babb, Lawrence. *The Elizabethan Malady: A Study of Melancholy in English Literature from 1580 to 1642*. East Lansing: Michigan State College Press, 1951.
Barroll, Leeds. *Politics, Plague, and Shakespeare's Theater: The Stuart Years*. Ithaca: Cornell University Press, 1991.
Benjamin, Walter. "Theses on the Philosophy of History." In *Illuminations*, translated by Harry Zohn, edited by Hannah Arendt, 253–64. New York: Schocken Books, 1968.
"Berkeley Rep Picks Bold New Plays and Beloved Artists for 2008/09." *Berkeley Repertory Theatre*. 5 March 2008. http://www.berkeleyrep.org/press/pr/0708/Berkeley_Rep_0809_Season.pdf (accessed 20 March 2008).
"Berkeley Rep to End 2008-2009 Season with 'You, Nero.'" *BroadwayWorld.com*, 10 July 2008. http://www.broadwayworld.com/viewcolumn.cfm?colid=29826 (accessed 11 July 2008).
Berry, Dawn Bradley. *The Domestic Violence Sourcebook: Everything You Need to Know*. Los Angeles: NTC Contemporary, 1998. *NetLibrary*. Belmont University Lib., Nashville, TN. http://teach.belmont.edu:2076/ (accessed 30 November 2007).
Black Hills Passion Play. 10 December 2007. http://www.theblackhillspassionplay.com/.
Blanchard, Jayne. "Life Gets Scrubbing in 'Clean House.'" *Washington Times*, 18 July 2005, B05, Theater.
Boehm, Mike. "Quick Takes: Ruhl Wins an Award for Script." *Los Angeles Times*, 25 February 2004, E3. Calendar.
Bowlby, John. *Attachment and Loss, Volume III. Loss: Sadness and Depression*. New York: Basic Books, 1980.
Brock, Rita Nakashima. *Journeys by Heart: A Christology of Erotic Power*. New York: Crossroad, 1988.
Bromley, David G. "Constructing Apocalypticism: Social and Cultural Elements of Radical Organization." In Robbins and Palmer, *Millennium*, 31–45.
Brown, Michael F. "Dark Side of the Shaman." In Narby and Huxley, 251–6.

Burbank, Rex. *Thornton Wilder*. Twayne's United States Authors Series. Edited by Sylvia E. Bowman. New York: Twayne, 1961.
Burton, Robert. *The Anatomy of Melancholy*. 3 vols. Everyman's Lib. Philosophy and Theology, 886–888. London: Dent, 1932.
Butler, Judith. *Gender Trouble: Feminism and the Subversion of Identity*. New York: Routledge, 1999.
Byrne, Terry. "'X' Factor Missing in 'Orpheus.'" *Boston Herald*, 31 March 2006, E19, The Edge.
Calvino, Italo. *Six Memos for the Next Millennium*. Cambridge: Harvard University Press, 1988.
Campbell, Joseph. *The Hero with a Thousand Faces*. Bollingen Series XVII. Princeton: Princeton University Press, 1949.
Carpentier, Alejo. "On the Marvelous Real in America." In Zamora and Faris, 75–88.
Castronovo, David. *Thornton Wilder*. New York: Ungar, 1986.
Chaudhuri, Una. *Staging Place: The Geography of Modern Drama*. Ann Arbor: University of Michigan Press, 1995.
Chave, Anna C. *Mark Rothko: Subjects in Abstraction*. New Haven: Yale University Press, 1989.
Chekhov, Anton Pavlovich. "Anna on the Neck." In Chekhov, *The Portable Chekhov*, 268–85.
———. "The Lady with the Pet Dog." In Chekhov, *The Portable Chekhov*, 412–33.
———. *The Portable Chekhov*. Edited by Avrahm Yarmolinsky. New York: Viking, 1947.
"Chicago Humanities Festival." *Chicago Reader*, 8 November 2007, Readings & Lectures. http://www.chicagoreader.com/features/stories/sidebars/readings/humanities/ (accessed 28 May 2008).
Clark, James M. "The Dance of Death in the Middle Ages and the Renaissance." In *Death and the Visual Arts*, 1–131. New York: Arno, 1977.
"Clean Room." In *Random House Unabridged Dictionary*. 2nd ed. 1987.
Cohen, Patricia. "Rethinking Gender Bias in Theater." *New York Times*, 24 June 2009. http://www.nytimes.com/2009/06/24/theater/24play.html?emc=eta1 (accessed 29 April 2010).
"A Conversation with Sarah Ruhl and Blair Brown." *Lincoln Center Theater*. 15 November 2006. http://www.lctstudentix.org/content/platform/CleanHousePlatform.pdf (accessed 17 August 2008).
Cox, Gordon. "Gotham's Golden Ruhl." *Variety*. 30 Oct. 2006: 63. Legit.
Creamer, Tom. "Queen, Fuehrer, President: Politics, Passion and Play." *OnStage* (Goodman Theatre) 23.1, September–December 2007, 6–9.
Crowley, Evelyn. "The Golden Ruhl." *W Magazine*, June 2007, 110.
Dake, Finis J. *Dake's Annotated Reference Bible: The New Testament*. Grand Rapids: Zondervan, 1961.
Danaher, David S. "The Semantics of *Pity* and *Zhalost'* in a Literary Context." *Glossos*, Spring 2002. The Slavic and East European Language Resource Center. http://selrc.org/glossos (accessed 12 November 2007).
"The Dance of Death: Books and Prints from the Collections of Swarthmore and Bryn Mawr Colleges." Swarthmore College. http://www.swarthmore.edu/x5358.xml (accessed 14 November 2007).
Dawson, Paul. *Creative Writing and the New Humanities*. London: Routledge, 2005.
Dead Man's Cell Phone. By Sarah Ruhl. Dir. Rebecca Bayla Taichman, 20 June 2007. Woolly Mammoth Theatre Company, Washington, D.C.
"Demeter." *Grolier Multimedia Encyclopedia*. 2008. Grolier Online. http://teach.belmont.edu:2309/cgi-bin/article?assetid=0082900-0 (accessed 20 March 2008).

"Directing *Passion Play*: An Interview with Mark Wing-Davey." *OnStage* (Goodman Theatre) 23.1, September–December 2007, 10–12.
Drewer, Lois. "Fisherman and Fish Pond: From the Sea of Sin to the Living Waters." *The Art Bulletin* 63.4, December 1981, 533–47.
Drostova, Lisa. "Never Look Back: The Berkeley Rep Turns Orpheus Inside Out." *East Bay Express* [California], 3 November 2004, Culture/Reviews.
Drukman, Steven. "In Guare's Art, Zero Degrees of Separation." *New York Times*, 11 April 1999.
D'souza, Karen. "Embracing the Inexplicable." *Knight Ridder Tribune Business News*, 22 January 2006.
"Duck Duck Goose." *Wikipedia*, 12 November 2007, 20:32 UTC. Wikimedia Foundation, Inc. *http://en.wikipedia.org/w/index.php?title=Duck_Duck_Goose&oldid=171032192* (accessed 13 November 2007).
Erasmus. "Praise of Folly." Translated by Betty Radice. In *Collected Works of Erasmus*, vol. 14, 77–153. Edited by A.H.T. Levi. Toronto: University of Toronto Press, 1986.
_____. "Sileni Alcibiades." In *Collected Works of Erasmus*, vol. 34, 262–82. Translated by R.A.B. Mynors. Toronto: University of Toronto Press, 1992.
Esslin, Martin. *The Theatre of the Absurd*. 3rd ed. London: Penguin, 1980.
Eurydice. By Sarah Ruhl. Dir. Les Waters, 16 June 2007. Second Stage Theatre, New York.
Evans, G. Blakemore, ed. *Elizabethan-Jacobean Drama: The Theatre in Its Time*. New York: New Amsterdam Books, 1988.
"Farce." In *Random House Unabridged Dictionary*. 2nd ed. 1993.
Faris, Wendy B. "Scheherazade's Children: Magical Realism and Postmodern Fiction." In Zamora and Faris, 163–90.
Fausto-Sterling, Anne. *Sexing the Body: Gender Politics and the Construction of Sexuality*. New York: Basic Books, 2000.
Frank, Glenda. "*Passion Play, a Cycle*." Performance review. *Theatre Journal* 58.3, October 2006, 500–1.
Freud, Sigmund. *Jokes and Their Relation to the Unconscious*. 1905. Translated by James Strachey. New York: Norton, 1960.
_____. "Mourning and Melancholia." In *The Standard Edition of the Complete Psychological Works of Sigmund Freud*. Vol. 14, 243–58. London: Hogarth Press, 1957.
Frye, Northrop. *Anatomy of Criticism: Four Essays*. Princeton: Princeton University Press, 1957.
Gaensbauer, Deborah B. *The French Theater of the Absurd*. Twayne's World Authors Series: French Literature. Edited by David O'Connell. Boston: Twayne Publishers, 1991.
Garner, Stanton B. Jr. "*Angels in America*: The Millennium and Postmodern Memory." In Geis and Kruger, 173–84.
Gates, Anita. "Love and Loss, in This Life and the Next." *New York Times*, 8 October 2006, late ed., section 14CN.
Geis, Deborah R. and Steven F. Kruger, eds. *Approaching the Millennium: Essays on Angels in America*. Ann Arbor: University of Michigan Press, 1997.
Gianopulos, Peter. "The Passion of Sarah Ruhl." *North Shore Magazine*, September 2007. *http://www.northshoremag.com* (accessed 8 March 2008).
Gilligan, Carol. *The Birth of Pleasure*. New York: Alfred A. Knopf, 2002.
_____. "When the Mind Leaves the Body ... and Returns." *Daedalus* 135.3, Summer 2006, 55–66.
Gilligan, Carol, and David A. J. Richards. *The Deepening Darkness: Patriarchy, Resistance, and Democracy's Future*. Cambridge: Cambridge University Press, 2009.

Gilman, Charlotte Perkins. "The Breakdown." In Golden, *The Captive Imagination*, 58–63.
———. "The Yellow Wallpaper." In Golden, *The Captive Imagination*, 24–42.
Goetschius, Elissa. "Poetry at Play: An Interview with Playwright Sarah Ruhl." *Stagegram: Dead Man's Cell Phone*, June 2007, 10–12.
Golden, Catherine, ed. *The Captive Imagination: A Casebook on* The Yellow Wallpaper. New York: The Feminist Press at the City University of New York, 1992.
Golden, Janet. *A Social History of Wet Nursing in America: from Breast to Bottle*. Cambridge: Cambridge University Press, 1996.
Goodman, Jordan, and Vivien Walsh. *The Story of Taxol: Nature and Politics in the Pursuit of an Anti-Cancer Drug*. Cambridge: Cambridge University Press, 2001.
Goodman, Lawrence. "Playwright Laureate of Grief." *Brown Alumni Magazine*, March/April 2007. http://www.brownalumnimagazine.com/march/april-2007/playwright-laureate-of-grief.html (accessed 22 March 2008).
Gray, Channing. "Sarah Ruhl's *Melancholy Play* Opens at Leeds Theatre." *The Providence Journal*, 8 Nov. 2007. http://www.projo.com/theater/content/wk-melancholyplay_11-08-07_TF7OGIT_v12.15d4988.html (accessed 9 November 2007).
Greenwood, Paul. "Ancient Yew in Upland and Cliff Habitats in the UK—New Research." *Ancient Yew Group*, 3 June 2007. http://www.ancient-yew.org/
Guare, John. *Bosoms and Neglect*. New York: Dramatists Play Service, 1980.
———. *Four Baboons Adoring the Sun*. New York: Dramatists Play Service, 1995.
———. "In Fireworks Lie Secret Codes." In *The Best Short Plays 1982–1983*, edited by Raymond Delgado. Radner, PA: Chilton Book Co., 1982.
———. Introduction. In Wilder, *Collected Short Plays*, xv–xxvii.
———. *Landscape of the Body*. New York: Dramatists Play Service, 1978.
———. "The Loveliest Afternoon of the Year." In *Something I'll Tell You Tuesday. The Loveliest Afternoon of the Year. Two Plays by John Guare*. New York: Dramatists Play Service, 1967.
———. *Marco Polo Sings a Solo*. New York: Dramatists Play Service, 1977.
———. *Six Degrees of Separation*. New York: Dramatists Play Service, 1992.
Gurewitsch, Matthew. "Wild Woman." *Smithsonian*, Fall 2007: 70.
Haigh, Christopher. *Elizabeth I*. London: Longman, 1988.
Hammer, Paul E. J. *Elizabeth's Wars: War, Government and Society in Tudor England, 1544–1604*. Houndmills, Eng.: Palgrave Macmillan, 2003.
Harrell, Jeremy. "Blood Ties in the Underworld." *American Theatre* 20.7, September 2003, 9.
Heartney, Eleanor. "The Strategist: Balancing His Photo-Appropriations with Large, Lush Paintings Steeped in Modernist Ambition, a Major Richard Price Retrospective Tweaks His Reputation for Artistic Brinksmanship. Or Does It?" *Art in America* 96.3, March 2008, 144.
Hegerfeldt, Anne C. *Lies That Tell the Truth: Magic Realism Seen through Contemporary Fiction from Britain*. Amsterdam—New York: Rodopi, 2005.
Helmetag, Charles H. "Mother Courage and her American Cousins in *The Skin of Our Teeth*." *Modern Language Studies* 8.3, Autumn 1978, 65–9.
Hitchcock, Laura. "Orlando." *CurtainUp*, 9 March 2003. http://www.curtainup.com/orlando.html (accessed 8 March 2008).
Holiday Inn. Dir. Mark Sandrich. Perf. Bing Crosby, Fred Astaire, Marjorie Reynolds, and Virginia Dale. Paramount, 1942.
Holman, Peter. *Dowland: Lachramie (1604)*. Cambridge: Cambridge University Press, 1999.

Horowitz, Helen. "Hysteria, Mysteria." *Lincoln Center Theater Review* 51, Fall 2009, 21–2.
Howard, Patricia. "Gluck, Christoph Willibald." *Encyclopedia Americana*. 2008. Grolier Online. *http://teach.belmont.edu:2307/cgi-bin/article?assetid=0177700-00* (accessed 24 March 2008).
Hurwitt, Robert. "Awash in a Young Writer's Bracing, Lucid 'Eurydice.'" *San Francisco Chronicle*, 22 October 2004, E2, Daily Datebook.
In the Next Room (or the vibrator play). By Sarah Ruhl. Dir. Les Waters, 31 January 2009. Berkeley Repertory Theatre.
In the Next Room or the vibrator play. By Sarah Ruhl. Dir. Les Waters, 16 December 2009. Lyceum Theatre. Lincoln Center Theater, New York.
Isherwood, Charles. "Always Ready with a Joke, If Not a Feather Duster." *New York Times*, 31 October 2006, late ed.—final, E1.
———. "A Comic Impudence Softens a Tale of Loss." *New York Times*, 3 October 2006, late ed.—final, E1.
———. "The Life and Times of Theater's Life and Times of Jesus." *New York Times*, 12 September 2005, late ed.—final, E5.
———. "A Nagging Call to Tidy up an Unfinished Life." *New York Times*, 5 March 2008, late ed.—final, E1.
It's a Wonderful Life. Dir. Frank Capra. Perf. James Stewart, and Donna Reed. RKO, 1946.
Jackson, Holbrook. Introduction. In Burton, vol. 1: vii–xvii.
Jesus of Montreal [*Jésus de Montréal*]. Dir. and screenplay by Denys Arcand. Max Films Productions, 1989.
Jones, Chris. "Steppenwolf Plans 'Crucible' Revival." *Knight Ridder Tribune Business News*, 5 March 2007.
Jones, Wenzel. "Demeter in the City." *Backstage.com*, 15 June 2006. LexisNexis Academic. Belmont University Lib., Nashville, TN. http://teach.belmont.edu: 3026/ (accessed 20 March 2008).
Kaplan, Lila Rose. "In Dialogue: Inhabiting *The Clean House* with Sarah Ruhl." *The Brooklyn Rail*, October 2004. http://www.thebrooklynrail.org/theater/oct04/cleanhouse.html (accessed 15 March 2007).
Kato, Kazumitsu. "Some Notes on *Mono no Aware*." *Journal of the American Oriental Society*, 82.4, October–December 1962, 558–9.
Kennedy, Louise. "A Season of Grief." *Boston Globe*, 24 Dec. 2006, first ed., N1. Living Arts.
Klaus, Carl H., Miriam Gilbert, and Bradford S. Field, Jr. "Henrik Ibsen." In *Stages of Drama: Classical to Contemporary Theater*, 5th ed., 547–9. Boston: Bedford/St. Martin's, 2003.
Klibansky, Raymond, Erwin Panofsky, and Fritz Saxl. *Saturn and Melancholy: Studies in the History of Natural Philosophy, Religion, and Art*. New York: Basic Books, 1964.
Knight, Denise D. Introduction. In *"The Yellow Wall-Paper" and Selected Stories of Charlotte Perkins Gilman*, edited by Denise D. Knight. Newark: University of Delaware Press, 1994.
Kolve, V. A. *The Play Called Corpus Christi*. Stanford: Stanford University Press, 1966.
Krieger, Murray. "Orpheus 'mit Glück': The Deceiving Gratifications of Presence." *Theatre Journal* 35.3, October 1983, The Poetics of Theatre, 295–305.
Kushner, Tony. *Angels in America: A Gay Fantasia on National Themes. Part One: Millennium Approaches*. New York: Theatre Communications Group, 1993.
———. *Angels in America: A Gay Fantasia on National Themes. Part Two: Perestroika*. Rev. version. New York: Theatre Communications Group, 1996.

_____. *A Bright Room Called Day*. New York: Theatre Communications Group, 1994.

_____. *Homebody/Kabul*. Rev. version. New York: Theatre Communications Group, 2000.

_____. "Hydriotaphia or the Death of Dr. Browne: An Epic Farce about Death and Primitive Capital Accumulation." In *Death & Taxes: Hydriotaphia & Other Plays*, 25–226. New York: Theatre Communications Group, 2000.

_____. "On Pretentiousness." In Kushner, *Thinking about the Longstanding Problems of Virtue and Happiness*, 55–79.

_____. "Slavs!: Thinking about the Longstanding Problems of Virtue and Happiness." In Kushner, *Thinking about the Longstanding Problems of Virtue and Happiness*, 81–185.

_____. *Thinking about the Longstanding Problems of Virtue and Happiness*. New York: Broadway Play Publishing, 1996.

Kushner, Tony, book and lyrics, and Jeanine Tesori, music. *Caroline, or Change*. New York: Theatre Communications Group, 2004.

Lahr, John. "Gods and Dolls: Sarah Ruhl Reimagines the Orpheus Myth." *The New Yorker*, 2 July 2007, 80–1.

_____. "Surreal Life: The Plays of Sarah Ruhl." A Critic at Large. *The New Yorker*, 17 March 2008. http://www.newyorker.com/arts/critics/atlarge/2008/03/17/080317crat_atlarge_lahr (accessed 11 March 2008).

Linhart, Sepp. *The Culture of Japan As Seen Through Its Leisure*. SUNY Series in Japan in Transition. Albany: State University of New York Press, 1998.

Lovelace, Maud Hart. *Betsy and the Great World*. New York: Thomas Y. Crowell Co., 1952.

"MacArthur Foundation. (AWARDS & PRIZES)." *American Theatre* 23.9, November 2006, 19.

Maines, Rachel P. *The Technology of Orgasm: "Hysteria," the Vibrator, and Women's Sexual Satisfaction*. Baltimore: Johns Hopkins University Press, 1999.

"Mandorla." *The Complete Dictionary of Symbols*. San Francisco: Chronicle Books, 2005.

McKillop, James. "Yew." *A Dictionary of Celtic Mythology*. Oxford University Press, 1998. *Oxford Reference Online*. Oxford University Press. Belmont University. http://www.oxfordreference.com/views/ENTRY.html?subview=Main&entry=t70.e3775 (accessed 20 May 2010).

McNichol, Tom. *AC/DC: The Savage Tale of the First Standards War*. San Francisco: Jossey-Bass, 2006.

"Melancholy." In *Random House Unabridged Dictionary*. 2nd ed. 1993.

Miller-McLemore, Bonnie J. *Also a Mother: Work and Family as Theological Dilemma*. Nashville: Abingdon, 1994.

Moore, Michael Scott. "One Step Beyond: A Greek Legend Made Modern Traces a Miniature Map of the Female Psyche." *SF Weekly* [San Francisco, CA], 3 November 2004, Culture/Stage.

Moote, A. Lloyd, and Dorothy C. Moote. *The Great Plague: The Story of London's Most Deadly Year*. Baltimore: Johns Hopkins, 2004.

Morreall, John. Introduction. In *The Philosophy of Laughter and Humor*, 1–7, edited by John Morreall. Albany: State University of New York Press, 1987.

"Most Memorable Theatrical Production: *Eurydice* at the Berkeley Rep." *East Bay Express* [California], 6 April 2005, Bestarts/Arts & Culture.

Narby, Jeremy, and Francis Huxley, eds. *Shamans through Time: 500 Years on the Path to Knowledge*. 2001. 1st trade paperback ed. New York: Jeremy P. Tarcher/Penguin, 2004.

New American Standard Bible. 1995. *http://www.biblegateway.com* (accessed 23 February 2008).
"Nostalgia." In *Random House Unabridged Dictionary.* 2nd ed. 1987.
"Oberammergau Passion Play." *Oberammergau. http://www.oberammergau.de/ot_e/passionplay/* (accessed 10 December 2007).
O'Leary, Stephen D. *Arguing the Apocalypse: A Theory of Millennial Rhetoric.* New York: Oxford University Press, 1994.
Oliva, Renato. "Re-Dreaming the World: Ben Okri's Shamanic Realism." In *Coterminous Worlds: Magical Realism and Contemporary Post-Colonial Literature in English.* Cross/Cultures: Readings in the Post/Colonial Literatures in English 39, 171–96. Amsterdam—Atlanta: Rodopi, 1999.
Ortiz-Griffin, Julia L., and William D. Griffin. *Spain and Portugal Today.* Studies in Modern European History 32. New York: Peter Lang, 2003.
Ovid. *The Metamorphoses of Ovid.* Translated by David R. Slavitt. Baltimore: Johns Hopkins University Press, 1994.
Parkes, C. Murray. "'Seeking' and 'Finding' a Lost Object: Evidence from Recent Studies of the Reaction to Bereavement." *Social Science and Medicine* 4, 1970, 187–201.
Partridge, Tim. "Trees in Mythology, Legend, Symbolism and Religion." *Ancient Yew Group.* 1993. *http://www.ancient-yew.org/* (accessed 3 June 2007).
"A Passion for Theater: Interview with Sarah Ruhl." *OnStage* (Goodman Theatre) 23.1, September–December 2007, 2–5.
Passion Play: A Cycle in Three Parts. By Sarah Ruhl. Dir. Mark Wing-Davey, 11 October 2007. Albert Theatre. Goodman Theatre, Chicago.
"Paula Vogel, Anne Fausto-Sterling." *New York Times,* 26 September 2004.
"Paula Vogel: Remembering through Language." Narr. Susan Stamberg. *Morning Edition.* Scenes I Wish I'd Written. Natl. Public Radio, 7 December 2004.
PEN America Center. http://www.pen.org/ (accessed 22 March 2008).
"The Perfect Arrangement." *The Internet Movie Database. http://www.imdb.com/title/tt0067569/* (accessed 21 April 2007).
Pinka, Patricia Garland. *This Dialog of One: The* Songs and Sonnets *of John Donne.* Alabama: University of Alabama Press, 1982.
Piven Theatre Workshop. http://www.piventheatre.org/ (accessed 22 March 2008).
"Playwright Sarah Ruhl Entertains with Big Ideas." Narr. Susan Stamberg. *Morning Edition.* Natl. Public Radio, 21 October 2005.
Plunka, Gene A. *The Black Comedy of John Guare.* Newark: University of Delaware Press, 2002.
———. "Freud and the Psychology of Neurosis: John Guare's *Bosoms and Neglect.*" *Papers on Language and Literature* 36.1, Winter 2000, 93–108.
Porter, Stephen. *The Great Plague.* Phoenix Mill, Eng.: Sutton, 1999.
Pressley, Nelson. "The Golden Ruhl: Playwright Has a Midas Touch." *Washington Post,* final ed.: N01, Sunday Arts.
"Production Notebook: Sarah Ruhl's *Eurydice* at Yale Repertory Theatre." *American Theatre* 23.10, December 2006, 36–7.
"Profiles." *Passion Play: A Cycle in Three Parts.* Program, Goodman Theatre. Oct. 2007, 9–18.
"A Promising Playwright's Summer Reading." Narr. Liane Hansen. *Weekend Edition Sunday.* What Are Your Summer Reads? Natl. Public Radio, 15 July 2007. *http://www.npr.org/templates/story/story.php?storyId=11979557* (accessed 28 May 2008).
The Pulitzer Prize. http://www.pulitzer.org/ (accessed 15 April 2007).

Robbins, Thomas and Susan J. Palmer. "Introduction: Patterns of Contemporary Apocalypticism." In Robbins and Palmer, *Millennium*, 1–27.

_____, eds. *Millennium, Messiahs, and Mayhem: Contemporary Apocalyptic Movements*. New York: Routledge, 1997.

Raine, George. "Creating Reagan's Image: SF Ad Man Riney Helped Secure Him a Second Term." *San Francisco Chronicle*, final ed., 9 June 2004, C1, Business.

Raskin, Victor. *Semantic Mechanisms of Humor*. Dordrecht, Holland: D. Reidel, 1985.

Redpath, Theodore, ed. *The Songs and Sonnets of John Donne*. 2nd ed. New York: St. Martin's Press, 1983.

Reid, Kerry. "Truth on a Slant." *PerformInk Online*. 26 May 2006. http://www.performink.com (accessed 15 March 2007).

Renner, Pamela. "Spiritual Cleanliness: An Interview with the Playwright." *American Theatre* 21.9, November 2004, 50.

Rilke, Rainer Maria. "Orpheus. Eurydice. Hermes." In *New Poems*, translated by J. B. Leishman. New York: New Directions, 1964.

Ritchie, David. "Frame-Shifting in Humor and Irony." *Metaphor and Symbol* 20.4, 2005, 275–94.

Ritter, Kurt and David Henry. *Ronald Reagan: The Great Communicator*. Great American Orators 13. Bernard K. Duffy and Halford R. Ryan, Series Advisers. New York: Greenwood Press, 1992.

Rivera, José. "Cloud Tectonics." In *Marisol and Other Plays*, 131–84. New York: Theatre Communications Group, 1997.

_____. "The Winged Man." In *Giants Have Us in Their Books: Six Naive Plays*, 61–72. New York: Broadway Play Publishing, 1997.

Rizzo, Frank. "Allen Stars an Upcoming 'Little Dog Laughed.'" *Hartford Courant*, 20 December 2007.

_____. "The Clean House." *Daily Variety*, 4 October 2004, 121, Legit Reviews.

_____. "Eurydice." *Daily Variety*, 3 October 2006, 16, Reviews.

Robbins, Emmet. "Famous Orpheus." In *Orpheus: The Metamorphoses of a Myth*, edited by John Warden, 3–23. Toronto: University of Toronto Press, 1982.

Robertson, Campbell. "Nine Writers See If the Fate of the Earth Can Be Any More Dramatic." *New York Times*, late ed.—final, 19 April 2008, sect. B: 7.

_____. "Paula Vogel Goes to Yale." *New York Times*, late ed.—final, 18 January 2008, sect. E: 6.

_____. "The Virtues of a Messy House." *New York Times*, late ed.—final, 3 October 2004, sect. 14CN: 11.

Rombauer, Irma S. and Marion Rombauer Becker. *Joy of Cooking*. New York: Signet, 1973.

Rooney, David. "The Clean House." *Daily Variety*, 1 November 2006, Reviews.

Roop, Eugene F. *Ruth, Jonah, Esther: Believers Church Bible Commentary*. Scottsdale, PA: Herald Press, 2002.

Rose, Phyllis. "The Source of Happiness." *Lincoln Center Theater Review* 51, Fall 2009, 4–7.

Rougeot, Jonathan. "'Eurydice' an Emotional Take on Greek Myth." *Stamford Advocate*, 8 October 2006.

Royce, Graydon. "OnStage: 'House' Proud." *Star Tribune* [Minneapolis-St. Paul, MN], 18 October 2007.

Ruhl, Sarah. "Anna around the Neck." In Ruhl, "*The Lady with the Lap Dog*," 40–70.

_____. "*The Baltimore Waltz* and the Plays of My Childhood." In *The Play That Changed My Life: America's Foremost Playwrights on the Plays That Influenced Them*, edited by Ben Hodges, 119–27. New York: Applause, 2009.

———. *The Clean House and Other Plays*. New York: Theatre Communications Group, 2006.
———. "The Clean House." In Ruhl, *The Clean House and Other Plays*, 1–116.
———. *Dead Man's Cell Phone*. Preview ed. USA: First Look Press, 2007.
———. *Dead Man's Cell Phone*. New York: Theatre Communications Group, 2008.
———. *Demeter in the City*. Unpublished script, 2006.
———. *Dog Play*. Unpublished script, 2002.
———. "Eurydice." In Ruhl, *The Clean House and Other Plays*, 325–411.
———. *In the Next Room or the vibrator play*. New York: Samuel French, 2010.
———. *"The Lady with the Lap Dog" and "Anna around the Neck:" Two Stories by Anton Chekhov*. Unpublished script, 2000.
———. "The Lady with the Lap Dog." In Ruhl, *"The Lady with the Lap Dog,"* 1–39.
———. "Late: a cowboy song." In Ruhl, *The Clean House and Other Plays*, 117–220.
———. "Melancholy Play." In Ruhl, *The Clean House and Other Plays*, 221–324.
———. *Orlando*. Unpublished script, 2003.
———. *Passion Play*. New York: Theatre Communications Group, 2010.
———. "Playwright's Note." In Ruhl, *Passion Play*, ix–xii.
———. "Program Notes." In Ruhl, *Demeter*, 4–5.
———. "Re: A Request: Dog Play, etc." E-mail to the author. 5 March 2008.
———. "Re: Checking in." E-mail to the author. 24 April 2007.
———. "Re: Eurydice." E-mail to the author. 24 March 2008.
———. "Re: Melancholy question." E-mail to the author. 10 November 2007.
———. "Six Small Thoughts on Fornes, the Problem of Intention, and Willfulness." *Theatre Topics* 11.2, September 2001, 187–204.
———. *Snowless*. Unpublished script, 2008.
———. *Virtual Meditation #1*. Unpublished script, 2002.
"Sarah Ruhl." *New Dramatists*, 29 October 2006. http://newdramatists.org/sarah_ruhl.htm.
Savage, William W., Jr. *The Cowboy Hero: His Image in American History and Culture*. Norman: University of Oklahoma Press, 1979.
Savran, David. "Ambivalence, Utopia, and a Queer Sort of Materialism: How *Angels in America* Reconstructs the Nation." In Geis and Kruger, 13–39.
———. *In Their Own Words: Contemporary American Playwrights*. New York: Theatre Communications Group, 1988.
Schalch, Kathleen. "The Marlboro Man." *Present at the Creation*. National Public Radio, 21 October 2002 http://www.npr.org/programs/morning/features/patc/marlboroman/ (accessed 27 November 2007).
Scheper-Hughes, Nancy. *Death without Weeping: The Violence of Everyday Life in Brazil*. Berkeley: University of California Press, 1993.
Schmidt, Kerstin. *The Theater of Transformation: Postmodernism in American Drama*. Postmodern Studies 37, edited by Theo D'haen, and Hans Bertens. Amsterdam–New York: Rodopi, 2005.
Schneider, Ronald M. "Brazil." In *The New Encyclopedia Britannica: Macropaedia*. 15th ed. 2007.
Scott, Susan, and C. J. Duncan. *Biology of Plagues: Evidence from Historical Populations*. New York: Cambridge University Press, 2001.
Segal, Charles. *Orpheus: The Myth of the Poet*. Baltimore: Johns Hopkins University Press, 1989.
Sforza, John. *Swing It! The Andrews Sisters Story*. Lexington: University Press of Kentucky, 2000.

Shirer, William L. *The Rise and Fall of the Third Reich: A History of Nazi Germany.* New York: Simon and Schuster, 1960.
Shteir, Rachel. "Home Fires." *Chicago Magazine*, May 2006. http://www.chicagomag.com/Chicago-Magazine/May-2006/Home-Fires (accessed 8 March 2008).
Shuchter, Stephen R. and Sidney Zisook. "The Course of Normal Grief." In *Handbook of Bereavement: Theory, Research, and Intervention*, edited by Margaret S. Stroebe, Wolfgang Stroebe, and Robert O. Hansson, 23–43. Cambridge: Cambridge University Press, 1993.
Simonson, Robert. "There's Little Doubt in New York Theater Circles That the Young American Playwright of the Hour Is Sarah Ruhl." *Playbill*, 13 December 2006.
Smith, Dinitia. "Playwright's Subjects: Greek Myths to Vibrators." *New York Times*, 14 October 2006, B7.
Smith, Michael C. *Jung and Shamanism in Dialogue: Retrieving the Soul/Retrieving the Sacred.* New York: Paulist Press, 1997.
Snyder, Diane. "Fit to Be Tidy: MacArthur 'Genius' Sarah Ruhl Opens up *The Clean House*." *Time Out New York*, 5 October 2006.
Solomon-Godeau, Abigail. "Living with Contradictions: Critical Practices in the Age of Supply-Site Aesthetics." *Social Text* 21, Universal Abandon? The Politics of Postmodernism (1989): 191–213.
Sontag, Susan. "Notes on 'Camp.'" In *Against Interpretation and Other Essays*, 275–92. New York: Farrar, Straus & Giroux, 1964.
Speake, Jennifer. *The Dent Dictionary of Symbols in Christian Art.* London: J. M. Dent, 1994.
Sponsler, Claire. *Ritual Imports: Performing Medieval Drama in America.* Ithaca: Cornell University Press, 2004.
Strauss, Walter A. *Descent and Return: The Orphic Theme in Modern Literature.* Cambridge: Harvard University Press, 1971.
Stroebe, Margaret S. and Wolfgang Stroebe. *Bereavement and Health: The Psychological and Physical Consequences of Partner Loss.* Cambridge: Cambridge University Press, 1987.
The Susan Smith Blackburn Prize. http://www.blackburnprize.org/ (accessed 15 April 2007).
Svitch, Caridad. "In Conversation with Sarah Ruhl." *The Dramatist* 4.3, 2002, 36–9.
Sweet, Frederick A. "Hopper, Edward." *Encyclopedia Americana.* 2007. Grolier Online. http://teach.belmont.edu:2307/cgi-bin/article?assetid=0205860-00 (accessed 28 November 2007).
Tedlock, Barbara. *The Woman in the Shaman's Body: Reclaiming the Feminine in Religion and Medicine.* New York: Bantam, 2005.
Test, George A. *Satire: Spirit and Art.* Tampa: University Press of Florida, 1991.
The Third Man. Dir. Carol Reed. Screenplay by Graham Greene. Perf. Joseph Cotton, Alida Valli, Trevor Howard, and Orson Welles. Rialto Pictures, 1949.
Traina, Cristina L. H. "Maternal Experience and the Boundaries of Christian Sexual Ethics." *Signs* 25.2, Winter 2000, 369–405.
"Troika VI." *Library of Congress Online Catalog.* LCCN Permalink. http://lccn.loc.gov/95062152 (accessed 21 March 2008).
"Turning the World Upside Down: Sarah Ruhl and Les Waters on *Eurydice*." *Yale Rep Newsletter*, October 2006, 3–5.
Varley, H. Paul. *Japanese Culture.* Honolulu: University of Hawaii Press, 2000.
Virgil. *The Georgics of Virgil.* Translated by David Ferry. New York: Farrar, Strauss and Giroux, 2005.

"Virtual Meditation #1." *Carnegie Mellon University Entertainment Technology Center.* *http://www.etc.cmu.edu/projects/atl/index.htm* (accessed 19 March 2008).
Vitello, Barbara. "Ruhl Rings It Up." *Daily Herald* [Chicago], 3 Apr. 2008. *http://www.dailyherald.com/column/?id=164850* (accessed 15 April 2008).
Vogel, Paula. "The Baltimore Waltz." In *The Baltimore Waltz and Other Plays*, 1–57. New York: Theatre Communications Group, 1996.
_____. "Sarah Ruhl." *Bomb* 99, Spring 2007, 54–9.
Webber, F. R. *Church Symbolism*. 2nd ed., rev. Cleveland: J. H. Jansen, 1938.
Weber, Carl. "I Always Go Back to Brecht." In *Tony Kushner in Conversation*, edited by Robert Vorlicky, 105–24. Ann Arbor: University of Michigan Press, 1998.
Weckwerth, Wendy. "More Invisible Terrains: Sarah Ruhl, Interviewed by Wendy Wentworth." *Theater* 34.2, 2004, 28–35.
Wessinger, Catherine. "Millennialism with and without the Mayhem." In Robbins and Palmer, *Millennium* 47–59.
Wilder, Thornton. *The Collected Short Plays of Thornton Wilder*. Vol. I. Eds. Donald Gallup and A. Tappan Wilder. New York: Theatre Communications Group, 1997.
_____. "The Long Christmas Dinner." In Wilder, *Collected Short Plays*, 3–25.
_____. "Our Town." In Wilder, *Three Plays*, 1–64.
_____. Preface. In Wilder, *Three Plays*, vii–xii.
_____. "Pullman Car Hiawatha." In Wilder, *Collected Short Plays*, 41–59.
_____. "The Skin of Our Teeth." In Wilder, *Three Plays*, 65–137.
_____. *Three Plays: Our Town, The Skin of Our Teeth, The Matchmaker*. New York: Bantam, 1957.
Williams, Tennessee. "Orpheus Descending." In *Plays 1957–1980*, 1–97. New York: Library of America, 2000.
Wilson, Frank Percy. *The Plague in Shakespeare's London*. 1927. Oxford: Oxford University Press, 1999.
Wood, Robert E. *Placing Aesthetics: Reflections on the Philosophic Tradition*. Athens: Ohio University Press, 1999.
Woolf, Virginia. *Orlando: A Biography*, edited by J. H. Stape. Oxford: Blackwell, 1998.
Worthen, W. B. "Bertolt Brecht." In *The Wadsworth Anthology of Drama*. 5th ed., 725–7. N.p.: Thomson Wadsworth, 2007.
Wortman, Camille B. and Roxane Cohen Silver. "The Myths of Coping with Loss Revisited." In *Handbook of Bereavement Research: Consequences, Coping, and Care*, edited by Margaret S. Stroebe, Robert O. Hansson, Wolfgang Stroebe, and Hank Schut, 405–29. Washington: American Psychological Assoc., 2001.
Wren, Celia. "The Golden Ruhl." *American Theatre* 22.8, October 2005, 30.
Wroe, Ann. *Pontius Pilate*. New York: Random House, 1999.
"Yew." Def. 4. In *Random House Unabridged Dictionary*. 2nd ed. 1987.
Zamora, Lois Parkinson. "Magical Romance/Magical Realism: Ghosts in U.S. and Latin American Fiction." In Zamora and Faris, 497–50.
Zamora, Lois Parkinson, and Wendy B. Faris, eds. *Magical Realism: Theory, History, Community*. Durham & London: Duke University Press, 1995.
Zimmerman, Mary. *Metamorphoses: A Play*. Evanston: Northwestern University Press, 2002.

Index

Numbers in ***bold italics*** indicate pages with photographs.

absurdism 57–9, 97
Actor's Gang 179
Actors Theatre of Louisville 183, 197
AIDS 30, 43, 44, 138, 139, 187
Albee, Edward 58–9, 153; *The Goat, or Who Is Sylvia?* 58–9; *Who's Afraid of Virginia Woolf?* 153
alienation effect 60, 184, 187
almond 5, 67, 68, 70, 74, 75, 76, 77, 79, 82
the American cowboy *see* cowboy
amygdala 76
Anatomy of Criticism 117–8
The Anatomy of Melancholy 68, 70–1
The Andrews Sisters 22
androcentric 145, 150, 176
Angels in America 28, 30, 137–9, 187, 194, 195
"Angelus Novus" 138
Anna Around the Neck 180–1, 197
Anouilh, Jean 16
anti-Semitism 114, 120, 133
apocalypse 115–8, 121, 122, 131, 134–5, 137, 139; comic 116, 132; tragic 116, 118
Arcand, Denys 136–7
archetype 98, 104, 109, 128, 168, 187, 189, 190, 193
Arena Stage 112, 137, 197
Aristaeus 18
Aristotle 8, 11, 20, 61
Armageddon 115, 117, 132, 134–5
ascension *113*
Astaire, Fred 104
Aston, Elaine 10–1
awards 1; Fourth Freedom Forum Playwriting Award 1, 112; MacArthur Fellowship 1; Pulitzer Prize 1, 7, 42, 143; Susan Smith Blackburn Prize 1, 42; Tony Award 1, 143

The Baltimore Waltz 42–4, 200
"*The Baltimore Waltz* and the Plays of My Childhood" 42–3

baptism 122, 124
Barchiesi, Franca *41*, *58*
basherts 48
bedroom farce 69
Benanti, Laura *154*, *158*, *162*, 176
Benjamin, Walter 138
bereavement 8, 11, 14, 24, 25, 109, 178, 196; obsessive review during 25, 37; psychology of 32–6; seeking and finding stage of 35–6, 75, 80; *see also* grief
Berkeley Repertory Theatre 13, 28, *142*, 143, *156*, *165*, *166*, *173*, 175, 197
Berlin, Irving 104
Bernstine, Quincy Tyler *154*
Betsy and the Great World 111
The Birth of Pleasure 158–9
the Black Death *see* the plague
Black Hills Passion Play 114
"Blue Moon" 178
Bogart, Anne 84, 88
Bosoms and Neglect 191–2, 193, 196
Bradley, Scott 24
Brecht, Bertolt 60, 187
Brechtian 176, 184, 194
A Bright Room Called Day 194, 195
Brock, Rita Nakashima 170
Brown, Blair 42
Brown, Harold P. 146
Brown University 7, 10, 43, 69, 106, 111, 112, 199
Brundibar 195
Buried Child 153
buried child 153–5, 176
Burke, Kenneth 116
Burton, Richard 68, 71, 78
Bush, George W. 136
Bush, Kristen *126*, *128*
Butler, Judith 105–6

Cabell, Hannah *156*, *165*, *166*, *173*
Calvino, Italo 6, 22, 81

camp 22–3
Campbell, Joseph 66
cancer 6, 10, 19, 39, 41, 43, 66, 75
Carnegie Mellon University 177, 183
Caroline, or Change 195
Carousel 94
Carpentier, Alejo 49, 199
catastrophic millennialism 115–6
Catholicism 9, 114, 133, 136, 190
Cerveris, Michael *158*, 159, 171–2
Chaikin, Joseph 97
Champa, Russell H. 144
Charuvastra, Anthony 10, 42
Chaudhuri, Una 143, 153–4, 156–7
Chekhov, Anton 9, 10, 11, 177, 180–2, 183, 191, 201
Chekhov: The Stories 180, 197
Chicago Dramatists 177, 197
Chicago Humanities Festival 185, 197
Chorus of Stones 19, 24, 25, *27*, *28*, *29*, *32*, 34, 192, 199
Cincinnati Playhouse 181, 197
Civil War 153, 155
The Clean House 10, 37, 38–67, 84, 85, 96, 97, 100, 102, 109, 152, 163, 176, 181, 189, 190, 193, 194, 195, 196, 197; and absurdism 57–9; and *The Baltimore Waltz* 40, 42–4; cleaning, significance of 44–7; and community 47, 57; double casting in 51–2; and ghosts 52–3; and humor theory 60–4; inspiration for 40–2; and literalization of metaphor 53–4; and logos 56–7; and magic realism 49–59; and matter-of-factness 50–1; and metamorphosis 51–2; and mirroring 51–2; and mythos 56–7; and overlapping space 54, *55*, 56; and shamanism 64–7; themes of 44–9; tonal shifts in 59–60; tree in 66–7
clean room 49
Clubbed Thumb 100, 197
Corley, Richard 8, 13, 197
Cornerstone Theater 184, 197
cowboy 98, 99, 104–6, 110
Crosby, Bing 104
crucifixion *112*, 119, 123, 124, 127, 129, 136
Cruz, Nilo 7, 8

DAH 45
Dance of Death 68, 79–81
Dead Man's Cell Phone 37, 82–3, 84–98, 102, 107–8, 109, 155, 164, 174, 181, 186, 189, 190, 193, 194, 196, 197; cell phone, significance of 86–7; character relationships in 90–3; and Hopper, Edward 106; and postmodernism 94–8; revisions of 87–8; social Darwinism in 88–90, tone in 93–4; Woolly Mammoth production of 84, 87, 93–4
"Death in Another Country" 8
The Deepening Darkness 167
Demeter in the City 177, 184, 190, 192, 196, 197

depression 69, 70, 73, 82, 195
Derrida, Jacques 108
Dickens, Charles 88, 90, 164
Dickinson, Emily 5
Dionysus 15, 53
Dizzia, Maria *32*, *142*, *165*, *166*
Dog Play 37, 177–9, 181, 183, 196, 197
A Doll's House 156–7, 165
domestic abuse 101, 108
Donne, John 92–3
"Don't Sit Under the Apple Tree (with Anyone Else but Me)" 22
double-casting 51–2
Doyle, John 181, 197
duck duck goose 72, 78, 82
duck hunting 36–7, 178

Eckert, Rinde 16
Edison, Thomas Alva 146, 147, 163
electric chair 146
Electrocuting an Elephant 146
Elizabeth I 110, 114, 131, 133, *134*, 135, 178, 179
Elizabethan sailing ships 110, 132, 196
Erasmus 118, 127
Esslin, Martin 57
Eurydice 8, 11, 13–37, 38, 67, 68, 84, 85, 100, 102, 109, 110, 142, 155, 176, 177–9, 181, 186, 189, 190, 192, 194, 195, 196, 197; and camp 22–3; critical response to 13–4, 28, 36; dualities in 14, 19–32, 143; hair imagery in 18–9; and nostalgia 36–7; and psychology of bereavement 32–6; raining elevator in 24, 30–1, *32*; and Rilke 14, 17–9; and time 31–2
Eurydice (Legend of Lovers) 16
Eve 119, *126*, 172, 175, 189

Fausto-Sterling, Anne 10, 106; *Sexing the Body* 106
femme fatale 96
film noir 81, 88, 96–7
Finnigan's Wake 189
fish puppets 110, 118, 124, *125*, 130, 131, 132, 196
food (in Ruhl's plays) 109
Fornes, Maria Irene 8
Forster, E.M. 196
Foucault, Michel 86
Foucheux, Rich *85*, 94
Four Baboons Adoring the Sun 192, 193
the four elements *see* the Greek elements
the four humors 71–2, 78–9
Fourth Freedom Forum Playwriting Award 1, 112
Franklin, Benjamin 146–7, 175
Freud, Sigmund 33, 39, 57, 61, 167, 193, 199
Frye, Northrop 117–8, 125, 128, 132

Gates, Anita 14
gender roles, Victorian 149–53, 156

Gender Trouble 105–6
geopathology 143, 148, 157
The Ghost Sonata 157
Gianino, Gian-Murray *29*
Gilligan, Carol 176; *The Birth of Pleasure* 158–9; *The Deepening Darkness* 167; "When the Mind Leaves the Body ... and Returns" 167, 175
Gilman, Charlotte Perkins 151–2; "The Yellow Wallpaper" 151
global warming 5, 177, 185
The Goat, or Who Is Sylvia? 58–9
Goodell, William 145
Goodman Theatre 111, *112*, *113*, 119, *120*, *121*, *125*, *126*, *128*, 129, *134*, *135*, 197
Goodnight Moon 185
Gorbachev, Mikhail 134
the Greek elements 23–5, 117, 125, 132
grief 11, 13–14, 17, 23, 24, 25; *see also* bereavement
Guare, John 103–4, 187–8, 190–4, 195, 201; *Bosoms and Neglect* 191–2, 193, 196; *Four Baboons Adoring the Sun* 192, 193; *In Fireworks Lie Secret Codes* 103–4; *Landscape of the Body* 192, 193; *The Loveliest Afternoon of the Year* 191; *Marco Polo Sings a Solo* 191; *Six Degrees of Separation* 191, 192, 193

Hades (god) 15, 184
Hades (place) 24
Hagen, Uta 182
"Hansel and Gretel" 119, 130
The Happy Journey to Trenton and Camden 188
Harger, Brenda 197
Harting, Carla *29*
Hawthorne, Nathaniel 167
Hébert, Mitchell *41*, *58*
Heisler, Laura *21*, *26*, *27*, *31*
The Hero with a Thousand Faces 66
heroism of departure 157
Highmore, Nathaniel 145
historification 176
Hitler, Adolf 110, 111, 112, 114, 115, 117, 119, 120, 129, 133–4
Holbein, Hans 80
Holiday Inn 104
Homebody/Kabul 99, 194, 195
Hopper, Edward 106
How I Learned to Drive 7
Humana Festival of New American Plays 183, 197
humor theory 39–40, 60–4; applied to jokes in *The Clean House* 62–3; and frame-shifting 61–2
the humors *see* the four humors
Hurwitt, Robert 13, 28
Hydriotaphia 194, 195
hysteria 141–2, 151, 153, 201

Ibsen, Henrik 156–7
Iizuka, Naomi 112

Illinois 9, 68, 69, 70, 73
"I'm Dreaming of a White Christmas" 104
improvisation 9–10
In Fireworks Lie Secret Codes 103–4
In the Next Room or the vibrator play 8, 140, 141–76, 186, 196, 197; and America, figure of 154–5; clothing in 172–3; curtains in 151–2; dualities in 143, 148–9, 160, 161–4, 174, 175; and electricity 142, 145, 146–7, 159, 161, 171, 174, 175; and the Eucharist 170; grape arbor in 152; and hands 171–2; home as shelter and prison in 151, 156–8, 174; and hysteria 141–2, 151, 153, 201; Madonna and Child in 144, 148, 155, *156*, 169; and male hysteria 142, 144; and maternal sexuality 168–9, 176; and naturalism 164; precipitation in 158–9; and race 153–5; and realism 164; and sexual intelligence 141; and the sexual voice 167–9, 171, 175; and vibrator, history of 145–6; and Victorian gender roles 149–53, 156; and walking 158; and wet nursing 144, 145, 147–8, 149, 153; woman-centered religion in 169–71, 175, 176
intersexual 106, 155, 180
Iraq 136
Isherwood, Charles 14, 28, 36
It's a Wonderful Life 100–2, 108
"I've Got Rhythm" 20, 23, 34

Jacobean drama 67, 70–1, 81
Jacobson, Naomi *41*, *45*, *90*, *92*
Jesus of Montreal 136–7
Johannesburg 96
John of Patmos 115
Johnson-Neshati, Kristin 182
joke theory *see* humor theory
The Joy of Cooking 99–100, 200
Joyce, James 189
Jungian 57, 126, 193

Kabuki 8, 199
Kennedy, Adrienne 108
Kennedy, Louise 14
Kennedy Center American College Theatre Festival 112
King Lear 21, 24
Klee, Paul 138
Kurup, Shishir 197
Kushner, Tony 28, 30, 99, 137–9, 187–8, 194–5; *Angels in America* 28, 30, 137–9, 187, 194, 195; *A Bright Room Called Day* 194, 195; *Brundibar* 195; *Caroline, or Change* 195; *Homebody/Kabul* 99, 194, 195; *Hydriotaphia* 194, 195; *Slavs!* 195

The Lady with the Lap Dog 180–1, 197
Lahr, John 36–7, 93, 111, 196
Landscape of the Body 192, 193
Langer, Susanne K. 116
the Last Supper 119, *120*

Late: a cowboy song 98, 99–110, 155, 180, 183, 197; and the American family 100–2, 106; and domestic abuse 101, 108; and gender 104–6, 107–8; and holidays 102–4; and myth of American cowboy 104–6; and Rothko, Mark 106–7; title of 107
Lear see *King Lear*
Lemos, Guenia *41, 45, 48, 58*
Lenertz, John *26, 31*
The Life of the Bee 108, 185
lightness 6–8, 20, 22–3, 31, 38, 43, 44, 81–3, 96, 107–8, 110, 160, 162, 186
Lincoln Center Theater 42, 60, 143, *154, 158,* 159, *162,* 176
"Little Red Riding Hood" 119
The Long Christmas Dinner 103
Long Day's Journey into Night 153
the Lord of the Underworld 25, 26, *27,* 28, 31
The Loveliest Afternoon of the Year 191
Luther, Martha 151
Lyceum Theatre 143, *154, 158, 162,* 175
Lyotard, Jean-François 56, 97

MacArthur Fellowship 1
MacArthur "Genius Grant" *see* MacArthur Fellowship
Madison Repertory Theatre 8, 13, *21, 26, 27, 28, 31,* 197
Madonna and Child 144, 148, 155, *156,* 169
Maeterlinck, Maurice 108, 185
magic realism 7, 38, 39, 42, 49–59, 85, 97–8, 185, 186; and absurdism 57–9; and community 57; and double-casting 51–2; and ghosts 52–3, 152; and literalization of metaphor 53–4; and logos 56–7; and matter-of-factness 50–1; and metamorphosis 52; and mirroring 51–2; and mythos 56–7; and overlapping space as metaphor 54, *55,* 56
magical realism 199; *see also* magic realism
Magritte, René 106
male hysteria 142, 144
mandorla 76, 200
Marco Polo Sings a Solo 191
Marlboro Man 105, 107, 108
Marshall, Sarah *41, 48, 58, 90, 91,* 93–4
Marx, Karl 135
maternal sexuality 168–9, 176
McMahon, David Andrew *21*
Medusa 6, 186
Meier, Josef 114
melancholy, cult of 70–2
Melancholy Play 10, 37, 59, 67, 68–83, 102, 105, 109, 192, 195, 197; and almond 5, 67, 68, 70, 74, 75, 76, 77, 79, 82; and *The Anatomy of Melancholy* 68, 70–1; and Dance of Death 68, 79–81; as farce 69–70; and the four humors 71–2, 78–9; and Jacobean drama 68, 70–1, 81; and Magritte, René 106; and *mono no aware* 72, 73, 74, 75, 76, 82–3; and plague 69, 75, 76–9; and *saudade* 73, 74, 75, 76; and *The Third Man* 81–2; and *zhalost'* 74
Mendoza, Zilah *40, 55*
Metamorphoses 16, 199
Michelangelo 164, 171
millennialism 115–6, 201
millennium 115, 117, 129, 134–5, 138; deferred 137–9
Miller-McLemore, Bonnie 170–1
Miss Julie 164
mono no aware 72, 73, 74, 75, 76, 82–3
Monsef, Ramiz *29*
Morse, John Lovett 147
Morton, Scot *26, 27*
mourning *see* bereavement
"Mourning and Melancholia" 33

the Nasty Interesting Man 18, 24, 25, *26,* 31, 109, 189
Nazi 110, 111, 119, 129, 130, 138, 195
Nelson, Bruce *91*
Neville, Meg 28
New York University Humanities Festival 185
Niebanck, Paul *142, 173*
Noonan, Polly 9, *27, 28, 85, 90, 91, 92, 120, 121*
Norment, Elizabeth *55*
nostalgia 17, 36–7, 87, 109
"Notes on 'Camp'" 22–3
Nurse, Karlie *27*

Oberammergau passion play 111, 112, 114, 119, 133
obsessive review 25, 37
Ohio Theatre 100, 197
O'Neill, Eugene 153
organ trade 88–9
Orlando 10, 177, 179–80, 181, 197
Orpheus: myth 15, 17, 18, 19–20, 67; stage adaptations 15–7
Orpheus Descending 16
"Orpheus. Eurydice. Hermes." 16, 17–9
Orpheus X 16–7
Our Town 103, 188, 189, 190, 192
Ovid 8, 15, 16, 199
Owens, Rochelle 95

Parker, Mary-Louise 84, 88
Parks, Joseph *32*
Parks, Suzan-Lori 95, 98, 108
Passion Play 102, 105, 110, 111–40, 178, 179, 186, 187, 190, 196; and anti–Semitism 114, 120, 133; and apocalypse 115–8, 121, 122, 131, 134–5, 137, 139, and Armageddon 115, 117, 132, 134–5; and ascension *113*; and baptism 110, 122, 124, 196; and Catholicism 114, 133, 136; Christian symbology 121–31; and crucifixion *112,* 119, 123, 124, 127, 129, 136; and dove 122, 129–30; fish puppets in

118, 124, *125*, 130, 131, 132; and *Jesus of Montreal* 136–7; and the Last Supper 119, *120*; and millennialism 115–6, 201; and millennium 115, 117, 129, 134–5, 138; and Oberammergau 111, 112, 114, 119, 133; production history of 111–2, 197; and rapture 116, 130, 131, 132, 139; and Revelation 115, 116, 121, 122, 127; and tribulation 116, 130, 135; and wise fool 118–20, 127
patriarchy 167, 176
The Perfect Arrangement 44
Persephone 15, 184
Perseus 6, 186
Pilate, Pontius 111, 114, 115, 118–9, 123–4, 131; death of 124
Pinter, Harold 58, 103
Piven, Joyce 9, 179, 180, 182, 197
Piven Theatre Workshop 9–10, 69, 97, 179, 197
the plague 69, 75, 76–9, 114; countermeasures against 79, 81; presumed causes of 78–9
Plato 39, 61, 118
"Platonic Love" 92
Playwrights Horizons 84, 88
pornography 176
postcolonial 39, 49, 56
postmillennialism *see* progressive millennialism
The Postmodern Condition 56
postmodernism 56, 94–8, 105, 110, 138–9; and asynchronicity 95–6, 98, 110, 186; and intertextuality 95–6, 98, 107, 108, 153, 186; and magic realism 97–8
Powers, Melle *156*
"Praise of Folly" 118
premillennialism *see* catastrophic millennialism
Prestininzi, Ken 69
priestly mode 116, 135, 137
Prince, Richard 105
progressive millennialism 115
prophetic mode 116, 135, 137
Pulitzer Prize 1, 7, 42
Pullman Car Hiawatha 103, 194

Queen Elizabeth I *see* Elizabeth I

raining elevator 24, 30–1, *32*
rapture 116, 130, 131, 132, 139
Rauch, Bill 42, 197
Reagan, Ronald 105, 110, 114, 115, 117, 132, 133–6, *135*, 139, 195
REDCAT 184, 197
Reed, Donna 100
reincarnation 129
Reiss, Judy *27*
religious authority: priestly 116, 135, 137; prophetic 116, 135, 137
Revelation 115, 116, 121, 122, 127
Reynolds, Marjorie 104

Richards, David A.J. 167
Rilke, Rainer Maria 14, 16, 17–9
"Ring Around the Rosie" 77–8
River Lethe 24, 195, 199
River of Forgetfulness 21, 24, 25, 30, 31, 34; *see also* River Lethe
River Styx 5, 24, 75
Rivera, José 50
Rizzo, Frank 13–4
Robinson, Charles Shaw *32*
Rodgers and Hammerstein 94
Roh, Franz 49
Rostova, Mira 182
Rothko, Mark 98, 106–7, 183
Ruhl, Kate 9, 36–7, 41–2
Ruhl, Kathy Kehoe 9
Ruhl, Patrick 6, 7, 9, 10, 19, 36–7, 41, 43, 85
Ruskin, John 201

sailing ships *see* Elizabethan sailing ships
Saivetz, Debbie 100, 197
Sands, Emily Glassberg 199
saudade 73, 74, 75, 76
Savage, William W., Jr. 104–5
Scheherazade 97
Schmidt, Kerstin 94–8, 108
Second Stage 28
September 11, 2001 14, 36
Sexing the Body 106
sexual intelligence 141
the sexual voice 167–9, 171, 175
Sgambati, Brian 119, *125*, *126*
Shakespeare, William 21, 24, 34, 81, 118, 179
shamanism 39–40, 42, 56–7, 60, 64–7; and magic realism 65
Shange, Ntozake 108
Shepard, Sam 153
Shklovsky, Victor 43
"Sileni Alcibiadis" 118
Six Degrees of Separation 191, 192, 193
"Six Small Thoughts on Fornes, the Problem of Intention, and Willfulness" 8
The Skin of Our Teeth 189
Slavs! 195
Smart, Annie 143–4
Smith, Molly 112, 197
Smith, T. Ryder *134*, *135*
Snowless 59, 108, 177, 185, 197
social Darwinism 88–90
Socrates 118
Sontag, Susan 22–3
South Dakota 114
Soviet Union 134, 138
Spearfish 114, 133, 135
Spolin, Viola 9, 97
Stage Kiss 197
Staging Place: The Geography of Modern Drama 143
Stein, Gertrude 188, 189
Steppenwolf Theatre Company 88
Stetson, Charles Walter 151

220 Index

Stewart, James 100
Strindberg, August: *The Ghost Sonata* 157; *Miss Julie* 164
subtracting weight *see* lightness
Sundance Theater Laboratory 112
Susan Smith Blackburn Prize 1, 42
Symposium 118

Taichman, Rebecca Bayla 84, 197
A Tale of Two Cities 88, 90
Taxol 66
Terry, Megan 95
Tertullian 122, 129
Tesla, Nikola 147, 163
Thales 160
The Theatre of the Absurd 57
Thebus, Jessica 10, 69, 197
"There's No Place like Home" 21
The Third Man 43–4, 81–2, 96, 200
36 Views 112
Thorntree Press 8
Thoron, Elise 181–2
The Thousand and One Nights 97
The Three Sisters 177, 180–2, 197
Tony award 1, 143
Torres, Joaquín *112*, *113*, *120*, *156*
Traina, Cristina L.H. 168–9, 170
transcendentalism 107
tribulation 116, 130, 135
Trinity Repertory Company 111, 197
Tristan Bates Theatre 112, 197
Troika VI 8

"The Undertaking" 92
University of Chicago 188

van Itallie, Jean-Claude 95
vibrator, history of 145–6
victimage of location 157, 172
Vietnam 5, 110, 115, 131–2, 135–6, 186, 196
Virgil 15, 18
Virgin and Child with the Angels 164, 171
Virgin Mary 111, 114, 123, 126–7, 133, 169, 170, 200
Virtual Meditation #1 177, 183–4
Vogel, Paula 7, 8, 10, 43–4, 53, 106, 111, 177, 199; *The Baltimore Waltz* 42–4, 200; *How I Learned to Drive* 7

Walker Bros. Original Pancake House 37
Waters, Les 8, 13, 24, 28, 37, 143, 175, 197
Weber, Carl 187
Wellman, Mac 8
Westinghouse, George 146
wet nursing 144, 145, 147–8, 149, 153
"When the Mind Leaves the Body ... and Returns" 167, 175
whimsical realism 50
Who's Afraid of Virginia Woolf? 153
Wiesner, Nicole *113*, *128*
Wilder, Thornton 103, 187–90, 191, 194–5; *The Happy Journey to Trenton and Camden* 188; *The Long Christmas Dinner* 103; *Our Town* 103, 188, 189, 190, 192; *Pullman Car Hiawatha* 103, 194; *The Skin of Our Teeth* 189
Williams, Chandler *162*
Williams, Tennessee 16, 103
Wilmette 9
Wing-Davey, Mark 112, 196, 197
wise fool 118–20, 127
woman-centered religion 169–71, 175, 176
women and playwriting 10–11
Woodruff, Robert 16
Woolf, Virginia 10, 74, 177, 179; *see also Orlando*
Woolly Mammoth Theatre Company *41*, *45*, *48*, *58*, 84, *85*, 87–8, *90*, *91*, *92*, 93–4, 197
the "Worthies" 92–3

Yale Repertory Theatre 13, 28, *29*, *32*, *40*, 42, *55*, 197
Yale School of Drama 199
"The Yellow Wallpaper" 151
yew 54, 66–7
"You'll Never Walk Alone" 94
Young, Stark 182

zhalost' 74
Zimmerman, Mary 16, 199
Zinn, David 144
Zola, Émile 164, 172

www.ingramcontent.com/pod-product-compliance
Ingram Content Group UK Ltd.
Pitfield, Milton Keynes, MK11 3LW, UK
UKHW041953140426
5217IPUK00015B/777